NTA

Trapping Handbook

a GUIDE for better trapping

DEDICATION: The contributors to this book salute the beaver, and the brave men who pursued the resource through a hostile and uncharted land to pioneer the development of our country. We salute the brave men who laid down their lives over the years so that we might enjoy both rights, and freedoms, to this very day. We salute those men today who cherish their heritage, and choose to be different, and choose to sacrifice so that others might have the right to decide whether or not they will trap. We salute those who will follow us, and wish them every good wish.

Author
Tom Krause

Artist
Bob Anderson

Editors
Norman Gray
Lloyd R. Hassler, M.D.
Don Hoyt, Sr.
Willis Kent
Charles Poches, Jr.
C. Pete Rickard

ISBN 0-9620698-0-9

Printed by
United Graphics, Inc.
Mattoon, IL 61938

Table of Contents

A Letter To Parents

THE National Trapper's Association, Incorporated, is an organization of Americans who have joined together to promote and protect the appropriate conservative use of our many furbearing species. The NTA was established in 1959, when a small group of trappers met in the Upper Peninsula of Michigan to form a defense against legislative bills designed to ban the harvest of our annual surplus of animals. A threat to a heritage, a way of life, and the best interests of wildlife has since attracted many people, from all walks of life, to build upon the humble foundation to encourage conservation in its purest form — "Wise Use".

The NTA Constitution and By-Laws provide a democratic government, with representation by a State Director from each state. Every member has the opportunity to vote for elected officers, and each member also enjoys the opportunity to comment on policies or other issues of concern. An official publication serves the membership with news, information, and pleasure. Finances are printed regularly, and audited regularly. NTA members have every right to be proud.

One of the highest priorities of the NTA is trapper education. Trappers are best equipped to help others who would consider trapping as a sport.

The intent of this book is not to recruit new trappers, but rather, it is an honorable attempt to help those who will trap. The accumulated information in this book is deliberately designed to be abundantly clear and easily understood by teenage readers, yet, valuable enough to serve as a ready reference for accomplished trappers. Our message is one of truth, ethics, honor and respect, both for the rights and opinions of others, and also to encourage pride and respect for our furbearers.

Literally millions of sportmen's dollars have been spent in this century to study the needs and problems of our wildlife. Properly, man feels a stewardship role towards our wild species, and scientific management objectives seek to recognize the needs of the species. Among other things, the quality and capacity of the available habitat must be evaluated, and compared to the population densities and reproductive capacities of the species. A regulated harvest is usually recommended. A primary objective is to allow the removal of excess numbers of the species, and controlling mechanisms include variable season lengths, license fees, and methods of harvest.

One thing is abundantly clear as a result of thousands of studies on wildlife species. Each species is its own worst enemy.

Each species is specific in its own needs, and the worst possible competition for food and shelter comes from others of the same species. Whenever the habitat is allowed to saturate with any species, that particular species is not served well. The inevitable result is a stressed species, and suffering is sure to follow.

Population densities above the supportive level of the habitat lead to malnourishment, and the inability of the species to sustain the stresses of winter. Resistance to diseases are greatly diminished with a malnourished species, and far too often entire populations have been devastated with nature's controlling mechanisms. To be accurate, natural population controlling mechanisms are far from kind. Suffering occurs, and bewilderment, internal disorders, blindness and pain are associated with several wildlife diseases.

It is altogether proper for a parent who has no knowledge of trapping to question whether or not the experience might benefit the child. Trapping is controversial in the minds of some people, and positive information might help you decide whether or not to encourage your child in his or her desire to learn to trap.

Interests are important in the character development of youths. While many youths develop interests in sports, or good grades in school, some do not when they realize that they can't excell. The so-called blood sports, including hunting, fishing, and trapping, do interest many youths, and one important thing to recognize is that the outdoor sports do offer equal opportunity for all to excell. Any young person, regardless of social advantages, can excell and be an achiever by catching the big fish of the day, or making a nice shot, or catching a mink.

Trapping can offer many advantages for our young people. Certainly, an awareness of the world around a young person opens up as he or she explores the woods and streams to see what manner of wildlife lives there.

At some point in time, every youngster must face reality. Lingering thoughts of furbearers as they are commonly portrayed in children's books, cartoons on television, or a teddy bear wearing clothes must be addressed.

People, and animals, are predators. The grocery store is not the source of food for man, and the cow that gives milk for years is finally eaten as its skin is put to further use as a pair of shoes.

Killing an animal is never agreeable. While many of us pay the butcher to do the killing for us, the end result differs little. Killing animals is addressed in this book, and our attempt is to teach methods that insure an honorable and humane death for the species.

Trapping is a responsibility, and teaches responsibility. There are laws to follow, private landowner permissions to seek, the rights of others to honor, fair chase rules to observe, and certainly, there is a responsibility to the species to help provide a reasonable and needful harvest.

Above all things, trapping is pure sport. Many species are not easily taken by novice trappers, and there is certainly a challenge to catch an elusive animal. A quality excitement abounds as a trapper looks toward his next set trap, and success is never assured.

Perhaps it is sad, but our young people have to struggle for an identity today. Spectator entertainment is constantly available, and there are many temptations thrust upon young people by a permissive society and the peer pressures of others. It is wise to consider that your child will develop an interest in something at some point in time, and that interest might not be the same as your own.

We seem to live in a programmed world, where routine is a way of life. The adventure of a trapline certainly changes that. Almost daily, there are new problems, challenges, responsibilities, opportunities, and lessons to be learned.

A sense of achievement is important in the character development of your child. Trapping certainly offers your child an opportunity to be an achiever. Both pride and confidence can be earned on a trapline, and these qualities may serve your child very well throughout life.

The membership of the NTA includes people who have an uncommon knowledge of furbearing animals. Some are professional trappers. Most are sport trappers. All have a common love, a common concern, and a common commitment to serve the best interests of the species, as well as our own.

If you determine that trapping might benefit your child, kindly allow us to help. We care too.

The memory of your child's first mink, or fox, or bobcat, will be a pleasant experience, and that memory will last to the grave.

"One need pay absolutely no attention to those who decry the blood sports, unless they have themselves, been from birth, logical vegetarians, for if it is right and moral to kill a beautiful animal for its food, it is also right and moral to kill a beautiful animal for its fur, or the trophy."—**Theodore R. Roosevelt.**

An American Heritage

THE value of furs has long been known to all men from every age in history. Garments made of fur were essential to protect early man from cold weather, and there is little doubt that furs served many prehistoric people as money to trade to others for necessities of life.

The American fur trade began with the Pilgrims at Plymouth Colony. The very first Indian encountered by the Colonists was Samoset, who wore a beaver robe. With sign language, the Pilgrims urged Samoset to bring them beaver robes for trade, and the American fur trade was born.

The values of beaver were known long before the discovery of the New World. The Greeks named the beaver, **Castor**, meaning "stomach", in reference to the unique stomach glands which produce oil. This oil is combed by the beaver through its fur as a waterproof process, and castor deposits also mark territorial boundaries. According to Greek mythology, Castor, one of the twin sons of Leda, was the protector of travelers and the guardian of hospitality. Castor glands have long been thought to have medicinal value, and even Solomon was thought to take castor twice a year to the weight of a gold pence to improve his memory. For generations castoreum was an accepted cure for such ailments as earache, deafness, gout, headache, colic, toothache, and tumors of the liver. It was also thought to be helpful in the treatment of madness, particularly if the victim was taken to the quiet beaver ponds for recuperation.

The American Indians too were wise to the value of beaver castor. Medicine bundles used in ceremonials to bring in game often contained a smaller hunting bundle with beaver castor. The odors of castor, or beaver oil, are strong, and the Indians knew full well that the smell was attractive to other beavers as well as lynx, fisher, marten, wolverine, and bear. The Algonquin Indians even mixed dried castoreum in their tobacco to sooth the fragrance of their pipes.

During the 1500's, a number of explorers from Europe continued to search the North American waterways for the passageway to China that Columbus had hoped to find. Harsh winters discouraged early settlement in the wild new world, and many more of the immigrating pioneers would have died without the help of native American Indians.

Paris fashion led to a boom in the beaver trade during the late 1500's, which was to last more than 200 years. Beaver hats became very stylish, and grew in popularity all across Europe.

The popular beaver hats were not made with skins, but rather, the fur was used to make felt which was then formed into felt hats. The felting process uses pressure with steam or hot water, and beaver fur had long been known for its superior felting qualities. A single particle of beaver fur shows scales that overlap when viewed through a microscope, and this quality makes a beaver fur felt hat look good, fit well, and last well.

With the boom in the value of beaver pelts, an effort was made by England, France, Spain and Holland to settle and claim parts of the new world known as America in 1600. Settlement began in earnest, and many immigrants came seeking religious freedoms, freedoms from oppressive laws, and opportunities. Prisoners, even convicted murderers, were pardoned to settle the new land in the name of their king.

The first white men to penetrate the American wilderness were known as "bush lopers". Many of these men, seeking adventure or escape from society, were never heard from after striking out into the vast wilderness. Some returned after long absences with piles of beaver furs to sell, before buying more articles and liquor to trade again for more furs in the wilderness. Many different tribes adopted these independent men, and many of the bush lopers took one or more Indian wives.

The native Americans were certainly impressed with the arrival of white men. As surely as they were impressed with guns that killed at a distance, they were impressed with clothing not made of leather, and of mirrors, metal knives, and trinkets offered in trade for their beaver furs. And as surely as they were impressed with the possessions of the newcomers, the Indians must have been confused by the never ending quest of the white man for more and more pelts of their friend, the beaver.

Prior to the arrival of men with beards, and white skin, the beaver was recognized as a brother, and even as a god to several Indian tribes. The American Indian was not in the habit of killing beavers, or other animals, simply because the opportunity presented itself. Killing to sustain life was a necessity for Indian people, but killing animals was not viewed lightly, lest the spirits be offended. Many tribes believed that the spirits of departed ones lived on in animals, and religious purification rites were required by some native cultures before an animal could be killed, even for food. Thanking ceremonies after the hunt were also common, and contrary to the ways of the Europeans, only the animals needed were harvested.

While all living things were held in respect by Indians, the beaver enjoyed a special reverence. Legends of very large beaver did exist in many Indian tribes when white traders appeared to buy skins, and these legends might be based in fact because skeletons of a very large species of beaver have since been found from Newfoundland to California, and from near the Arctic Circle in Alaska to Florida. Some of these large beaver skeletons measure more than seven feet in length, and indicate weights of 400 pounds and more.

Still, the beaver enjoyed a special place in the hearts of Indians. Surely, an animal as innocent as a beaver harbored the spirits of special loved ones. Respect and honor were important, and even when beavers were killed and eaten, the bones were not broken, and the bones were oftentimes returned to the deep water above the beaver dams so that wolves or magpies could not dishonor them.

The arrival of the white man provided a real shock to Indian cultures. Early explorers reported that many Indians roasted beavers whole, on spits above a fire, with the fur being burned off during the cooking process. Religions of the white man were introduced, and these were very confusing to the natives. With the talk of heaven and the eternal soul of man — and only man — how could it be that a creature as intelligent, useful, responsible, sober, and peaceful as a beaver would have no soul? The white man did not honor living things, and troubled the spirits by wasting lives foolishly. The white man killed for money.

But the white man had power. He brought guns that roared and killed without reason. He brought metal points for spears, and arrows. He brought cloth, paint, mirrors, brightly colored beads and he brought firewater that gave visions and dreams.

The demand for beaver furs presented the Indians with many problems. The offers of trade were too valuable to ignore, and many Indians accepted the ways of the white men to kill honored animals for profit. Religions were accepted to please the powerful and magic white men. With the destruction of many beliefs and traditions, the American Indian began to hunt the beaver in earnest.

The Indian methods of harvesting beavers varied with the region and season. One of the most widespread methods used by Indians to kill beavers called for a community effort. Stakes were driven in beaver dams to act as fences, and the beavers were dislodged from their lodges by chopping and pounding. With avenues of escape cut off, the animals were usually speared, shot with an arrow, or clubbed. Dogs joined in the hunts, and oftentimes they were able to sniff out undercut banks and bank dens holding beavers.

The snare was seldom used for animals with thick necks, but the beaver was often netted, largely by the fishing tribes who were expert in weaving fish nets. Netted beavers were usually clubbed to death before the nets were badly damaged by the trapped beavers.

Some woodland Indian tribes were expert with deadfall traps, but it appears that these deadfall traps were used mostly for other species.

Hunting from a canoe with a bow and arrow was also common. Usually, these hunts took place in the early morning or late evening when the beavers were actively feeding on shore. The hunter sat quietly in the front of the canoe while a silent partner in the back of the canoe directed the canoe toward a vulnerable beaver. There was an attempt to reach the beaver quickly after being shot to prevent the wounded beaver an escape in the water.

Progress into the American wilderness was slow during the 1600's. Rivers flowing easterly hampered the progress of men in boats trying to go upstream, and there were numerous obstacles in the new land.

Champlain was one of the first early and successful explorers to probe the fur rich Iroquois country along the St. Lawrence river valley and, in 1608, he established the first fur post at the mouth of the St. Lawrence in Quebec. In 1610, Etienne Brule discovered Lake Huron, and in 1611 Champlain established a fur post at what is now known as Montreal. Brule reached Lake Superior in 1622, and Jean Nicolet was sent out by Champlain in 1633 to find new beaver trade regions. Nicolet traveled through the land south of Lake Superior, down through the Illinois country and brought back a tale of a great river that flowed to a faraway sea.

Other important explorers of the 1600's include Radisson and Groseilliers, LaSalle, Marquette and Joliet, and Henry Hudson, who was set adrift by a mutinous crew in what is now known as Hudson's Bay.

The first of several major fur trading companies was established and chartered on May 2, 1670. The Company of Gentleman Adventurers, as the organizers called themselves, was known as the Hudson's Bay Company, and the HBC continues as a significant fur market power to this very day. The original charter granted practically absolute power over the domain, for which the HBC was to pay "His Majesty two Elks and two Black Beavers whenever he happened to enter the country."

With a prime beaver pelt as a standard unit of money in the wilderness, values fluctuated somewhat for many years depending upon the demand for pelts as well as increasing offerings by other traders. A value of $2 per pelt was established as early as 1626. Beaver prices were the standards for other product values, and one winter prime adult beaver pelt usually had the trade value of each of the following: 3 martens; 1 fox; 1 moose; 1 weejack (fisher); 1 bear cub; 2 queequehatches (wolverines); 2 ordinary otters (1 if exceptionally fine); 2 deerskins; 1 lb. castoreum; 10 lbs. feathers; 8 moose hoofs; or 4 fathoms of netting.

East of the buffalo ranges, Indian women often overscraped the leather side of beaver pelts to loosen the roots of the long guard hairs, which were then pulled from the pelt leaving just the dense underfur. These pelts were then sewn together, and worn with the fur side in for several months until they became semi-tanned, and soft as silk. These pelts were highly prized by the fur trade, and they brought special prices until the desire for more rum and brandy caused the sale of pelts soon after the skinning.

The native Indians certainly placed great values upon the trinkets, such as mirrors, beads, and ribbons offered in trade for beaver skins. Competition from more and more buyers drove beaver values up for the Indians, and virtually guaranteed a supply of the miraculous alcohol. Reasonable prices were almost never paid to the Indians for skins. Finally, when desperation and depleted beaver supplies forced the traders to offer guns in trade for beaver skins, a standard measure of trade was a pile of beaver skins as tall as the rifle. That caused the production of rifles with extremely long barrels, much longer than needed for accuracy, and the intent was to simply get more furs at cheaper prices yet.

Steel traps can be documented as being used as early as the 1650's in Massachusetts. These early traps were all hand forged, and copied after the larger gin traps used to catch poachers of game in England and France. Most early traps were of the single long spring design, and steel traps for beaver trapping were used very sparingly for many years because they were so costly to make, and not nearly as sure as a well placed bullet. Some of the early bush lopers did take a few hand forged traps with them on their hunting and trading journeys, and these traps were never traded to the Indians.

The pursuit of beaver continued throughout the entire 1700's, as new and promising hunting and trapping areas were needed to supply the constant demand for more furs. Entire tribes of Indians moved about seeking the one thing that they could offer for trade, and there were many conflicts between uprooted Indians as well as conflicts between Indians and whites. Scurvy plagued many white explorers, and tribes of Indians were decimated by a dreaded enemy which could not be fought — smallpox.

The American frontier advanced during the 1700's as white men settled further and further west in lands now known as Tennessee, Kentucky, Pennsylvania and Ohio, and by the end of the century hardy souls were fighting Indians, and clearing land for farming as far west as Illinois and Missouri. St. Louis became a fur trading center, and the North West Company was formed in 1784 by French and Montreal traders to compete for beaver furs.

David Thompson, of the North West Company, wrote about a meeting with an older Indian in 1794, and recorded these words: "We came to an aged Indian, his arms folded across his breast with a pensive countenance, looking at the beavers swimming in the water and carrying their winter provisions to their houses..." "We are now killing the beaver without labor; we are now rich, but shall soon be poor, for when the beaver are destroyed we have nothing to depend on to purchase what we want for our families; strangers now overrun our country with their iron traps and we and they shall soon be poor."

Strong beaver values continued into the 1800's, and the historic trip of Lewis & Clark up the Missouri River in 1804 proved that the bush lopers had long preceded them. The warring Sioux were unimpressed with a gift of an American flag, for they had received another some 13 or 14 years earlier, and it was only a piece of cloth. Further up the river, in what is now known as Montana, the Lewis & Clark expedition encountered several French traders of the North West Company who had settled, taken Indian wives, and raised children. Further upstream, some of the children, and adults, were actually fair-haired. Lewis & Clark were generations behind the obvious evidence of the early bush lopers.

Hand forged beaver traps were taken along on the Lewis & Clark expedition, and the reports of many beavers in the Rocky Mountains encouraged young settlers from Missouri and Illinois to seek their fortunes as mountain men and beaver trappers in the Rockies. Most of these young men were hardened from clearing farmland, and experienced in Indian fighting, and many reputations were to be gained in the pursuit of Rocky Mountain beavers.

Many of these trappers were hired by companies, and most banded together in small trapping parties for protection from warring Indians. Steel traps were popular with the mountain men, and the average trapper had 4 or 6 traps to use. Fortunes were made and lost in the mountains during the early 1800's, and roughly one half of the trappers survived bouts with bitter weather, hostile Indians and robbers.

Andrew Henry and William Ashley led a party of young trappers up the Missouri in 1822 with recruits that had answered a notice in the St. Louis **Republican**. Names in this party included Jedediah Smith, William and Milton Sublette, Robert Campbell, Etienne Provost, James Clyman, David Jackson, Jim Bridger and Thomas Fitzpatrick. These men were to form yet another fur company, the Rocky Mountain Fur Company, and all of these names became places scattered throughout the west.

In 1826, Kit Carson joined a wagon train leaving St. Louis to Sante Fe, and Carson was to become a famous Indian fighter as well as a trapper. His pursuit of the beaver took him to California, and through the mountain states as far north as Idaho.

Many other names became famous during this era, including: John Colter, Pierre Menard, Thomas James, Manuel Lisa, John Reed, John Clarke, Liver-eating Johnson, and John Jacob Astor, who formed the Pacific Fur Company.

Ashley and the Rocky Mountain Fur Company managed to get the first fur rendezvous together at Henry's Fork of the Green River, Wyoming, in 1825. Although this first mountain trapper's rendezvous was small, it was successful and led to a number of others. There certainly was an incentive to gather with others to sell, trade and celebrate. Other important fur trading rendezvous were held in Pierre's Hole, the Wind River valley, and Ham's Fork.

The 1830's were the death knell of the beaver trapping mountain men. The harvest of beaver dwindled as every stream was explored, and trapped, and European wars had devastated the European continent, destroying the market for beaver pelts. A cheaper substitute for beaver fur had been found in South American nutria, and the market of 250 years for beaver was destroyed.

Without a market, many trappers went west in pursuit of gold in Oregon and California, and goodly numbers went to hunt the still plentiful buffalo on the plains.

A significant improvement in traps began in 1823, at the hands of a 17 year old trapper in New York state. Sewell Newhouse, not having the money needed to buy traps, began to make his own in Oneida County. The iron parts for 50 or more were fashioned in the blacksmith's shop, and the springs were forged from the blades of old axes. A friend showed the young man how to temper the springs, which proved to be a success; for the traps would catch and hold. After Newhouse used these traps for one season, he sold them to local Indians for 62 cents each, and the making of a new supply was begun.

During the next 20 years, Newhouse worked both alone, and with hired help to produce from one to two thousand traps a year to supply the demand that was building for better quality traps. Trap production was mostly during the off season, as Newhouse continued to trap. Newhouse was

Beaver Distribution 1600

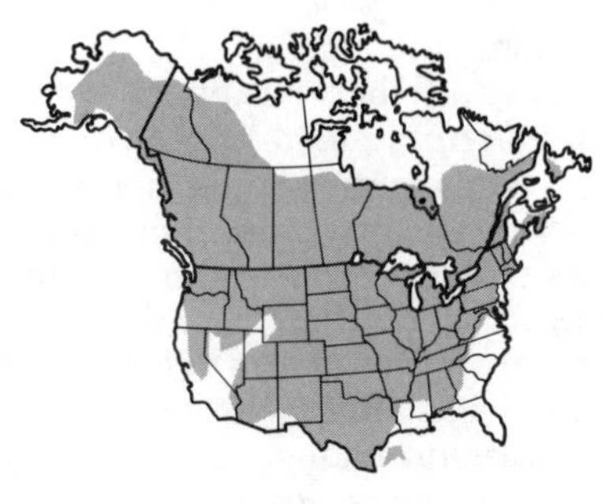

Beaver Distribution 1980

determined to make faultless traps, and his traps would catch animals whether they caught customers or not.

The Oneida Community, a religous group, established itself about 2 miles from the home of Sewell Newhouse in 1848, and the Newhouse family entered its membership the next summer. For several years, Newhouse continued to make and sell traps, and in 1855, orders for traps from New York and Chicago caused the Oneida Community to become involved in the trap making business, and a power punch was the first machine introduced to help streamline the trap making operation. One by one, the difficulties of hand production were changed to machine operations, and the Newhouse trap was the first trap to be mass produced and uniform in quality.

Many small companies were encouraged to make traps during the late 1800's, and early 1900's. Hawley & Norton traps were introduced in 1874, by the Oneida organization, and the Oneida Community also introduced the Victor line of traps in 1887.

The Animal Trap Company, of Abingdon, Illinois, made traps before 1900. This company bought out the J.M. Mast Company, a mouse trap producing company, in 1923 and moved all operations to Lititz, Pennsylvania. The Oneida Community bought out the Animal Trap Company almost immediately, and in 1924, C.M. Woolworth and two partners bought out the entire Oneida Community and changed the name back to the Animal Trap Company, later to be known as Woodstream Corporation.

There were a number of significant trap producing companies during the early 1900's, and Triumph introduced the first underspring jump traps. W.A. Gibbs, a retired railroad worker, tried to sell his idea of a better muskrat trap to Triumph, and when Triumph was not interested, Gibbs decided to produce his own traps. Within a few years, Gibbs traps were outselling Triumphs, and Gibbs bought the Triumph Trap Company. Gibbs introduced several new ideas to trap designs, including the first coilspring traps.

Other significant trap companies during the late 1800's and early 1900's include Blake & Lamb, Diamond, Eclipse, Bell Spring, Sargent, Nisbet, Champion, Hector, and Trailsend, to name a few.

A significant idea for a different design of trap was invented by a British Columbia trapper during the mid 1900's. This new design proved to be effective for certain species as a body gripping trap, and bears the name of the inventor, Frank Conibear.

At the turn of this century, Americans began to realize that the many resources of our land were vulnerable to exploitation. The great white pine forests in the northern states were being denuded, soil erosion from plowed prairies became obvious, and many species of wildlife were becoming increasingly more scarce. Although Yellowstone National Park had been established by Congress in 1872, little land had been set aside for preservation, and conservation practices were virtually unknown.

Gifford Pinchot became head of the forestry division of the Department of Agriculture in 1898, under President McKinley. Vice-President Theodore Roosevelt inherited the presidency upon McKinley's death, and the team of Pinchot and Roosevelt was to have a significant impact on conservation practices in this country.

During Roosevelt's presidency, from 1901-1909, the U.S. Forest Service was established, and conservation in timber harvesting was begun along with reforestation practices. Farmers were urged to plow and plant on the contour to minimize soil erosion, and 125 million acres were added to the National Forests.

The conservation of wildlife was recognized by Roosevelt, and he called a conference of governors in 1908 to address the problems of wildlife. Within two years, 27 states established conservation commissions, and seasons were set to prevent over harvests of wildlife.

The accomplishments of the game commissions have been significant, and plenty, over the years. Exploited species, like beaver, were reintroduced in many states, and many habitat problems were addressed with land and wetland purchases, and habitat improvements. Hunters, fishermen, and trappers eagerly supported the sensible management of wildlife, and paid the costs in license fees and taxes on sporting equipment.

The story of wildlife management is one of the great successes of our nation. As biologists and scientists studied the needs and problems of our many wildlife species, solutions were found, and implemented. Regulations, closed seasons, bag limits, and curtailment of market hunting were enacted in places, based on the needs of the species. Tree nurseries, fish hatcheries, and game farms were established in many areas, and even foreign species and hybrids were introduced into the wild.

Trapping remains today as a valuable management tool in the management and control of our many furbearing species. Harvesting is essential to the best interests of all abundant species, and the steel trap is needed today as much as ever to serve the best interests of the species, and the best interests of man.

Management

AMERICANS are fortunate to live in a land with abundant natural resources. These natural resources are known as "renewable" resources, and "non-renewable" resources. Non-renewable resources include such things as oil, coal, and the mineral ores used to make materials. These resources are important to the well being of people, and management of these non-renewable resources is planned to provide supplies for generations to come.

Our renewable resources are also valuable, and examples of these renewable resources include forests, wildlife, and fertile lands to grow crops. The management of our natural renewable resources recognizes that there is a surplus which can and should be harvested, or it will be wasted.

Wildlife, including furbearers, are an **annually** renewable resource. Most species produce more young in a year than can survive, and good management plans allow for the harvest of excess numbers of furbearers, fish and game.

Habitat is a real key to furbearer management. The word "habitat" describes the environment — things both seen and unseen. Vegetation is an important part of the habitat, and is easily seen. Things not so easily seen, such as water temperatures, acidity, or the presence of agricultural or industrial chemicals also have a dramatic effect on the habitat, and alter the ability of the habitat to support different wild species.

Although many types of habitat seem obvious, such as mature forests, marshes, prairies, farmlands and lakes, wildlife and furbearer biologists need to study many things to determine the real ability of the habitat to support different species. This is the first goal in furbearer management, and before man can manage furbearers wisely, he must be able to know and recognize the ability of the habitat to support wildlife throughout the entire year. Habitat study is a science.

All furbearers are habitat dependent. Although some species can adjust to different climates and habitat types, the furbearers still have needs for survival, including a suitable and available food supply, denning sites to raise young, and a degree of protection from enemies. Whenever the habitat cannot meet one of these needs, that particular species cannot survive.

Populations of furbearers are also considered by game managers, and these estimates are accomplished by a variety of methods. Many game departments send out survey questionnaires to fur harvesters, or fur buyers, and this information can be used from year to year as a data base, and adjusted according to season lengths, trapper and hunter numbers, and even weather conditions. Spotlight surveys of furbearers are taken in some states, as are track and sighting counts. One relatively new method of estimating the size and health of furbearer populations is called population modeling, and very accurate estimates of a species health and status is now being gained in many states by putting harvest data into a computer for analysis.

Dense populations of furbearers and predators are not in the best interests of man and this must be addressed by wildlife managers. Expensive problems do occur when an abundance of beavers flood valuable timber, killing the trees and complicating harvests. An abundance of muskrats create many problems in farm ponds and dikes as a result of burrowing habits, and coyotes certainly take a toll of sheep on western range lands. All of these problems are very real to the person who owns the timber, farm ponds, or sheep.

There is an abundance of information on what happens to furbearers when they are neither managed or controlled. While some people think that animal populations will grow and stockpile when no harvest is allowed, such is not the reality. Nature has its own controlling mechanisms, and they are far from kind.

Entire populations of furbearers are threatened every time furbearing species are not controlled within the supportive level of the habitat. Virtually every animal is territorial during parts of the year, which means that the animal stays, feeds and lives within a certain area. As populations increase, territories decrease in size, and even overlap. These dense populations cause competition for the available food as well as denning sites, and fighting becomes common as the animals become stressed. Malnourishment also occurs as more and more of the same species compete for the available food supply, and these stresses combine to make all of the affected animals very vulnerable to sickness, exposure and death.

Winter is often cruel to over populated and malnourished species. Many individuals with an inadequate coat of fur, or a lack of energy, simply die of exposure in wet or cold weather. During extreme weather conditions, survivors can be few because virtually all suffer identical stresses.

Disease is oftentimes a controlling factor with dense furbearer populations. In fact, many young animals are innoculated by their mothers shortly after birth with a variety of disease organisms. Many times, these diseases remain as "latent infections", and do not grow and attack the seemingly healthy animal until it is stressed. Even mother's milk can and does infect newborn furbearers.

Dense populations of furbearers create a huge potential for disease spread. As territories become smaller, and touch each other or overlap, diseases can and do run rampant. Entire species can be devastated, and this has happened many times with several diseases and several species. Whether the disease happens to be tularemia, distemper, parvo enteritis or mange really doesn't matter a great deal to the infected animals. Most die a slow death after suffering from internal disorders, fever, pain, and even blindness.

Each species is its own worst enemy when its population is not controlled.

Good furbearer management programs seek to control species populations so territories do not touch or overlap during the period of year when the animals are territorial. Diseased animals can then die without opportunity to spread the diseases, and a reasonable food supply will allow both strength and health during the time of year when the species disburse to seek mates, and new territories.

The needs of man are also recognized by good furbearer management programs. Furbearers certainly have a value, and it is absolutely right for people to enjoy the value of excess numbers of furbearers. Indeed, one of the major management problems is to encourage an adequate harvest during the years that furs have little value.

Sales of furbearer pelts are significant, and amount to hundreds of millions of dollars annually for American fur harvesters. That income is important for hundreds of thousands of people, and America is by far the largest producer for the world wide demand for wild furs. These raw furs are usually purchased by manufacturers in Europe or the Far East, and bring new money into virtually every community in our land. Furbearer managers recognize this value, and that is why harvest seasons are open during the time of year when the pelts have most value.

Human health is another concern for furbearer managers. Several significant diseases also are spread by furbearers, including tularemia, bubonic plague, leptospirosis, and rabies. Rabies is a particular concern at present, and there is evidence to suggest that skunks can and do spread rabies without dying of the dreaded disease.

The role of trapping in furbearer management is essential if both the best interests of the species and man are to be served properly. Many species are not hunted for sport, and poisoning is far less desirable for population control.

The foothold trap is a particularly valuable tool for game managers. These traps are live holding traps, when used as such, giving opportunity for the release of unwanted catches. In fact, several species cannot be captured efficiently in other types of traps. Foothold traps also allow the benefit and opportunity to release nontarget catches.

Before furbearer managers are able to recommend trapping seasons, there are many factors to consider. Other than the current wild populations, and habitat quality surveys, there are some unknown factors to consider. Trapping pressures vary a great deal due to prices paid for furs, and trapping seasons must be set far in advance of actual fur markets. Weather conditions during the trapping season also have a great bearing on the harvest, as an early freeze up or heavy snow falls significantly decrease the harvest, and this cannot be known when the seasons are set.

Furbearer management programs are not an exact science, and cannot be an exact science. Animal densities vary from county to county, township to township, and stream to stream. Harvest pressures also vary a great deal, and fluctuating fur prices encourage both greater harvest pressures and lesser harvest pressures. Still, an adequate harvest is necessary to protect the health of the entire resident species, and attempts are made to keep harvest levels within acceptable and reasonable boundaries.

The single most important furbearer manager is the trapper. Seasons are one thing, but the ability of the individual trapper to manage furbearer populations on his or her own trapline is far more important. The ability to know when to stop trapping is a skill enjoyed by many of our better trappers who recognize the needs of the species as well as the carrying capacity of the available habitat. Some species can be trapped more intensively than other species, and the wise trapper is careful to only crop the excesses without damaging a healthy breeding stock.

Some furbearers multiply much more rapidly than others, and for that reason you will find information in each of the species chapters to help you achieve a safe and reasonable harvest on your own trapline.

Furbearer management is paid for with a combination of license fees and federal excise taxes paid on sporting equipment. Fur sales pay trappers, who buy licenses and equipment, and these fees and taxes are further used to study and manage the species.

In a sense, the furbearers pay for their own management, and benefit from it.

Laws and Rights

LAWS are a necessity for society, and the purpose and intent of law is to inform, identify and protect rights. Rights to be protected include the rights of the federal and state governments, and individuals.

The law since early times, as it relates to birds and animals, is that they are possessions of the king. Now it would be stated that they are possessions of the federal and state governments. Because of this, the taking and possession of animals is governed by our federal and state governements.

These laws are in the form of **enactment of law** by Congress and state legislators as well as **regulations** adopted by both federal and state agencies charged with administering the laws. Needless to say, as our environment, number of animals and people's attitude changes, the laws and regulations covering trapping also change.

Federal wildlife laws include the Lacey Act and the Black Bass Act. These laws are administered by the U.S. Fish & Wildlife Service, and are concerned with import and export of wildlife, endangered species, and other wildlife law violations when state or federal boundaries are crossed. The U.S. Fish & Wildlife Service is also concerned with the management of migratory species, such as ducks and geese. Trapping is permitted by the federal government on many federal wildlife refuges, but it is also governed by applicable state law and regulation.

Each state has the authority and responsibility to manage resident wildlife species on private land, state owned land and other federal lands. As a general rule, wildlife living on private lands or state owned lands are considered as property of the state. Wildlife living on federal lands, although managed by the state, are considered as property of the federal government.

Many state wildlife laws are legislated. That means that the laws were passed by the state legislature and became law after being signed by the governor of the state. Many legislated wildlife laws identify and classify game animals, game fish and furbearers. Hunting and trapping license fees and the means and methods by which game and furbearers can be taken is often addressed in legislative law.

The legislative process varies a little from state to state. Generally, a new law or a change of an existing law requires the introduction of a written bill, which is introduced by a legislator. After the introduction, the bill is assigned to an appropriate committee of legislators, who either decide to kill the bill by inactivity or decide to hold a public hearing to evaluate the opinions of concerned citizens. If the committee decides that the bill has merit, it is passed out of committee to the legislature for consideration. At times, these bills are amended or changed in either the committee process or in the legislature itself, to address the concerns of others.

Legislative law is a political process and there are two opportunities available to citizens to either support or protest the proposed law. One opportunity is available during the public hearing process, and if the bill is passed out of committee to the legislative body, there is also opportunity to lobby, or influence the legislators, before a vote is taken. The final step is a signing by the governor, who has power to veto or approve the bill.

Regulations are another form of law, and wildlife regulations are usually adopted by state game commissions. Game regulations are reviewed annually by the game commissions in each state, and input is usually sought from the state game department staff to determine if there is a need to alter the regulations. As a rule, there is opportunity for groups, or individuals, to comment on suggested regulation changes or to propose regulation changes. Trapping seasons are usually regulated by the state game commissions and the regulatory process allows needed changes without a prolonged and expensive political process.

Some people are of the opinion that wildlife should enjoy legal rights, such as a right to life, or a right to freedom. Animal rights arguments are new to law and most opinions are that animals and other wild species do not have legal rights. The proper relationship of animals and man is not one of equality. Man, as a superior being, cares about other living things and accepts a responsibility to help wildlife for the common good of both the species and man.

Landowners have very definite rights on their own lands. A landowner has every right to determine whether or not he or she will allow others to hunt or trap on their private lands. But the landowner does not own the wildlife and landowners when hunting or trapping are bound by the same laws and regulations of both the federal and state governments.

Most states recognize that landowners have a right to protect their private property from wildlife causing damage. In some states, a permit is required for the landowner or his agent to remove the offending animals, and a number of states provide trained people to help.

Individuals certainly have rights too. Each resident, as a citizen of that state, enjoys an equal ownership of our wild species, and individuals are entitled to decide for themselves whether or not they will hunt, fish or trap for the annual surplus of wildlife according to the laws and regulations of that state.

Individuals have further rights, under the laws, including protection of their traps, equipment and themselves, so long as they comply with the other game laws and rights of the landowner. Each state varies in its respective laws, and it is the individual trapper's **duty** to be informed of the laws and regulations.

With each right in a party, there is a corresponding duty. Thus you have a right to trap and others assume the duty to not harm, molest or take your traps, equipment and animals. Likewise, the government has the right to regulate and control the animals, and you have the **duty** to obey those laws and regulations.

Respect others rights, but enforce your rights as well.

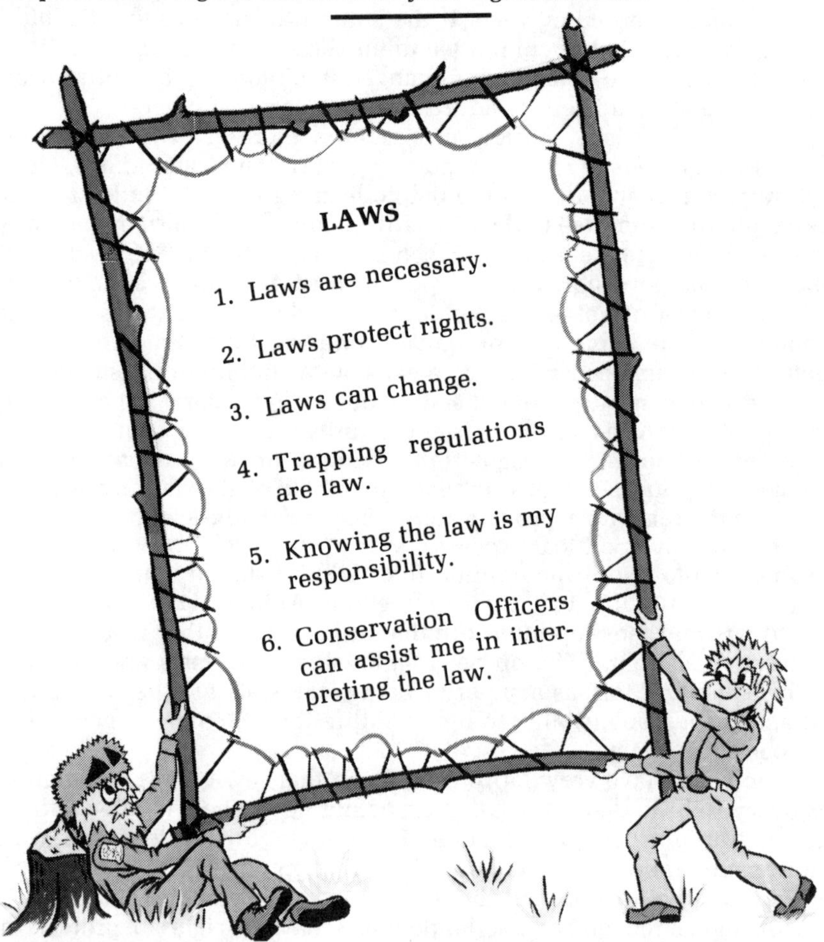

LAWS
1. Laws are necessary.
2. Laws protect rights.
3. Laws can change.
4. Trapping regulations are law.
5. Knowing the law is my responsibility.
6. Conservation Officers can assist me in interpreting the law.

Responsibility

AS stated in the chapter, **Laws and Rights**, every law identifies protection or rights on one side. On the other side, laws also identify duties and responsibilities.

The first of several responsibilities that trappers have is to know the law. Trapping laws vary considerably from state to state, and you **must** know your own laws. Printed regulations are usually available wherever trapping licenses are sold. Be absolutely sure that you get a copy, even if you have to ask for it. Study the regulations to be sure that you know the law, and abide by the law at all times.

If you should have a question about your trapping laws, call your area game warden. He will be pleased to help you, and answer any of your questions. Part of his job is to help you be aware of laws, and he will be your friend if you always obey the law.

Please be aware that some of the trapping information in this manual may be illegal in your state. Many laws do conflict from state to state, and our attempt is to provide you with good information in harmony with most state laws. But, this guide is only a guide, and you are expected and responsible to know and follow all of your state laws. There is no need, and no excuse, to break the law.

Just as there is a right and a responsibility to harvest excess numbers of furbearers, there is a responsibility to do the job legally, properly, and well. Proper traps for each species are recommended in this book to help you in your trap selections. The trap used is important, and it is just as important to check each single trap for flaws before it is set for an animal.

The ability to trap selectively is also a skill, and a responsibility. There are a number of ways to keep trap sets very selective in catching target animals, and our suggested methods are designed to minimize non-target catches. Still, you need to use good judgment at all times when trapping, and you must discipline yourself to avoid trapping in areas where problems are likely to occur, such as near homes or parks where pets might roam.

The treatment of captured furbearers is another responsibility. Traps must be checked frequently, and the captured animals deserve to be dispatched humanely, or released unharmed. The possibility of further entanglement after a catch is made greatly affects the plight of trapped animals, so care should always be taken when making trap sets to visualize just what might happen to the catch after it is caught. Many times, it is a real advantage to move a trap set a few feet one way or another to avoid possible entanglement problems. There are many places and ways to catch each animal, and skilled trappers learn to pass up trap set locations where problems might occur in favor of locations where problems **can't** occur.

A trapper should also feel a responsibility to those who don't harvest furbearers. All citizens of a state can claim a partial ownership of wild animals, and each person has a right to decide for themselves whether or not they will participate in the harvest. Some people believe strongly that wild animals should be totally protected at all times. These people are entitled to an opinion differing from yours, and you should feel a responsibility to not deliberately offend them. Your disposal of skinned carcasses is important in the consideration of other people, and please remember at all times that public opinion might determine whether or not we will continue to enjoy the right to trap.

There is also a responsibility to others who choose to trap. Many times, and in many places, trappers are forced to share in the harvests on both public and private lands. Trap theft is a common problem for most trappers, but there is never a just cause for you to steal another person's traps. If you suspect that another trapper is trapping without permission on private lands, or someone is trapping illegally, you still don't have the right to steal traps. Bring the problem to the attention of the landowner on private lands. You might just find that another trapper has permission to trap there too. If a violation of law is occurring, contact your game warden. Assist him if you are asked, but don't ever molest the traps of another.

Each trapper bears a responsibility to every other trapper. In a sense, we are our brother's keeper. Many times, there are opportunities to help each other, and you might find your competitor to be a good friend if you treat him fairly.

If you happen upon a live animal in the trap of another, it is perfectly acceptable to kill the animal for the other trapper. But, do not take the trap off of the animal. Should the trapper appear while you are doing this, he might suspect you of trying to steal his catch. Killing the furbearer is a consideration for the animal, and the other trapper will probably thank you for that.

If you trap on private lands, you have a large responsibility to honor every wish of the landowner. Follow his or her instructions carefully, and always be sure that you close every gate that you open. A good relationship with landowners is very valuable to you, and you should do everything within your power to keep your relationship a happy one. At times, the landowner or farmer might have need of your skill to catch a damage causing animal, and your offer of help is appreciated. But, before you set a trap out of season, call your game warden first. A permit or assessment of damage might be necessary before you can set a trap out of season in your state.

There are many responsibilities to trapping. Each one is important. Each time you face a temptation on your trapline, you have an opportunity to build your own self-respect. If you deliberately break the law, you harm yourself more than others, and bring reproach upon all trappers. On the other hand, if you resist temptation, and do what is lawful and right, you strengthen your own character, and prepare yourself better to lead a happy and productive life.

The choice is yours — Either you win, or we all lose!

1. Obey all laws;
2. Respect public and private property;
3. Honor the rights of others;
4. Check traps regularly and faithfully;
5. Use proper traps; and selective sets;
6. Consider the trapped animal's plight;
7. Properly handle pelts;
8. Dispose of carcasses properly;
9. Help others who need my skills;
10. Support and defend proper conservation practices.

Fur Handling

MILLIONS of dollars worth of pelts are wasted each year through ignorance or neglect. That is a sad, but true, fact. It makes little sense to kill a beautiful animal for its fur, and then allow the pelt to disintegrate into worthless rot.

One of the most important things to realize is that furs begin to deteriorate shortly after the death of the animal, and that heat speeds up the process. For that reason, make an attempt to cool the animals and keep them shaded from direct sunlight. Never pile warm animals. Separate them to allow cooling until they can be skinned.

If you have freezer space, you might consider freezing smaller furbearers for skinning or selling at a later date. Be sure to wrap the animals in one or two airtight garbage bags, or a freeze drying process known as "freezer burn" can damage the frozen pelts.

Larger animals can also be skinned and frozen for later processing or sales. It is to your advantage to not flesh, or scrape the hides to be frozen. The layer of fat found on most skins will act as protection against freezer burn. You may further safeguard the furs from freezer burn by wetting the flesh side before they are wrapped tightly and frozen.

If you elect to freeze skins or small animals, be sure that the freezer temperature is set around zero degrees. Distribute the furs in the freezer. Do not lump them together or the skins in the middle of the pile may actually spoil before the cold temperatures freeze them. Furs are top quality insulation, and keep out both heat and cold temperatures.

Never use an old refrigerator with the thermostat turned as cold as possible. While an old refrigerator may freeze the pelts, they will only be very lightly frozen, and spoilage can still occur.

Learning to properly handle and finish your own furs is a skill that can give you pride. Your abilities will improve with practice, and you can certainly profit by watching a fur buyer or experienced trapper skin, scrape, and dry his furs. If you are not afraid to ask for help, you will find that many good fur handlers will be happy to help you.

The unhappy truth is that many furs are devalued by improper handling.

Different species are handled by different methods, and for that reason, you will find information in each of the species chapters in this book to help you handle that particular type of fur properly. Every single thing is important to observe and practice if you are to gain full value for your skins. Properly cared for pelts command higher prices, always.

The proper care of pelts begins immediately after the furbearer is removed from the trap. Muddy animals, such as muskrats, raccoons, or nutria, can often be washed in a stream or pond to remove much of the mud before they are suspended in a dark and cool place to air dry before skinning. An electric fan can be used to hasten the air drying process of wet animals if you wish, but do not use heat, or spoilage can occur.

A curry comb or pet grooming brush is needed to remove dirt and objects from furs.

It is always a good idea to comb or brush the fur before the animal is skinned to remove weed seeds, burrs, or other debris. Scotch combs, or curry combs, are useful for this purpose, and often available at farm supply stores.

The tools needed to handle furs properly depend upon the species being handled. Nevertheless, a well supplied fur handler will have all of the following tools available: a skinning gambrel, a single handled fleshing tool, a two handled fleshing tool, a tail stripper, a fleshing beam, fleshing boards in assorted sizes, a fur comb, proper sized stretchers, an electric fan, an apron, and an assortment of knives and knife sharpening equipment.

A skinning gambrel is useful to suspend a furbearer by the hind legs while skinning. Many trappers prefer a heavy duty gambrel, and use the hook on only one side to skin smaller furbearers, such as mink or marten. A swivel right above the gambrel is a convenience, and allows ease in turning the animal as it is being skinned.

Single handled fleshing tools are available from trapping supply dealers. A good substitute can be a

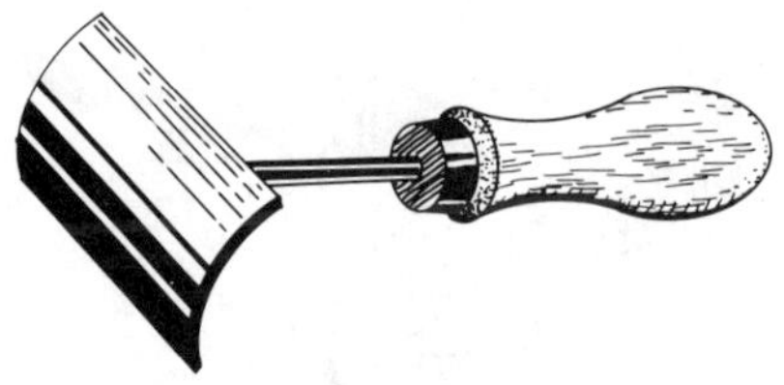

A single handled fleshing tool is an aid for many fleshing chores.

paint scraping tool that has been dulled by use. These tools are adequate and particularly handy for all of the fleshing required on muskrats, mink, marten, skunk, and opossum.

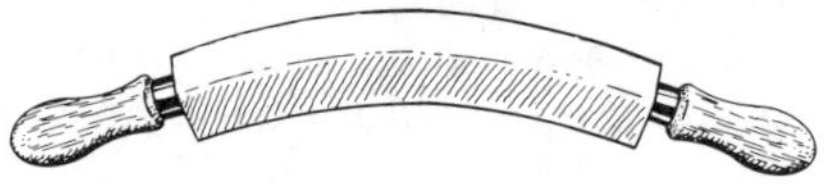

A two handled fleshing knife makes fleshing hard to flesh skins much easier.

Two handled fleshing tools are a great convenience in the proper fleshing of harder to flesh species, including beaver, badger, raccoon, otter, and coyote. These knives are used on pelts placed on fleshing beams, and allow greater pressures and better control while fleshing. Many two handled fleshing knives have a sharp edge on one side of the blade for slicing through gristle and fat, and a blunter side to allow greater pressures while scraping the pelts without cutting or tearing of the pelt. As a general rule, two handled fleshing knives with blade widths of two inches are easier to control than fleshing knives with blades of only an inch or so in width. Good two handled fleshing knives are somewhat expensive, but they are a great aid in the proper handling of raw furs, and last for many years with proper care.

A tail puller, or tail stripper, is another handy tool for pulling a furred tail off of an animal's tailbone. A clothespin can also work for this purpose, and many trappers prefer to use the gap in a pair of pliers to serve the same purpose. All furred tails must have the tailbone removed and should also be opened with a knife cut all the

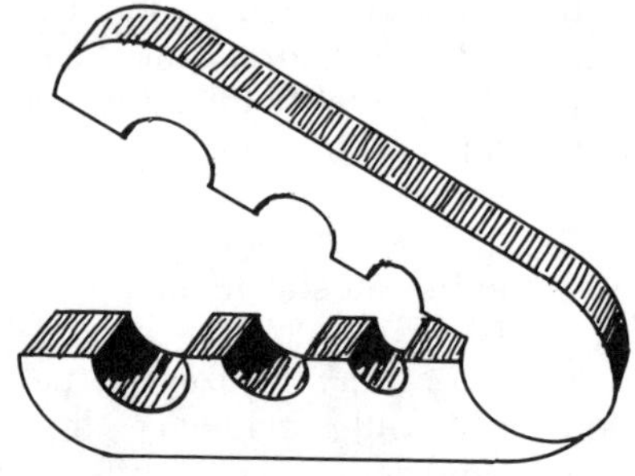

Most tail stripping tools have different sized notches for different sized tailbones.

way to the tip of the tail, with the knife cut on the underside of the tail.

A fleshing beam is a necessity for the use of a two handled fleshing tool, and the combination of a good beam and good two handled fleshing knife greatly speeds up the proper handling of many of the more difficult to flesh furs. Many trappers prefer tapered fleshing beams so that the furs can be slipped over the beam for the fleshing process. Some trappers prefer wider logs for a fleshing beam. With log beams, the fur is simply placed on the log for the scraping process to remove all fat and tissue right down to the leather.

Fleshing beams are sometimes available from trapping supply dealers, and they can be homemade with a proper shaping of a 2x8 board, four or five feet long. It is important to have a smooth surface on the fleshing beam to prevent nicks and cuts during the fleshing process.

Fleshing boards are often used

A fleshing beam can be homemade and is necessary for two handled fleshing knives.

with the smaller one handled fleshing tools. The object is to provide a flat surface under the pelt being scraped. Smaller stretching boards can be used for this purpose, and smaller than normal stretching boards will allow the fur handler to rotate the pelt as it is being scraped.

Proper sized stretchers are also important in the appearance of the finished pelt. Commercial wire stretchers are available for most species, but hand made wooden stretchers do an equally good job when they are shaped properly. When solid stretching boards are used to dry the furs to the proper shape, a wedge shaped belly board must be used between the stretching board and the pelt on the belly side. Furs shrink as they dry, and the belly board prevents the fur from shrinking too tightly and adhering to the stretcher.

Plywood does not make a good wooden stretcher because the edges of the stretchers have to be beveled, and sanded smoothly. Stretchers should be as thin as possible, and of a type of wood free from knots. Cedar siding boards are easily worked into stretchers with hand tools. Siding boards are thicker on one side than the other, so get them wider than needed, and many times, a wedge or two can be cut from the excess on the thicker side of the board.

Different types of furs are handled with different methods, and it is very important to handle the furs exactly the way that the fur trade wants them handled. Most pelts are skinned with a method called "cased", which does not allow a cut up the belly of the skin. Some cased furs are handled with the fur side to the outside, and others are handled with the fur side to tho inside. There are good reasons for this.

Beaver and badgers are properly handled with a skinning method called "open". With this method, the animal is opened with a knife cut from the bottom of the chin all the way down the middle of the belly to the tail. After skinning and fleshing, the pelts are stretched with an oval shape for beaver, and a rectangular shape for badger.

Many good fur handlers wash dirty or bloody pelts to clean and brighten them. Coyote and badger furs, in particular, command better prices when they are clean. If you elect to wash dirty furs, use cold water only, and a liquid or powdered soap. Never use a detergent, or warm water to wash furs, or the fur may slip from the skin, completely ruining it. An old washing machine can be used for this purpose, or a five gallon bucket

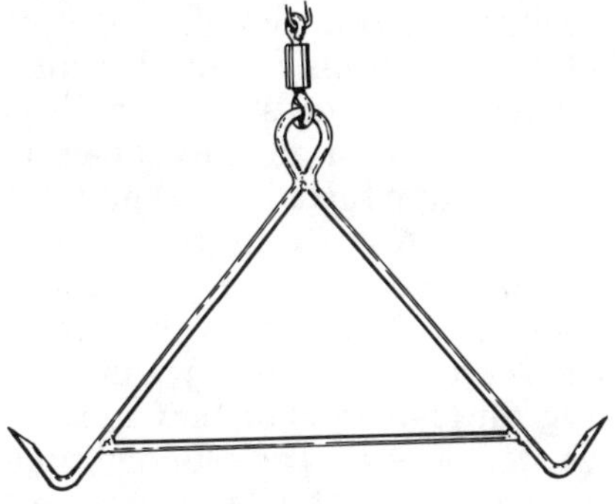

A gambrel is commonly used to suspend a furbearer while skinning.

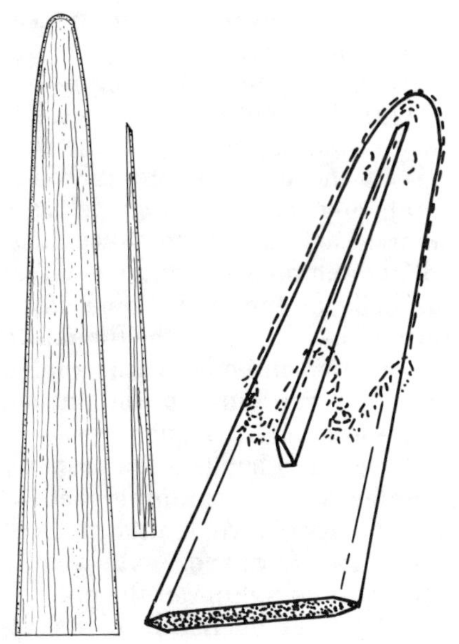

Solid stretching boards must be beveled on the edges and used only with a wedge shaped belly board.

can also be used to wash one skin at a time. Always be sure to rinse the pelt well, and use an electric fan to speed the drying of the wet furs.

Never apply salt to a furbearer's pelt. Furs that are tanned for coats are tanned with a quick tan process, and salted furs will not tan with this method. These pelts may be worthless to the furrier trade. Salted skins can be tanned by taxidermists, who use a completely different method of tanning.

Two basic knife designs are most helpful in skinning. One is a long and narrow blade shape which is most helpful in making opening cuts, splitting furred tails, and most other cuts. Another useful shape is a drop blade, with a rounded cutting edge. These convex cutting blades are most helpful when skinning difficult to skin furs such as beaver and otter. The rounded edge helps to prevent skin punctures, and some trappers use these knife shapes to flesh animal pelts as well.

Knife prices vary a great deal, as do knife qualities. Generally speaking, the more expensive knives are tempered with higher heat, making them harder. This is an advantage in a knife's ability to keep or hold an edge, but the harder knives are also somewhat more difficult to sharpen easily.

A sharp knife certainly makes skinning more enjoyable and safer than trying to skin with a dulled blade. Fortunately, there are a number of knife sharpening aids available today, and all work when they are used properly.

Two factors greatly determine the sharpness of a knife. One is the bevel, or angle at which the cutting edge is sharpened. The other critical factor is the smoothness, or polish, of the cutting edge. Every

A - Muskrat
B - Weasel
C - Female Mink
D - Male Mink, Marten
E - Skunk, Female Fisher
F - Opossum
G - Raccoon, Bobcat
H - Fox, Male Fisher
I - Coyote, Large Bobcat
J - Otter

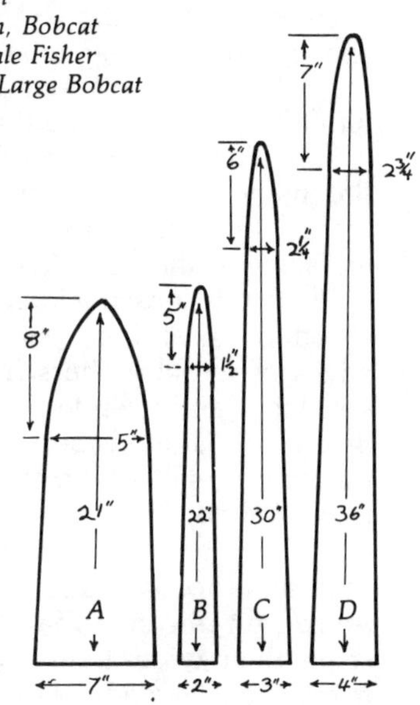

little microscopic nick or gouge dulls a knife, and for any knife to slice properly, the bevel must be exact on both sides of the blade.

New bevels can be most easily cut with hand held or bench rest carbide cutting tools. Simply, new bevels are shaved when the knife blade is stroked from the handle to the knife point. Both sides of the bevel are cut at the same time with these tools, and all nicked or gouged blades should have new bevels cut below the nicks in the blade.

Abrasive knife sharpening tools include whetstones, sharpening steels, and ceramic sticks.

Whetstones come in a variety of textures from coarse and soft to hard and fine. Oil should always be used freely when using whetstones, as the oil will prevent the stone from glazing over, and it will keep the knife blade cool as well. Coarser stones are an advantage for quicker grinding, and the finer stones are used to gain further sharpness by polishing away any tiny grooves left by the coarser stones. Whenever you are using a whetstone, keep the bevel in mind, and lift the blade 30 degrees before making equal numbers of strokes on each side of the knife blade.

Sharpening steels, or ceramic sticks, are usually used to touch up and polish knife blades. Again, keep the angle of bevel at 30 degrees before making sharpening slices against the steel or ceramic stick.

A washing with soap and water cleanses the metal filings from

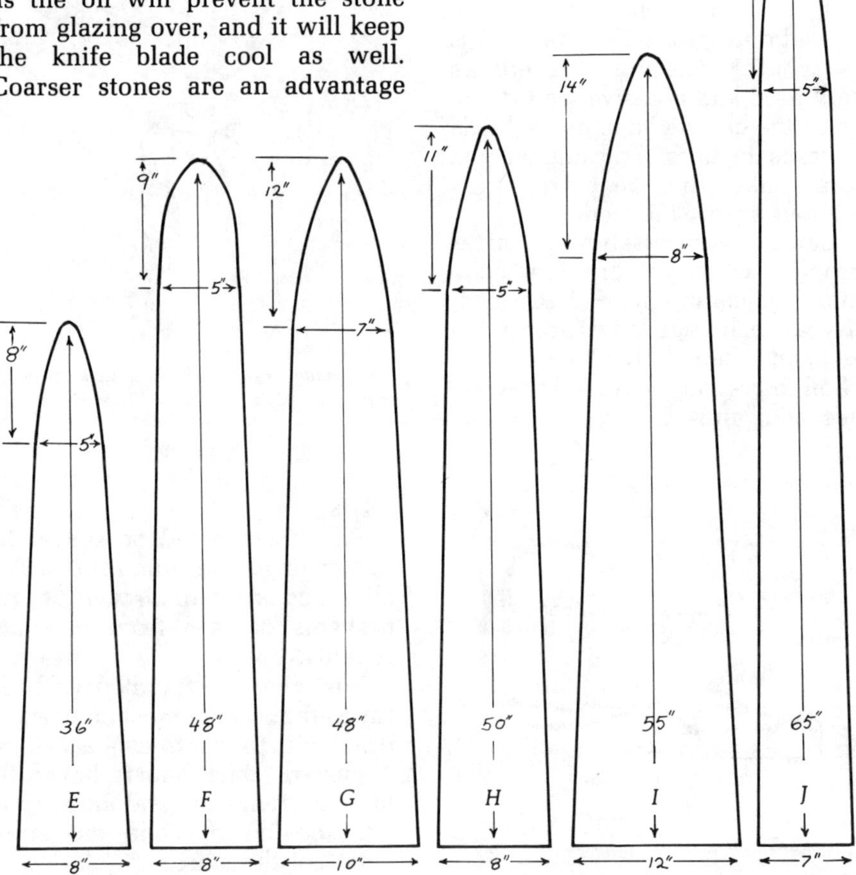

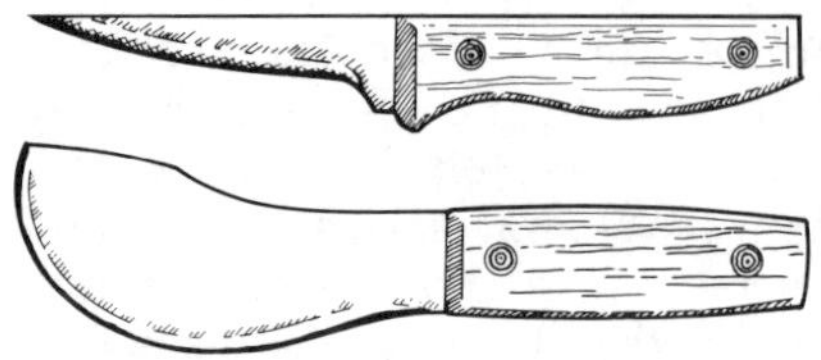

A narrow blade is best for most ripping cuts, and rounded blade is helpful with difficult to skin animals.

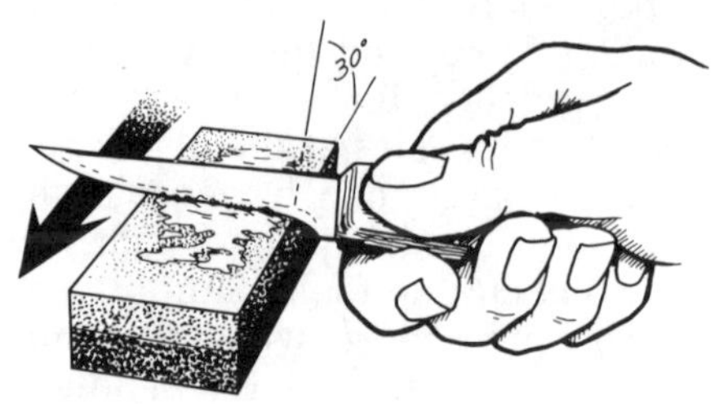

Whetstones should always be used with a light oil.

whetstones, sharpening steels, and ceramic sticks. It is a good idea to do this occasionally to keep the tools in top operating condition.

You can keep your skinning knives sharper while skinning if you insert the blade between the skin and the carcass as you are cutting. This will prevent abrasives in the fur from dulling the blade. Cutting into bones dulls a knife quickly, and one area to be careful in is the mouth of the animal. Teeth are very hard and abrasive, and if you point the cutting edge of the blade towards the nose of the animal, you can make the necessary cuts without hitting the teeth.

Care for your skinning knives properly when you are done skinning by cleaning them of all blood. If you wash your knives, dry them well, and then apply a thin coating of oil to protect them until they are needed again.

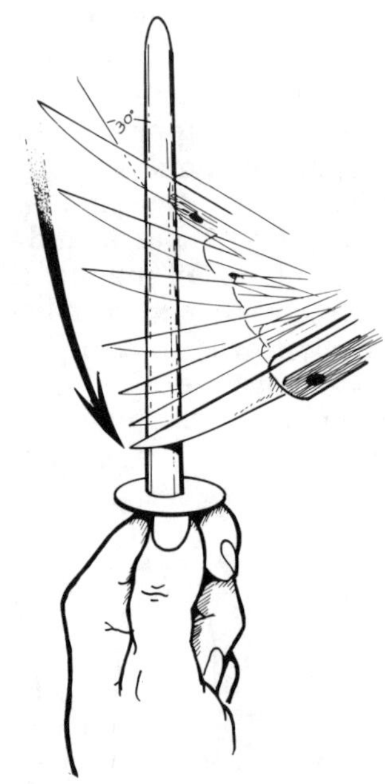

Sharpening steels and ceramic sticks are quick and easy to use.

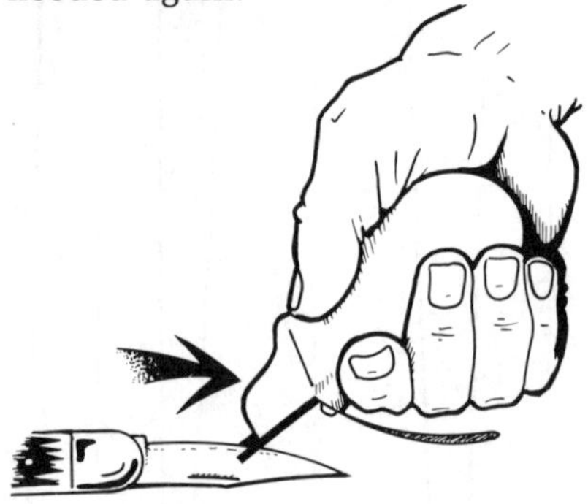

A carbid cutter removes gouges and nicks.

Tips

Raw furs should be suspended by hanging them from rafters. This allows constant air circulation, and prevents damage from pets and rodents.

Furs that are handled with the fur to the outside must be partially dried with the fur to the inside first.

Furred tails must have the tailbone removed, and an opening cut should be made the entire length of the tail.

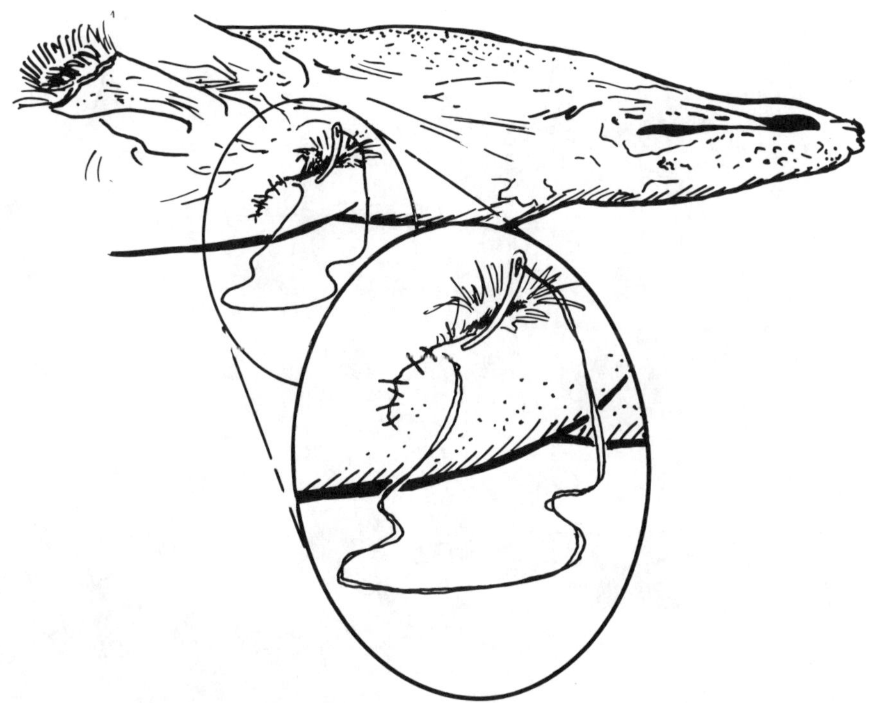

Holes need to be sewn shut while the skin is still pliable. A curved needle is helpful and available at taxidermy shops and veterinarians.

If insects appear to be attacking a pelt during mild weather, freeze the pelt overnight to kill the insects or their eggs before they do any real damage.

If humid weather prevents a wet furbearer from drying properly before it needs to be skinned, skin it wet and place it fur side out on a stretcher. Then, direct air from an electric fan on the wet fur overnight to dry it properly before you turn the fur to the inside on the stretcher.

Combing and brushing pelts greatly helps their appearance by cleaning them and fluffing them.

Do not overstretch pelts. Most pelts are wanted in a long and relatively narrow shape, which allows the fur in the middle of the back to appear as dense as is possible.

Furs that are to be frozen for several months or more should not be fleshed, and they should be wetted before they are wrapped air tight.

Furs stretched open, like badger and beaver, should be suspended in a fur to fur and skin to skin order to prevent the fur sides from getting greasy from the fur hanging next to it.

Wood stretchers can be coated with spar varnish, or shellac, to prolong the life of the stretcher.

Visit your local fur buyers to see how they handle their pelts.

Don't be afraid to ask a fur buyer or experienced trapper for help whenever you need it.

Never pile animals.

Keep animals and furs out of direct sunlight.

Trapping Equipment

THE selection of a suitable trap is an important decision made every time a trapper makes a set to catch an animal. A variety of traps are available for trappers, including foothold traps, body gripping traps, and cage type traps. Each type and style of trap has advantages, and disadvantages, for certain species and certain situations.

Cage type traps have value for the capture of several species. Some trappers use these types of traps where an accidental dog or house cat catch seems likely. These traps are efficient in capturing raccoons, opossums, and skunks. At times, bobcats and badgers are caught in them as well.

Cage traps are somewhat expensive, and they are also cumbersome. It is difficult to carry more than two cage traps at a time, but most trappers have a few cage traps to use to help people who are having trouble in cities with animals causing damage. With the use of cage traps, accidental nontarget catches can usually be released easily by simply opening the trap door.

Cage traps are more difficult to disguise than other types of traps, which makes them more vulnerable to thievery. Still, many

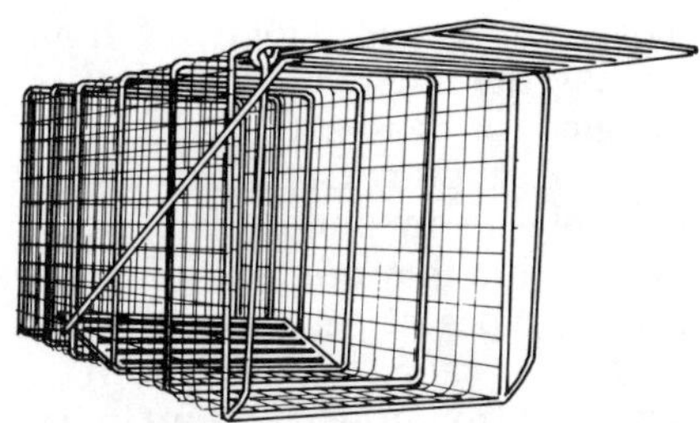

Cage traps are particularly useful in populated areas.

trappers use some where thievery is not likely, such as in or near old barns on private property. Fruit or fish baits are oftentimes used in cage traps to entice the furbearer into the trap. One good trick is to cover the floor of the trap with straw or dirt, which makes a comfortable and natural surface for the furbearer to walk on.

A submarine trap has doors that swing inwardly only.

One variation of a cage trap is known as the submarine trap. This type of trap has two doors that swing inwardly only, and these traps can be effective when used under the water for muskrats. At times they are placed in underwater runs or trails. They can be baited with an ear of corn, or a few carrots. Good locations for these types of traps aren't always available, but they are efficient in suitable locations. Multiple catches do occur at times. Submarine traps should always be submerged to allow a quick drowning of the trapped muskrats.

Body gripping traps are another important tool for trappers. These types of traps are available in different sizes for different species. These traps are oftentimes used submerged in water, and they also have value on dry land for some species. (Many states do regulate the sizes of body gripping traps allowed on dry land, so please be aware of the laws in your own state before you buy or use body gripping traps.)

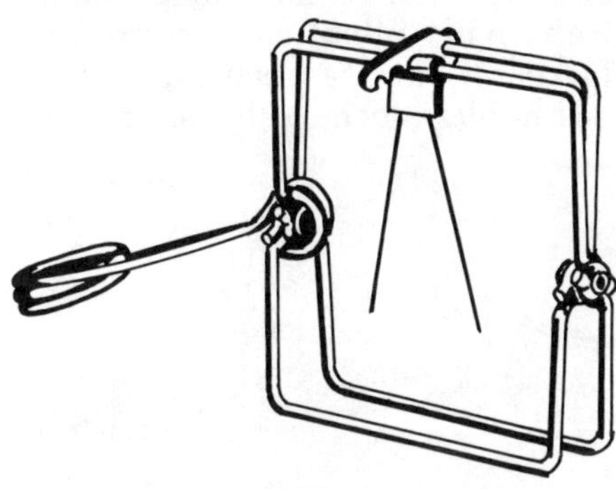

Small body gripping traps are useful for several different furbearers.

Body gripping traps have either one or two springs, and work with a scissor's like action when the trap trigger is fired. The wire triggers can be baited for species which commonly pick up food with their mouths, like muskrats and marten, but baited triggers should not be used with species which pick up bait with their paws, such as raccoon and beaver.

Many times, experienced trappers use body gripping traps by placing them where the furbearer is encouraged to try to go through the trap. This is done by attempting to guide the animal through the trap with the placement of brush or other debris. Many furbearers are caught in body gripping traps when the path through the trap appears to be the path of least resistance.

Some of the more suspicious species, like foxes and coyotes, refuse to enter or be forced into these traps, and avoid them regularly.

Properly set in dryland sets, body gripping traps should always be set so that the trap jaws close from top to bottom, and not from side to side. The object is to allow the trap jaws to strike the furbearer just behind the skull, and across the throat area at the same time. The striking force of the body gripping trap will oftentimes stun the furbearer, and a relatively quick death often occurs by strangulation.

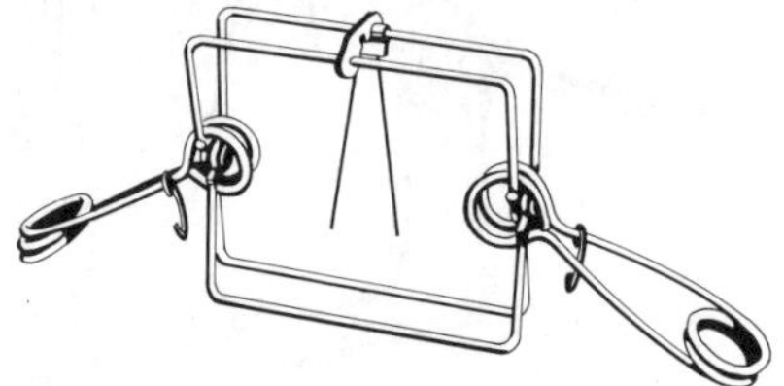

Large body gripping traps usually have two springs for additional power.

Contrary to some opinions, body gripping traps of the proper sizes do not break necks or backs.

When body gripping traps are set on dryland so that the jaws close from side to side, stunning and strangulation are not nearly so sure. Some furbearers might suffer more anxiety and stress than is necessary, and there is also a greater chance of escape from the trap when set in this manner.

When body gripping traps are submerged in water, with baited triggers, it doesn't matter as much if the trap jaws close from side to side or top to bottom. Semi-aquatic furbearers like muskrats and beaver often roll over on their sides to attempt to get the baits, and it is much more difficult to predict the position of the animal when the trap is fired. Contrary to dryland situations, death occurs in approximately the same amount of time whether the submerged animal is strangled, or drowned.

Body gripping traps are oftentimes placed in underwater runs, or trails, and they are very effective in these types of sets. These traps should be placed so that the trap jaws close from top to bottom to try for a stunning blow to the back of the animal's neck, and many furbearers do not appear to struggle in these traps before death occurs.

When these traps are set in underwater runs, it is usually an advantage to place the trap right on the bottom of the run, and then place some sticks for guides over the top of the trap to act as a guide. Most furbearers would prefer to dive, rather than surface, when presented with the alternative.

Foothold traps remain as the single most important tool for trapping. These tools can be used as live traps (or holding devices), or under certain circumstances, as effective killing devices. Properly, they are used both ways by experienced trappers, depending upon the situation, and the species being trapped.

There are many designs of foothold traps, including: longspring traps, coilspring traps, and underspring or jump traps. Some models have different triggering mechanisms, some have a double set of trap jaws, and some models even have a guard apparatus to prevent a captured furbearer from twisting after it is caught. Foothold traps are made in a number of different sizes for different species, and have smooth jaws to prevent injury to the trapped animal.

One extreme value of the foothold trap is the fact that the trap can be completely concealed

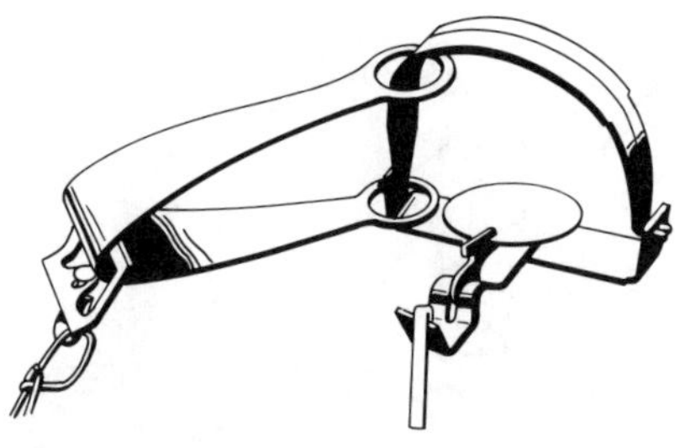

A longspring foothold trap in the closed position.

The same trap open, or set.

either in a water set or a dryland set. This advantage is important, and allows the capture of the more suspicious species.

The key as to how the animals are treated in foothold traps depends upon several factors. Most importantly, foothold traps should be of a proper size for the species. Traps that are much too large for the species oftentimes catch the animal too high on the leg. A foot catch is much more desirable, and lessens the opportunity for the animal to damage itself after it is captured. Relatively short trap chains are also an advantage as they prevent an animal from making long lunges after being caught. Swiveling is important, and a trap that is properly swiveled allows the captured furbearer to twist and roll without stressing the trap or the trapped foot.

The possibility of further entanglement after capture is another consideration in the treatment of the furbearer. Good trappers select trap set locations where the potential catch cannot wrap the trap chain around a small tree, or other solid object. But, the single most important thing for every trapper to realize is that foothold traps must be checked regularly, preferably, early in the morning.

Wild animals appear to be more concerned with a restriction of freedom, rather than any pain, when held in foothold traps. Numbness occurs in the affected limb as circulation is restricted. Many animals can be observed resting or taking naps with a quiet approach to the trap sets.

Occasionally, a skunk, raccoon or gray fox may attack its own foot in a foothold trap. Biting of the affected toes can occur underneath the trap jaws when there is no feeling in the foot, and the animal doesn't recognize it or separate it from the trap. Animals who recognize their own numbed foot do not bite their own foot, and trapped furbearers do not bite their trapped foot above the trap jaws where pain would occur.

Double jawed foothold traps seek to prevent animals like skunks, raccoons and gray foxes from biting numbed feet beneath trap jaws.

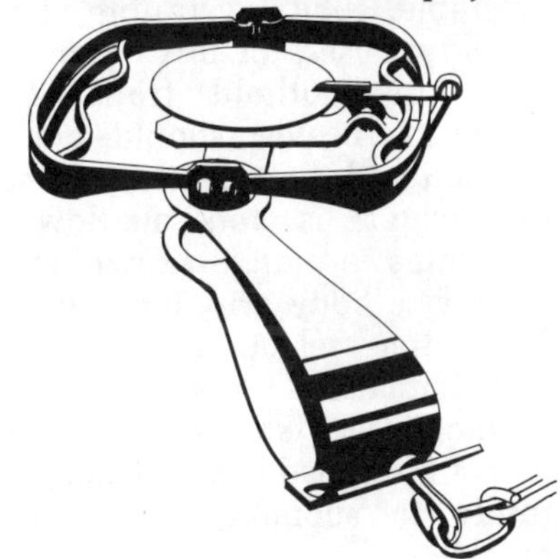

Double jaw models are available for species which might attempt to chew on their own foot.

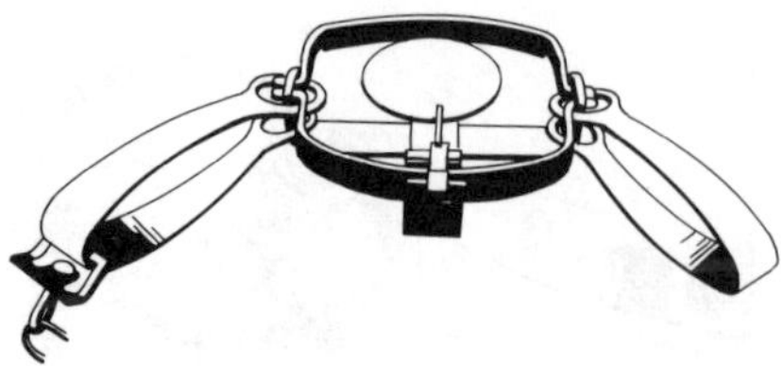

Longspring traps in size #2 and larger usually have two springs.

The second set of trap jaws acts as a barrier, and these designs of foothold traps make good selections for these species.

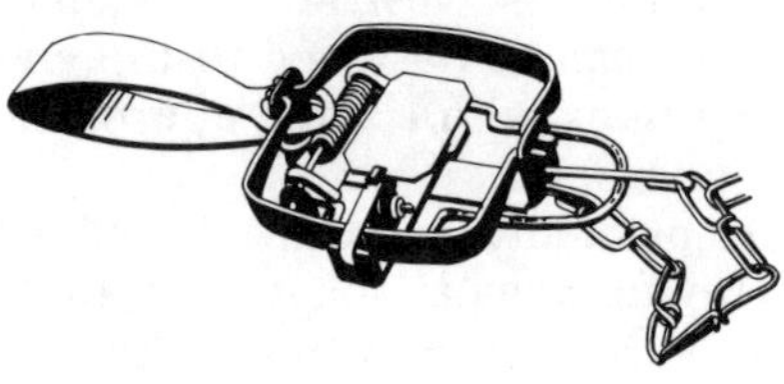

Guard type traps keep an animal from twisting after it is caught.

Muskrats and beaver have small wrists for their body sizes, and an occasional muskrat or beaver will twist out of a foothold trap. This is known as "wring-off", and it can be avoided with a little thought on the part of the trapper. Muskrats can easily be trapped where they have opportunity to drown in deep water, and if deep water is not available, body gripping traps should be used for this species instead of foothold traps. Like muskrats, beaver should not be trapped with foothold traps where the water is too shallow to guarantee a quick drowning. A large size body gripping trap is a far better selection in shallow water situations for beaver, and the foothold traps should be set only where a trapped beaver has opportunity to submerge and drown quickly.

The method of fastening traps is as important as the particular trap

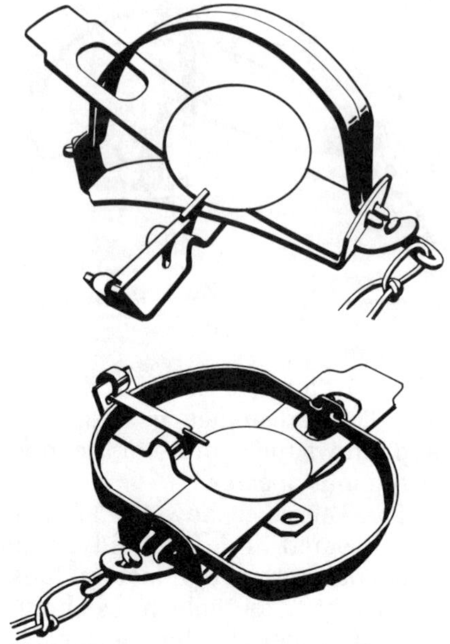

Underspring, or jump traps, in the closed and open positions.

being used. In all instances, the trap stake, or wire used to attach the trap, should be strong enough to hold the largest possible non-target catch. All muskrat trap fastenings should be strong enough to hold raccoons, and all fox traps should be strong enough to hold coyotes or bobcats if they are in the area. It is a mistake to try to economize with a fastening system that is too light. The last thing any trapper wants is for a furbearer to be running around with a trap on its foot.

Equipment needs vary with the species being trapped, the type of habitat being trapped, and the expected weather conditions. There is a lot of variation between mountain marten traplines and southern tidal marsh trapping for nutria and muskrats.

The following guide will suggest tools and equipment that many trappers have found handy for trapping water species, and dryland species.

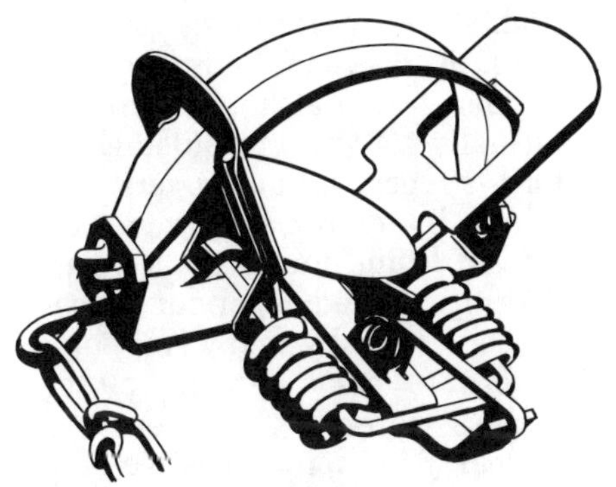

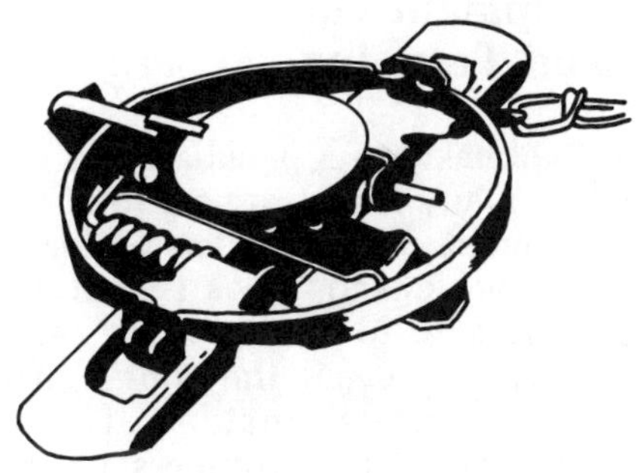

Coilspring traps are favored by many trappers.

Equipment For Water Trapping

Hip boots or chest waders - You will need good quality hip boots or waders to keep warm and dry while trapping in creeks, lakes and marshes. Keep your boots in a good state of repair, and store them away from sunlight for long life.

Packbasket - You will need something to carry your equipment with you on your trapline, and a packbasket is handy. Gear can also be carried in a clean five gallon pail, or a burlap sack.

Gloves - Rubber or neoprene gloves are available in different lengths. Shoulder high gloves, called gauntlets, are favored by many water trappers.

Wire - Strong wire is needed to attach traps. New baling wire or 14 gauge wire is oftentimes used for muskrat, mink and raccoon sets along the water's edge. Heavier wire is needed for beaver and otter sets, and many trappers use #9 wire for this purpose.

Pliers - A pliers is helpful on a trapline to cut wire.

Stakes - Wooden stakes are usually used for water trapping. Stakes can be made from dried lumber, or they can be cut from hardwood trees along the trapline.

Trowel - A trowel or shovel is used by many water trappers to level off places where traps are to be set, and also to dig bait holes.

Hatchet - A hatchet is often carried by water trappers, and is used to cut stakes, and to pound stakes. Many trappers prefer a heavy hatchet.

Clothing - Clothing for water traplines must be warm. Long underwear is a must. Wool shirts and pants are far superior to cotton and blue jeans, and wool will keep you warmest when you are wet. Hats should always be worn to conserve body heat, and many trappers use two pairs of medium weight wool socks when wearing hip boots or waders.

Lures and baits - Lures and/or baits are useful for water trappers.

Slide locks - Slide locks are often attached to traps for several species, including otter, beaver, and raccoon.

Hook stick - Many water trappers carry a stout stick of four or five feet in length. A hook is usually screwed into one end to aid in the search for traps in deeper or silty water. This stick is also used as a wading staff to determine water depth, and as an aid to prevent stumbling. A regular garden hoe can perform the same service, and the hoe blade is sometimes helpful in trap set constructions.

Equipment For Land Trapping

Packbasket - A packbasket is used by many land trappers to carry equipment. Some trappers prefer to attach pockets to the outside of the packbasket to hold lures and urines, to prevent the contamination of traps inside of the packbasket. Other trappers prefer to carry their equipment in clean five gallon buckets.

Gloves - Many land trappers prefer to use gloves while handling and setting land traps. Some land trappers prefer rubber or neoprene gloves, and others prefer leather or cloth gloves.

Trowel - Many trappers use a trowel to dig trap beds under the trap, and this tool is useful to dig bait holes in the ground. A 22 inch long model is very popular, and this tool is also handy to stun trapped animals.

Stakes - Hardwood stakes are used by some land trappers, and they must be driven under the dirt level to prevent a trapped animal from chewing them off. Most land trappers use metal stakes because these types of stakes take a lot of abuse, and most designs will allow a better swiveling action after a furbearer has been caught. Needed lengths vary with the species being trapped, as well as the soil types. Some land trappers also use grapples attached to traps instead of staking the trapped animals in one place. A chain length of four or five feet at least is needed between the grapple and the trap, and a swivel is usually placed somewhere near the trap.

Dirt sifter - A dirt sifter is used by many land trappers to sift dirt over the set traps. These tools are available from trapping supply dealers, or, they can be made with a wooden frame at home. Screens are usually 1/4" mesh welded wire.

Pan covers - Pan covers are preferred by many trappers to keep dirt from filling under the set pan of the trap. Waxed paper cut to proper size is used by many trappers, and others use canvas cloth, fiberglass screening, or even a large leaf. Another alternative is to place a piece of fiberglass insulation under the trap pan.

Hatchet - A hatchet is often used to drive stakes for traps set on dry land. The hatchet is also useful to chop away frozen dirt. A heavy hammer can also be used to drive metal stakes. Some trappers prefer to carry a single bit axe for both driving stakes and chopping frozen dirt.

Lures and baits - Lures, baits and urines are usually used to attract land animals to trap sets.

Catchers - Many land trappers carry a hog catcher (choke stick, catch pole, noose-stick) along on traplines to catch and release accidental or non-target catches. A piece of tubing about four feet can be used to make your own, and simply a cable or rope is inserted through the tube to form a loop at one end. To release an animal, simply place the loop over the animal's head, and hold it down to ground level while releasing the trap.

Preparation

GOOD trappers spend a lot of time preparing for their traplines. Trapping seasons are short, and successful trappers will have their traps ready, and every little thing organized so that they won't be slowed down or bothered by a shortage of any necessity.

If you do decide to trap, the one thing that you must have besides a trap is a trapline. In most states, you will have to have landowner permission to trap on private lands. If you are a farm boy or girl, you might be able to get permission on all the land that you want to with a few phone calls, but generally speaking, most trappers have to go out and request permission to trap.

The best time to contact farmers is not when they are in the field working, but during rainy days when they are more apt to be home and have more time to visit with you. They have every right to talk with you about what you hope to do on their lands, so you should give the landowners every consideration and opportunity to do so.

If you are going to meet a farmer for the first time, wear clean clothes. Clothes do not need to be expensive to make a favorable impression, but cleanliness helps a lot.

Don't be afraid to ask for permission to trap. Just walk up to the landowner and introduce yourself. Tell him where you are from, and ask him if he would mind if you tried to catch a few furbearers during trapping season on his land.

Always be polite, even if the landowner isn't. Never answer questions with "Naw" or "Nope". Your answers should be "No sir", and "Yes sir".

Little tricks that may help you include looking the landowner in the eye while you are talking. Smile a lot. If you have completed a trapper education course, say so. If the landowner fears for the safety of livestock or pets, show him or her a trap, and explain how it works.

Most landowners will appreciate the fact that you stopped to ask for trapping permission, whether they decide to let you trap or not. Expect some landowners to refuse your request to trap, and never argue. Thank them for considering your request anyway.

Many landowners will allow you to trap if you respect their requests. If the farmer or rancher asks you to not drive on a certain field, or not to trap in a certain area, or whatever, follow the landowner's request exactly. Always close gates that you open, and always carry your litter home with you to dispose of properly.

Always maintain a good relationship with your landowners. Farmers and ranchers appreciate it when you stop to show them your catch once in a while. You can always offer to help remove any damage causing animals when a problem arises for the landowner. (Check your laws first.) To show your appreciation, consider sending a Christmas card or taking a box of candy to the landowner after the trapping season is over. They will appreciate that consideration, and remember it the next time that you ask for permission to trap on their lands.

Never assume that you have landowner permission to trap from year to year. Stop and visit with the landowners each year to be certain that you are still welcome on their lands.

If you are aware that a farm may be owned by someone other than the person farming the land, it is always a good idea to check with the landowner as well as the farmer. Sometimes, both the farmer and the landowner will give trapping permission without checking with each other. It is an awful disappointment to be setting your traps on the first day of the trapping season only to find someone else also setting traps.

You should always prepare yourself by scouting your trapline before the season begins. You might find "fur pockets", where there is an abundance of animals. Then again, you might find that there are few animals, and it is to your advantage to know where to concentrate your trapping efforts.

Try to do your scouting a few weeks before the season starts so you will have a better idea where the animals are living, and feeding. Some trappers make mock sets, without a trap, and return a day or two later to see if furbearers responded to the sets as is evidenced by tracks. Most lures are attractive to a wide variety of furbearers, and a little application of lure at your mock sets can help you determine which species are present.

Scouting for furbearers on your trapline offers you further opportunity to prepare your trapline for trapping season. Cubbies can be constructed to hold a bait and trap later when the season opens. Oftentimes, a small stream can be nar-

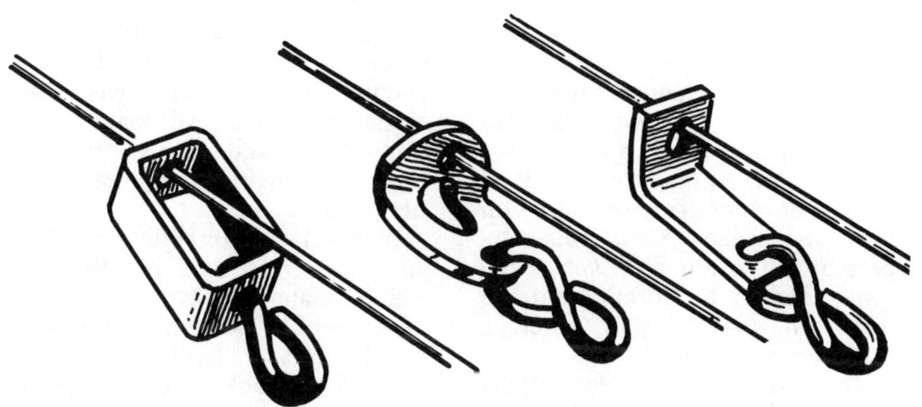

One way sliding locks can be purchased from trapping supply dealers, or made at home with basic tools.

rowed with rocks or brush to make a better natural set for later use. Any preparation of the trapline that you do before the season is to your advantage. It saves you time later on, and another advantage is that the set constructions have time to weather, and look more natural by the time that trapping season is open.

One scouting trick is to carry a notebook with you. Write down things that might help you later on; like where you notice trails, feeding areas, dens, or an abundance of tracks or other signs.

You must prepare your traps, even if they are new, in advance of the trapping season. New traps should be cleaned of oil. Some trappers do this by taking the new traps to a hose type car wash, and then wash the oil off of the traps with the pressured spray of hot water and soap. Older traps that are rusty must be cleaned of rust and caked on dirt. A wire brush is sometimes used for this purpose.

Every trap, new and old alike, must be checked for flaws. A good time to do this is right after the traps are cleaned up. Flaws to look for include nicked or damaged chains, sloppy trap pans, and any sharp metal edges. Pay close attention to swivels, and if they bind, you will have to shorten the crimped end with a hacksaw before you tighten the swivel loop back up in a vise, or with a strong pliers. Rough edges should be smoothed with a metal file, and sloppy trap pans can be adjusted on many traps with a screwdriver.

Set each trap to make sure that all parts are working properly. Trap pans that set too high or too low can be adjusted with a pliers by bending the arm with the trap dog on it inwardly or outwardly a little bit at a time until the desired level pan height is reached. Check out the end of the trap dog, and the notch in the trap pan to be sure that everything is smooth. A few licks with a good file will correct any problems.

If trap tags are required in your state, or you wish to have your name on your trap, now is a good time to apply the tags. Wire them on with a strong wire because some animals may attempt to tear them off after they are caught.

You might consider applying drowning locks to the traps you intend to use for beaver, otter, or raccoon at this time. They needn't be applied to the end of the trap chain, and work best when applied on the trap chain six or eight inches away from the trap.

Many land trappers cut the traditional ring off of the end of the trap chains on new traps, and attach a swivel connector, large sized S-hook, or other device for use with metal trap stakes. Also, some trappers attach another swivel in the trap chain to be certain that the trap will swivel freely when a furbearer is captured.

The vast majority of trappers prefer to dye their traps. Two purposes are served by dyeing traps. For one, a dyed trap is easier to conceal than a shiny trap. This does help to prevent thievery, and makes the trap appear to be more of a natural object to a furbearer. Another purpose in dyeing traps is to deodorize and protect them from rusting. Deodorizing traps is important for several land species of furbearers, especially foxes and coyotes.

Before the traps will "take" dye, they should be lightly rusted. There are a number of ways to speed up the rusting of traps. You might elect to bury your traps in a hole in the garden for a week or ten days, or the same result can often be achieved by just leaving the shiny traps in the grass where rain and dew speed up the rusting process. If you are in a real hurry to speed up the slight rusting of your new traps, you can immerse them overnight in a bucket filled with a ½ and ½ mixture of vinegar and water, or salt water.

Trap dyeing is usually accomplished by boiling the traps with a solution of water and dye in a bucket, tub, or the bottom half of a barrel. Trap dyeing compounds are available from many trap supply dealers, or you may elect to gather your own natural dyes.

Some natural trap dyes used by trappers include maple bark, hemlock twigs, sumac berries, walnut hulls, sweet ferns, and sagebrush twigs. All make good trap dyes, and many trappers economize by collecting their own native dyes.

If you decide to collect and use your own trap dye, put the collected materials in small cloth sacks, or old pairs of pantyhose. The natural dyes will be released through the sacks during the boiling process, and this will help a great deal in keeping the debris from attaching to your traps as you remove them from the boiling water.

Allow yourself plenty of time when you decide to dye your traps. Trappers usually begin the trap dyeing process by building a fire in the morning, and arranging concrete blocks or bricks in a position to hold the bucket or barrel above the fire to allow a continual feeding of the fire. The container, water and trap dye can be placed on the concrete blocks to begin heating as soon as the fire has been started. Be sure to fill the container no more than two thirds full. You must allow room for the water to boil, and further space will be taken up when traps are placed in the heated solution. If it is convenient, it is nice to have a water hose near the fire so that water can be added as needed. Do keep a pair of heavy gloves near by when boiling the traps to help prevent hand burns from heated water or hot traps.

If you wish, you can keep a piece of tin or sheet metal over the top of the container to speed up the water heating process. But, this piece of metal can become very hot, and it should never be handled without a heavy pair of gloves on your hands.

The slightly rusted traps can be lowered into the boiling solution

Wax fires must be smothered. Be sure to keep the end of the tin or plywood board nearest you lower to direct the flames away from body and face.

whenever you are ready to do so. The traps should never be thrown into the heated solution; to prevent the splashing of hot water. Instead, use a stick with a clothesline hook screwed into the end, or a similar tool. It is best to not tie the traps into bunches for the dyeing process. Tied traps can become entangled in the boiling container, and this complicates the safe removal of the traps.

The length of time it takes for the traps to take on a dark color varies with the condition of the traps and the quality of the dye. If your dye is strong, most traps will take on a dark color in twenty or thirty minutes of boiling. The addition of more dye or a longer time in the boiling dye water will also color the traps darker.

Before you remove the traps from the boiling water, you should lay down a piece of cardboard or plywood to lay the traps on. This will help keep the traps clean. Many trappers prefer to hang the newly dyed traps on a clothesline or tree branches to cool and air out for a few days. Remember to wear your gloves whenever you are handling hot traps. Burns are painful, and avoidable with a little thought.

Properly dyed traps can be packed away and stored for trapping as soon as they are perfectly dry. Dyed traps are odorless, or nearly odorless, and if you keep the dyed traps free from the contaminating odors during handling and storage, they will be in good enough condition to catch foxes and coyotes.

Some trappers prefer to treat their traps further after the dyeing process by waxing them. A thin coat of wax over a trap does serve as an odorless lubricant to speed up the action of the trap, and further protects the trap from moisture which can cause the trap to begin rusting again. One disadvantage of wax is that wax does pick up odors more easily than traps that are only dyed.

Body gripping traps should not be waxed. Waxing makes them slip-

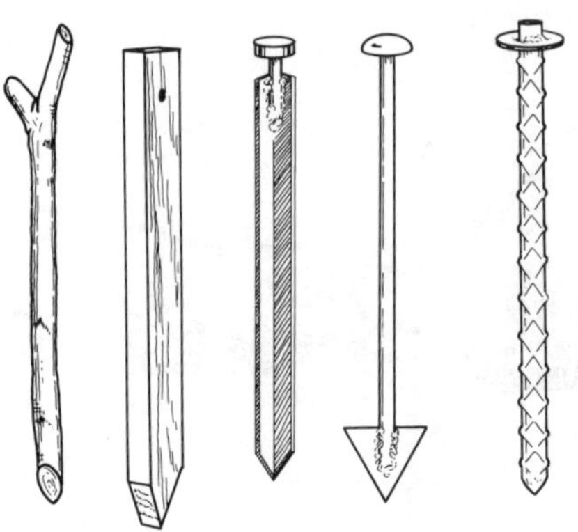

Wooden and metal trap stakes should be made or purchased before trapping season begins.

pery, difficult to set, and unpredictable in your hands. There is no reason, or need, to wax body gripping traps.

The waxing process for foothold traps is best accomplished with a separate process. But, before you decide to wax your traps, please be aware that wax is flammable. You must select a suitable place, outside, to wax traps, and importantly, you must be prepared to smother the wax fire safely in the event that the wax does catch fire. Wax fires can be dangerous, and trap waxing should only be done with adult supervision.

The container to hold the wax must have a smooth rim all around the top. Some pails have humped rims where the handles attach. Do not use these types of pails, as an accidental fire can be very difficult to smother whenever a piece of tin or sheet metal cannot be placed flatly over the top of the container.

A Coleman type camp stove is very handy for waxing traps, and it is somewhat safer than a wood fire because the flames can be more readily controlled. Either way, with a wood or stove fire under the wax container, keep the flames from rising along the sides of the container. Open flames are what might ignite the wax in the container.

If a wax fire does result, don't panic. Put on your heavy gloves, and smother the fire by laying the handy piece of tin or sheet metal over the container. As you lay the metal over the pail or bucket, keep the end nearest you lower at all times. This will direct the flames away from you.

Do not, under any circumstances, attempt to put out a wax fire with water. Water will only spread the fire.

Prepared trap waxes are available from trapping supply dealers. You can also get good results by melting pure canning wax in the container. (Canning wax is available at your local grocery store.)

Some trappers prefer to melt wax on top of a layer of water in the container, but the best waxing results are usually obtained with pure wax. The wax does need to get hot, and traps are usually immersed in the hot wax for thirty seconds or so, or until bubbles from the trap stop coming to the surface. This time allows the trap to become very hot, and allows a very thin coat of wax to form as the trap is removed from the pail with a hook. If the wax is not hot enough, or the trap is just dipped into the wax, it will take on a thick coat of wax which is prone to chipping and flaking.

Other preparations for a trapline include the purchases of supplies. State trapping association conventions often attract a goodly number of trapping supply dealers. Wise trappers shop around, compare prices, and evaluate new products. Most trapping supply dealers are friendly and helpful, so don't be afraid to ask questions. The chances are that the trapping supply dealer you ask is an experienced trapper, and he is in the trapping supply business because he enjoys helping other trappers.

Some trapping supply dealers send out catalogs regularly, and you can usually get on these mailing lists with a request, or with a nominal fee to send the catalog to you. Staying on these mailing lists is easy if you continue to buy supplies from these firms.

Several trapping publications carry ads from trapping supply dealers. If you start buying your supplies well in advance of the trapping season, and shop around, there is a good chance that you can get your supplies at bargain prices.

It is an advantage to cut and make your own wooden stakes far in advance of trapping season. Hardwood branches or saplings cut easiest in the early summer when the wood is softest. If you want to, you can peel the bark or whittle it away to allow your trap stakes to harden as they dry.

If you decide to trap on dryland during the winter in an area where the ground freezes hard, you will need to collect dry dirt during the summer, and store it away until you need it to cover your traps. Many trappers sift the clods out of the dry dirt as it is collected. This dry dirt can be stored in clean cans, buckets with lids, or two thicknesses of garbage bags as long as they are only partially filled.

Being prepared to trap is just about as important as knowing how to trap. Good trappers seem to be busy all of the time, making bait, cutting stakes, overhauling traps, scouting their traplines, or by doing any number of things to be sure that everything will be ready when it is needed.

Swiveling around the metal stake is an important consideration for the trapped animal. Lap link connectors and S-hooks are available at hardware stores, and several commercial products are available from trapping supply dealers.

OPOSSUM — Didelphis Marsupialis

Order — Marsupialia
Family — Didelphidae

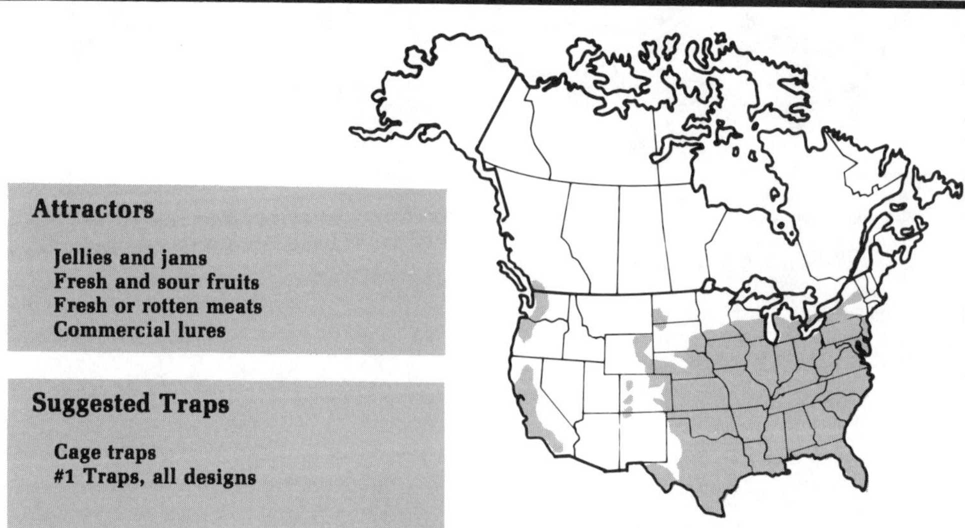

Attractors

Jellies and jams
Fresh and sour fruits
Fresh or rotten meats
Commercial lures

Suggested Traps

Cage traps
#1 Traps, all designs

The Opossum

FOSSILS of opossums have been dated at 70 million years of age, making the opossum a North American resident during the time of dinosaurs. A marsupial, opossums have pouches in which to incubate newborn offspring. The nearly hairless tail of the opossum is prehensile, making it the only native furbearer with an ability to grasp things with its tail. Opossums appear to have little intelligence, and opossums are commonly caught by novice and experienced trappers.

Description

Opossums are grayish animals with naked ears and nearly naked tails. Males are usually larger than females. The males may measure up to 36 inches in length, including the tail of 12 to 14 inches. Weights average around 7 pounds for males, and 5 for females. An occasional male might weigh as much as 10 pounds or a little more.

Ears are soft and leathery, and white tipped around the outer edge. Ragged ears are common in the northern parts of the opossum's range, and usually the result of frost damage.

Male opossums have a gland under their chins which secrete fluids that often stain their chests a yellow color.

There are 5 toes on each foot, and the hind feet have a toe that resembles a thumb. All toes have toenails except the thumbs of the hind feet.

Opossums have 50 teeth, more than any other American mammal. Four canine teeth are present.

An opossum brain is very small in comparison to body size, and opossums are thought to be less intelligent than many other species.

The only North American marsupial, female opossums have pouches on their stomachs, where young are incubated after birth.

Color variations do occur in the wild, and some opossums are darker in color. Rarely, opossums may be reddish or reddish brown in color.

Distribution

The opossum was a southern animal until the 1890's, when a range expansion began to occur. The opossum is now found as far north as New York and occasionally in Maine. The opossum does not thrive in arid regions, or the Rocky Mountains. The species thrive on the west coast states from Mexico to southern British Columbia.

Opossums can adapt to a variety of habitat types, including forests, swamps, prairies, and farmlands.

Opossums are presently harvested by trapping in 33 states.

Sign

Opossum tracks are different, and easily recognizable by the thumb print left by the hind foot. Opossum tracks may be found just about anywhere as opossums appear to wander many places, and they may or may not use trails for convenience in traveling.

Droppings are rarely found, and it appears that droppings are left indiscriminately as the opossum travels.

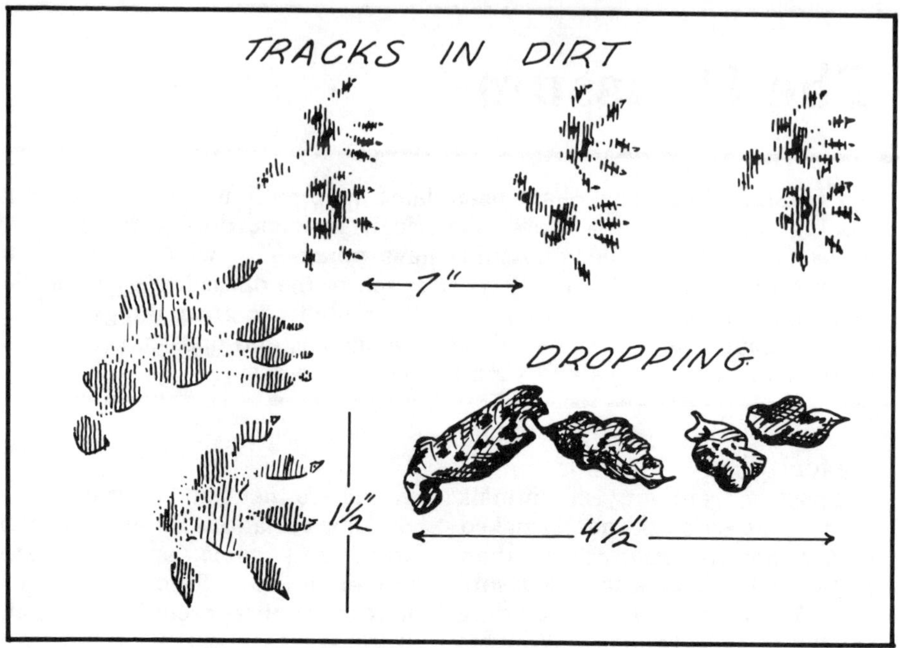

Good places to look for opossum sign are garbage dumps, old buildings, and log or brush piles.

Reproduction

Opossums have 2 annual litters over much of their range. In far northern areas, one litter per year is typical.

The two peak breeding times are February, and June, in much of the opossum range.

Birth is just 13 days after conception. After the newborn are cleaned by the mother opossum, they climb in a hand over hand fashion to the mother's pouch, where they attach themselves to a nipple. The newborn young are very tiny, smaller than honeybees. It takes 22 to 24 newborn opossums to equal the weight of a common penny.

The newborn young appear to be only partially developed, except for the front feet, which are needed to grasp to help the newborn travel the several inches to the pouch.

Once secured to the nipple, the newborn opossum does not let go for 6 or 7 weeks. After 80 days in the pouch, young opossums begin to venture outside of the pouch. They begin climbing on the mother's fur, occasionally riding there as the mother travels.

Young opossums grow rapidly, and the first litter of the year is weaned and off on their own by mid-May. The second litter is usually born about 4 weeks later.

Average litter sizes are about 7 or 8 in southern states, and 10 in northern states.

Six years of age is considered old for an opossum.

Habits

Opossums have an ability to feign death, called "playing possum". In this condition, the animal appears unconscious, the mouth opens slightly, drooling occurs, the feet clutch together, and the entire body becomes limp as in death. Not all opossums "play possum", and the condition is induced by fear, or other stresses.

Opossum sets can be very simple. If the trap is lightly covered, a more valuable furbearer might be captured.

Whether this condition is voluntary or involuntary is not known, nor fully understood. One theory is that the opossum suffers a short circuiting of the nervous system, known as catatonic shock. The condition is much more apt to happen during daylight hours, which suggests that the animal might be able to trigger the response deliberately as a defense mechanism.

Opossums are clean animals, and spend time grooming themselves.

Underground dens are favored by opossums, and the species commonly rake piles of leaves or grass for bedding, which they transport into the dens by grasping the pile with their tails, and carrying the bedding aloft to the nest.

Opossums are good tree climbers, and they seem to prefer to climb smaller trees where they can use their tails as an aid for grasping. If suitable underground den sites are not available, an opossum will often use a larger hollow tree for a temporary daytime den.

The use of dens is sporadic except when young are being reared, and it appears that opossums use any convenient den site as their nighttime activities are interrupted by dawn. Natal dens are an exception, and the female regularly uses the same den as the offspring are being reared.

Opossums do not hibernate, but they do store up layers of fat in northern ranges to sustain them during periods of severe cold and deep snow. When cold periods last for more than two weeks, the opossums do have to travel to seek more food, and both ear tips freezing and tail end freezing does occur at these times. These frozen appendages do separate, leaving many northern opossums with rather ragged ears and stubby tails.

The sense of smell is well developed in opossums, and helpful in the search for foods, which vary a great deal according to opportunity. Insects are a most important food, as are worms, eggs of ground nesting birds, and young mice or rabbits. Fruits are eaten when available, and opossums frequently scavenge any dead animals found. Roads serve the resource as an important source of food as traffic killed insects, birds, and small mammals are found regularly.

The home range of an opossum is about 50 acres. They are not territorial to the extent that they defend their ranges from other opossums. Many opossum ranges overlap, and good quality habitats may support 20 opossums to the square mile.

Opossums do frequent the edges of water for food, and they are rarely found more than 750 yards away from water of some sort.

Trapping

Because opossums are attracted to almost every type of bait or lure, they are commonly caught in traps set for other species.

Traps deliberately set for opossums should include either cage traps, or foothold traps no larger than size #1. Opossums will enter cage traps without hesitation, and they will step into uncovered foothold traps as well.

Opossum traps may be staked solidly, or attached to convenient clogs. The method of attachment should be as strong as is needed should a stronger animal be caught, such as a raccoon.

Set constructions to catch opossums can be simple. There is no need to dye traps to catch opossums. Baits can be placed in empty tin cans, in hollow logs, or in holes in the ground with a trap placed where it would be convenient for the opossum to stand while investigating the bait.

Lures are usually not used to capture opossums, because opossums are attracted to virtually every smell that might suggest food. Fruit baits, either fresh or rotting, are attractive to opossums and help to prevent accidental captures of free roaming dogs and cats. Good selective baits include apples, jellies and jams, and persimmons where they are available. The attractiveness of persimmons can be enhanced with an overnight freezing in sandwich bags, and if you take care to properly conceal your traps with this bait, you may be rewarded with a gray fox catch.

Do not leave your baits exposed. Cover them lightly, as the opossum has a good nose and will locate the bait. Exposed baits may attract birds, and should be avoided for that reason.

Due to the small ranges of opossums, they may be trapped without concern for over harvest. Even though opossum ranges are small, they are erratic in their travel habits, and it can take them days or weeks to happen by your sets.

Dispatch

Opossums are oftentimes dispatched by shooting in the head with a .22. Care should be taken to

Bait or lure can be placed under the crotch. Use a strong wire connection in case a raccoon is captured.

place the killing shot because opossum brains are small.

Opossums can be killed with a neck breaking technique. The animal is stunned first with a blow to the top of the head with a trowel, or trap stake. Then, a trap stake or trowel handle can be placed over the neck of the opossum while it is laying flat on its belly, and this stake or trowel handle is stood on with one foot on each side of the opossum's neck. Neck breaking occurs when the animal is pulled upwards by the tail and hind feet, and the neck separation can easily be felt.

Controls

More opossums are probably killed by cars than are harvested by man and natural predators put together. Roads do provide a significant supply of foods for the species, and their plight is compounded by the fact that they do not see well at distances.

Free roaming dogs and great horned owls probably kill more opossums than any other predators.

Predation by other natural predators is not thought to be significant.

Opossums are relatively free of parasites living on the outside of their bodies, possibly because they frequently change dens and this activity might keep them from reinfesting themselves from contact with infested bedding.

Roundworms, tapeworms, and flatworms do afflict the species however, and tapeworms can become so numerous that they fill the entire stomach area.

Values

Opossums are not serious predators upon any species, and they are more of a threat to ground nesting birds and their eggs than they are to other wildlife. The species does provide a service by cleaning up carrion.

Although opossum fur doesn't command a high price, annual harvests by man exceed one million animals, and the fur value does bring 2 or 3 million dollars to hunters and trappers in many states.

The meat of opossum is edible, and appreciated in some areas of America.

An occasional opossum will raid a chicken house.

Fur Handling

Opossum furs are handled cased, with the fur on the inside. The opening cut is made from the inside of one hind leg to the other. Two more cuts can then be made from the base of the tail, around the vent, to the opening cut. The fur can then be separated from the hind legs, and severed around the base of the furless tail. Hang the opossum from a gambrel, and pull the fur down over the shoulder area, where you will have to use finger and thumb pressure to skin each leg down to the forearms individually. The fur should be separated above the front feet with knife cuts, and then the skin can be pulled down to the ear area, where knife cuts will be needed to free the ears. Knife cuts will also be needed over the eyes, and the final knife cut should leave the nose attached to the pelt.

Opossum pelts are greasy and fatty, and they must be fleshed well. Most trappers prefer to use a fleshing beam and a two handled fleshing knife to properly flesh opossum skins. The skin is light and tender, especially around the pouch area of females, and care should be taken to prevent the tearing of the skin during the fleshing process.

An opossum pelt can be fleshed over a stretching board with a single handled fleshing knife. A dull edge is best, and care should also be taken with this process to prevent a tearing of the thin skin.

Opossum pelts may be stretched on wire stretchers or wooden stretchers. If wooden stretchers are used, a wedge shaped belly board should be inserted along the belly side of the fur to prevent the drying skin from shrinking too tightly to the stretcher.

Properly fleshed and stretched opossum furs take from several days to a week to dry under average cool temperatures.

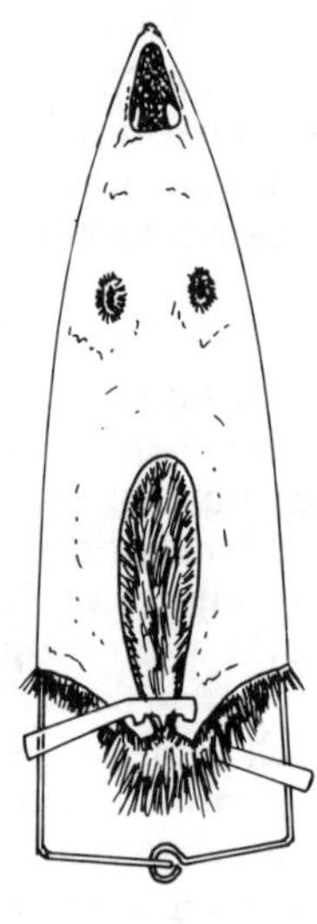

BEAVER — Castor Canadensis
Order — Rodentia
Family — Castoridae

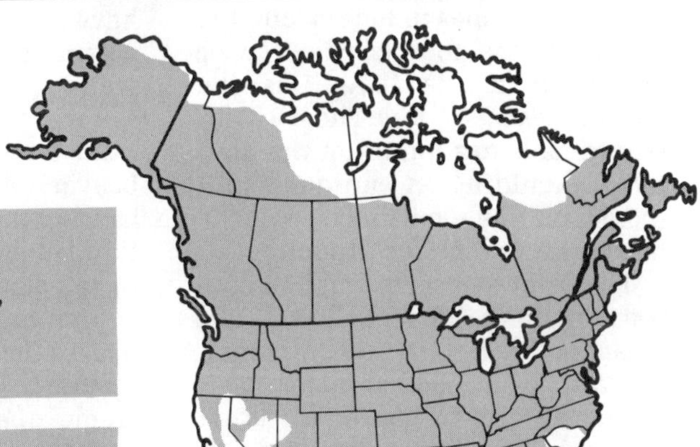

Attractors

Thumb sized sticks of poplar, cottonwood, willow
Commercial lures

Suggested Traps

Large sized body gripping traps
#4 Jump traps
#4 Longspring traps

The Beaver

THE beaver is the largest North American rodent. A common furbearer, the beaver inhabits waterways of every North American state and Canadian Province. A unique paddle shaped tail distinguishes the species, and self-sharpening incisor teeth allow beavers to mow down sizable trees. Beaver often alter the landscape with the construction of dams, canals and lodges. Beavers are territorial as long as the habitat will support family groups, called colonies.

Description

Beavers continue to grow in size throughout life, and weights in excess of 60 or 70 pounds do occur when foods are abundant and accessible during the entire year. Unlike many other species, females are as large as males of the same age, and they sometimes are heavier.

A paddle shaped, leathery tail, positively identifies the species. An adult's tail is usually about 10 inches long, and 5 or 6 inches wide, with a thickness of ½ inch in the middle.

The hind feet of beaver are fully webbed, and large. These feet often measure 6 inches in length, and the spread of the toes is equal to or greater than the length as the beaver swims. Five toes with strong nails are found on the hind feet, including a unique split toenail on one toe which serves the beaver as a comb for grooming.

The front feet seem small in contrast to the hind feet. These feet measure 2½ to 3 inches in length, and are not webbed at all.

Guard hairs in beaver fur are 2 inches in length, overlaying a soft and dense underfur about an inch deep. Colors vary from section to section, and from blonde colors to nearly black.

Both male and female beavers have large glands, called castors, beneath the skin on the lower bellies. These glands produce an oil which the beaver combs into its fur to waterproof it. This oil is also deposited by the beaver at selected locations as territorial markers or as a communication to other beavers.

Beaver have transparent eyelids which cover the eyes as the beaver submerges, enabling the beaver to see well when submerged as the eyeball is protected from abrasive particles suspended in the water.

The ears and nose of a beaver have valves that close as a beaver submerges, preventing the entry of water.

Two upper and two lower incisor teeth dominate the front of a beaver's mouth. The upper incisors overlap the lower incisors, and friction from chewing causes the teeth to self-sharpen to chisel sharpness.

Similar to birds and reptiles, beaver have a single lower body opening, known as a cloaca. This single opening serves the urinary and bowel tracts, the secreted oil from the castor glands, and covers the reproductive organs of both males and females.

Distribution

It is possible that beaver occupy more areas today than when the white men first came to this country. The total numbers of beaver can never be as high as it once was due to the destruction of habitat by man.

Beaver are adaptable to a wide variety of climates, and food types. The species prefers to eat the soft bark of various deciduous trees and shrubs, but it can survive on water plants and grasses in the northern tundra.

Beaver live in every North American state and Canadian Province. This species is currently harvested by trapping in 46 states.

Sign

Evidence of beaver is usually abundant. Lodges, dams and felled trees are positive proof that beaver were present.

When food is abundant and water levels stable, beaver leave very little sign at times, especially where bank dens are common. Still, cut and peeled sticks can usually be found, and chiseled tooth mark grooves around the finger and thumb sized sticks make positive identification easy.

Beaver tracks can often be found in muddy locations, and the hind foot track of a beaver is unmistakable. Drag marks from the flat tail are often obvious as well.

Beaver droppings are woody, with a large pellet shape, and they are always found in water.

Reproduction

Beaver usually live in family units, consisting of the older mated pair, young from the previous year, and young from the current year, called kits.

Breeding season takes place in late January or February in most states. Yearling beaver are about 22 months of age at this time, and they are evicted from the colony at this time to relocate and seek mates of their own.

The gestation period of beavers is 107 days and the adult male and kits usually take up a temporary residence in a bank den while the new litter is being born in April, May or June. The birthing process may take several days, and 3 to 5 kits are a typical litter size.

Beaver kits are fully furred when born, their eyes are open, and the incisor teeth are visible. Newborn beaver kits take to the water easily, and they might begin swimming, before they are one day old.

Most adult beaver are monogamous, and stay with their mate throughout life. A beaver is considered to be old at 12 years of age.

Habits

Beaver require deep water for protection from enemies, and they alter the landscape a great deal with dam building and flooding. Dams can be hundreds of feet in length, and vary in height from only a few feet to 7 or 8 feet, and even higher at times.

Permanent lodges are often constructed by piling layer after layer of sticks into a large conical form above the waterline. Two or more underwater tunnels are then chewed up into the pile, and an inner chamber hollowed out to serve as a living quarters. Finally, the outside of the lodge is plastered with mud and rocks, except for the peak, which is left porous enough to allow an air exchange to the inner chamber. There are two levels in the chamber. One is near the waterline near the "plunge" holes, where the beaver shed water before climbing to the higher resting or nesting areas.

In areas prone to flooding, or where strong currents may be present, beaver usually construct bank dens by digging tunnels from underwater up into banks. Bank dens often have two or more submerged entrances. Many times the beavers will construct a pile of sticks over the tops of the underground living chambers. These piles of sticks are sometimes called "caps".

Shallow pockets are sometimes dug into banks near the waterline, and these are known as "feed pockets" where beaver will often prefer to eat.

In northern areas, beaver construct "feed piles" by submerging large amounts of small trees and limbs to serve as a food source after ice prevents the beaver from activity above the ice.

These feed piles are usually constructed close to the den as a convenience to the kit beaver, who do not normally travel far from the den itself.

At times, solitary beaver will be found living all alone. These beaver are known as "bachelors", whether they are male or female.

Adult beaver mark out their territories in early spring by dragging up mud and debris from the bottom and depositing the debris in mounds along the shores, where they also deposit oil from their castor glands. These "castor mounds" often leave a reddish stain on the bank, and the odors are powerful enough for man to easily detect.

Beaver are very territorial, and territories seldom overlap. Generations of beavers may continuously inhabit a choice area, even building canals to help float food from inland cutting sites. If and when food supplies are exhausted, they do relocate to a better area.

Once beaver have determined to claim a territory, they are very difficult to dissuade. If the activities of the beaver flood roads or damage property, the beaver usually have to be removed to prevent reoccurring damages.

Beaver normally swim with their front feet held against their chest, and the large webbed hind feet provide the propulsion with the tail acting more as a rudder. If speed is needed, the beaver will use its tail in an undulating fashion to advantage.

Although beaver normally submerge for 3 or 4 minutes at a time, they are quite capable at holding their breath for 12 to 15 minutes. They exhale a little in spurts as they swim or work under water, and a large beaver is capable of traveling nearly ½ mile under the surface before it must surface for more air.

Migrations of beaver usually occur with the breaking up of ice in late winter or early spring as the 22 or 23 month old beaver are expelled just prior to birthing time for the new litter. These beaver may choose to go either up or downstream. Although these beaver are capable of reproducing, they usually do not until the next season, after a mate and a new territory have been established. Most new colonies are established within a few miles of the home colony.

Beaver are primarily vegetarians, although an occasional beaver may eat a dead fish. Preferred foods include the bark of aspen, willow, cottonwood, and dogwood, and many other varieties of trees and shrubs are also eaten. In early spring, beaver will often eat bark and twigs of evergreens.

In season, beaver also eat water lillies, leaves, grasses, roots, and a variety of crops including corn, wheat, oats, carrots, potatoes, apples, clovers and alfalfa.

Trapping

Beaver are powerful animals, both on land and in the water. Large sized body gripping traps make good selections for submerged locations, or where water is shallow.

Foothold traps must be strong to hold beaver, and many beaver trap-

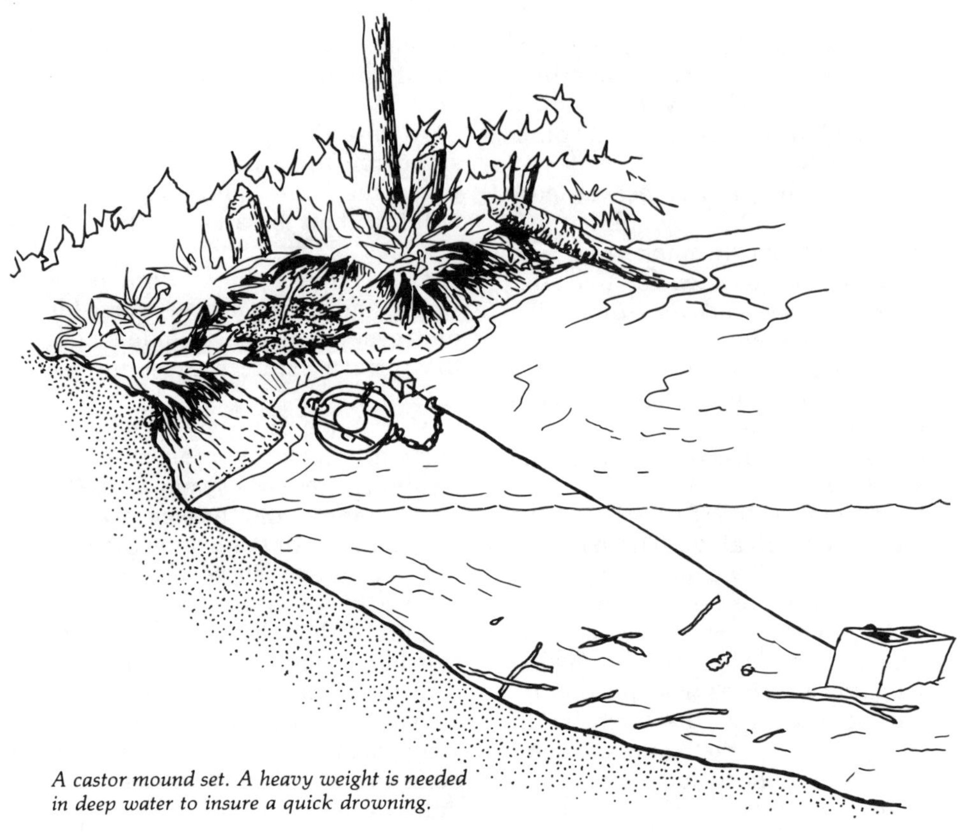

A castor mound set. A heavy weight is needed in deep water to insure a quick drowning.

pers prefer #4 traps in either the longspring or jump design. Foothold traps for beaver should only be set where the beaver has opportunity to drown in deep water, and better trappers insure a quick drowning with the aid of weights near the trap or using a set construction with a one way slide wire and slide lock to prevent the trapped beaver from surfacing for air.

Set constructions must be strong for beaver trapping. Beaver can cut off green stakes. Any wire used in the set construction must also be strong.

Weights at the bottom of slide wires are better than staking the trap in deep water. Beaver sometimes are able to pull the deep water stakes, and then reach shore where complications can result. On the other hand, the beaver seems content to drag the weight along the bottom until drowning occurs. These weights should be at least 10 pounds or more, and some trappers use sandbags filled with small rocks, or sand, to achieve the desired effect.

Channels or canals make good locations for the larger sized body gripping traps. These traps are usually set right on the bottom of the stream in the groove of the channel. Strong stakes should be placed through each spring of the trap, and at times, it is helpful to place a stick horizontally over the top of the submerged trap to encourage a beaver to dive into the set trap.

When deep water is present, many trappers prefer to use strong foothold traps, rigged on a slide

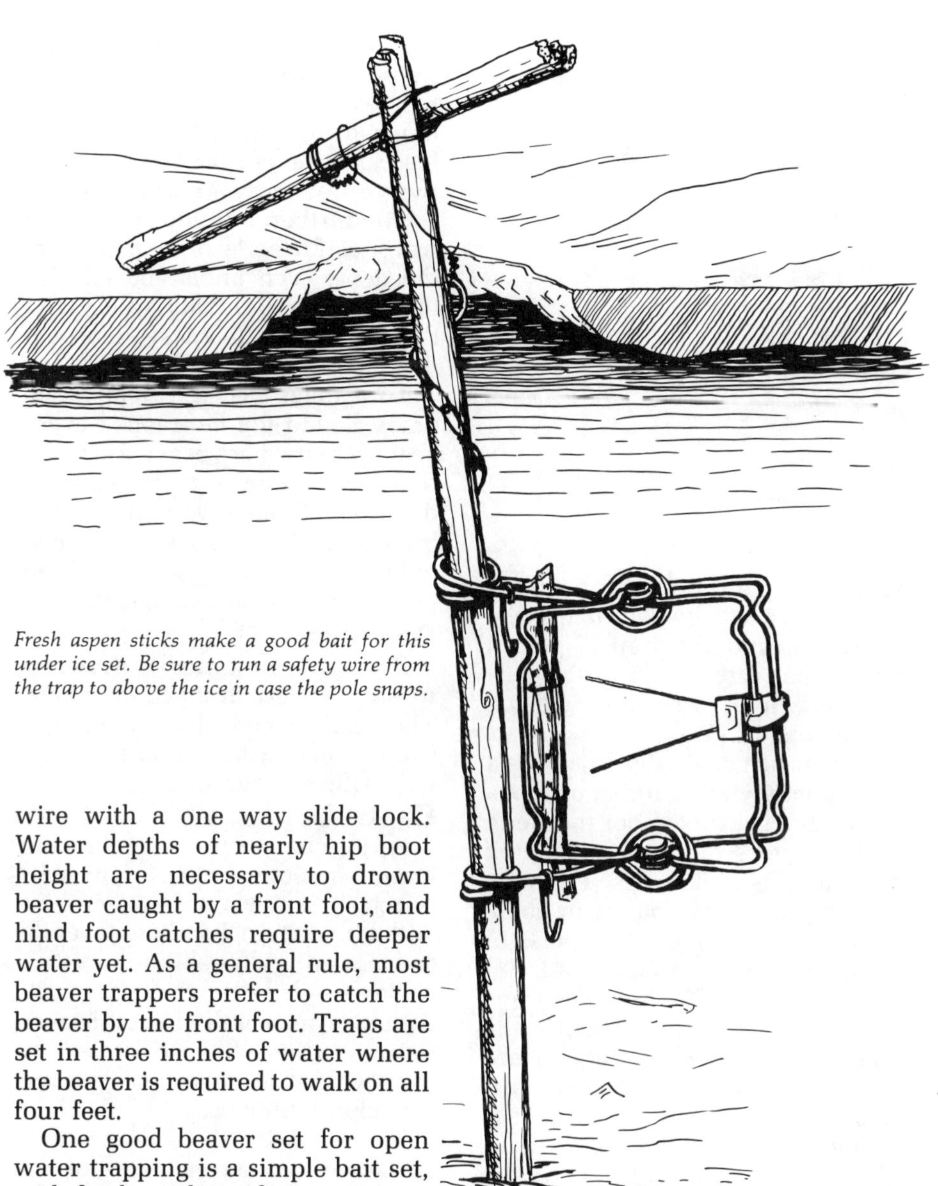

Fresh aspen sticks make a good bait for this under ice set. Be sure to run a safety wire from the trap to above the ice in case the pole snaps.

wire with a one way slide lock. Water depths of nearly hip boot height are necessary to drown beaver caught by a front foot, and hind foot catches require deeper water yet. As a general rule, most beaver trappers prefer to catch the beaver by the front foot. Traps are set in three inches of water where the beaver is required to walk on all four feet.

One good beaver set for open water trapping is a simple bait set, with fresh cut bait of aspen or cottonwood placed right at the shoreline, and either wired to a stake or pushed into the mud to make the bait look as if it was growing there. A knife or axe can be used to scrape the bark in places. This gives the bait added attraction. The trap is placed close to the bait in shallow water where the beaver can be expected to stand while attempting to cut down the bait.

A favorite set for after ice out is the castor mound set, made to simulate where a beaver has piled up a small mound of mud and debris to deposit its castor. Again, a site should be chosen where there is ample water depth to drown the catch quickly with a slide lock arrangement, or weights near the

A foothold trap can also be used near the bait in under ice sets.

trap. These imitation castor mounds are usually placed near the shoreline, and the trap is placed under the water close to the new mound, which is scented with an application of lure.

Beaver pelt quality is usually best during mid-winter, and many trappers catch beavers under the ice in both large sized body gripping traps and foothold traps. The body gripping traps can be set in channels or runs, or placed on poles of dead wood with fresh cut baits.

Favorite sets for foothold traps for under ice beaver include the use of baits, which the beaver are vulnerable to as the cached feed pile begins to sour with age. These foothold traps can be set on poles in deep water, or used right on the bottom in shallow water. As a general rule, it is wise to place the foothold traps quite close to the baits. All beaver traps set under ice should be attached to dry poles. A strong wire must also be attached to the trap and fastened above the ice.

Better trappers prefer to harvest the larger beaver in a colony, and this is done easily because the larger beaver travel further from the dens than the younger and smaller beavers. Kit beavers travel the least of all, and usually not much further than the submerged feed pile in northern states. The two year old beaver normally range a little further, and the adults may travel as far as ¼ or ½ mile from the dens, even under the ice. Kit beaver have little fur value, and traps should not be set close to dens in order to avoid them.

To manage beaver properly, colonies should not be trapped every year, except where beavers are particularly numerous or causing damages. Generally, two to four beaver can be removed from colonies every two years to keep populations stable and healthy.

Dispatch

Beaver are normally drowned when they are trapped properly. The best method of dispatching a live beaver is with a brain shot with a .22 rifle or hand gun.

Controls

Serious beaver predators include mountain lions, wolves, lynx and bobcats. At times, a bear can and will kill mature beavers. Juvenile beavers are vulnerable to coyotes, eagles, and large owls as well. Although instances of adult beaver being killed by coyotes are somewhat rare, many bobcats are skilled at killing beavers.

Tularemia can be a devastating disease in beavers, wiping out entire populations when conditions are good for disease transmissions. Tularemia infects livers, and is usually fatal to beaver of all ages.

Values

Beaver usually alter the habitat a great deal with the building of dams, and the resulting flooding of lowlands. The deeper water behind dams creates a better habitat for muskrats, and a variety of other wildlife species such as fish and waterfowl. Mink and otter hunt regularly around beaver dams. These locations often provide suitable denning sites as well for these furbearers.

Dam building on trout streams can have an adverse effect on trout survival by slowing the water and allowing it to warm to temperatures higher than the trout can tolerate. Dams also serve as barriers to migrating trout and salmon species.

At times, beaver cause a significant amount of property damage by cutting trees, and flooding large areas also killing the timber. Culvert plugging is common, and often causes roads to flood and wash out.

Beaver are also a host to an internal parasite, giardiasis. Water reservoirs inhabited by beaver can and do become contaminated by the giardiasis cysts, which are too small to be filtered out of the drinking water, and these cysts do hatch in the small intestines of people who drink the contaminated water, resulting in diarrhea, nausea, and stomach aches. Approximately 600,000 beaver are harvested annually in North America, yielding values of about 10 million dollars.

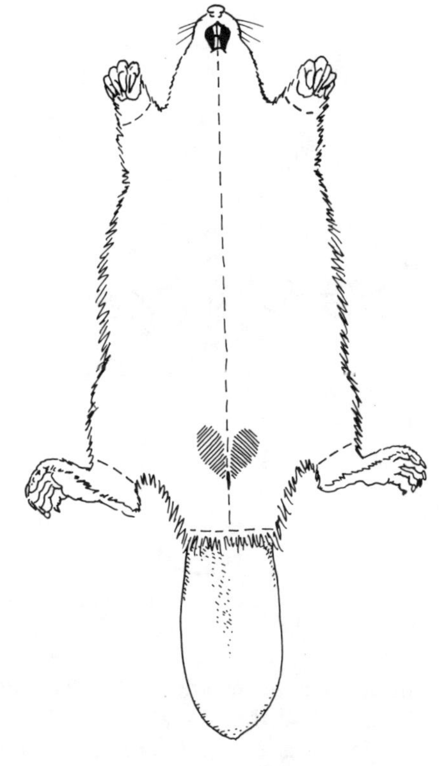

Fur Handling

Beaver are one of the more difficult animals to skin and flesh properly. The skins must be cut off of the carcasses. A knife with a drop blade or rounded end is a great aid to prevent cutting through the pelt.

Beaver are handled "open", and stretched to a round or slightly oval shape.

The opening cut is made with a pointed knife blade from the bottom of the chin down the middle of the belly to the tail. Many trappers pinch the vent closed with one hand, and cut around both sides of the vent. The feet can be removed with a knife by inserting the pointed blade between the tendon and the ankle or wrist bones, and cutting the tendons. Then the knife blade can be used to follow the

A drop point blade shape should be used when skinning beavers.

The skin on the lower back adheres tightly and must be freed with knife cuts.

bone sockets. A twisting of the foot is an aid as the feet are cut off.

Skinning usually begins at the chin area, as the pelt is freed with a sharp and rounded knife blade away from the belly cut. Care must be taken as the animal is being skinned, particularly around the leg areas as the pelt is freed over the ends of the cut off feet.

The skin must be cut around the base of the tail as the sides of the beaver are skinned. Many trappers prefer to skin the back by starting at the base of the tail and skinning toward the head. A layer of meat will often be attached to the pelt along the back. This is usually taken off of the pelt during the fleshing or scraping process, although some experienced beaver skinners prefer to "clean" skin the pelt during the entire skinning process.

After the belly, legs, and lower back have been skinned, you might be able to stand on the beaver tail and pull the pelt all the way to the

A strong man can pull the fur all of the way off of the back of the beaver.

head area, where severing cuts will be needed to free the ears, eyes and nose of the pelt.

The best way to flesh beaver pelts is on a fleshing beam with a two handled fleshing knife. Some trappers prefer to begin the scraping process right behind the ears, and fleshing off a strip down the middle of the back first, after which the pelt can be rotated on the beam as the entire pelt is fleshed free of all fat and meat. A sharp edge is useful to start the fleshing process, although the bulk of the fleshing should be done with the dull edge of the two handled fleshing knife.

Beaver pelts can be stretched on 4' x 4' plywood boards, and the first step is to use nails to shape the pelt to a rather loose diamond shape. More nails can then be added in an alternating fashion around the

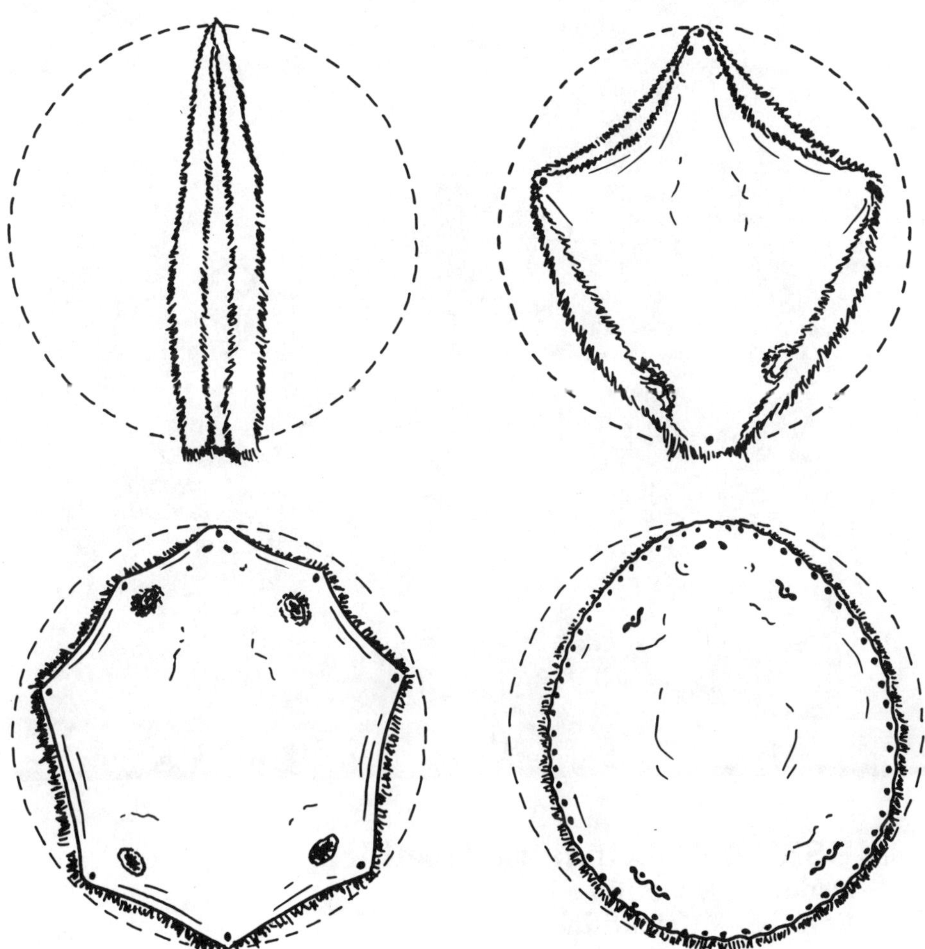

The various stages in stretching a beaver pelt on a board with nails. The finished shape should be slightly oval.

edge of the pelt until the nails are about one inch apart, and the pelt has a smooth oval shape.

After the proper shape has been fashioned, a screwdriver can be used to pry the pelt an inch or so off of the board up on the nails. This will allow air circulation to the fur side of the pelt and prevent the fur from matting as the pelt dries.

Stretching beaver pelts on hoops is also very popular. This can be done either by sewing or with the use of hog rings to hold the pelt to the wire hoop. The holes for the hog rings can be punctured with an awl. Pleasing oval shapes are quickly and consistently attained when using wire hoop stretchers.

Drying times vary according to humidity and temperatures. Pelts should be left on the stretchers until they are fully dry.

Some trappers prefer to close the leg holes on beaver pelts by sewing, and this does improve the appearance of the pelt. If oil should appear on the leather side of the pelt, it can be cleaned with a paper towel or rag.

MUSKRAT — Ondatra Zibethica

Order — Rodentia
Family — Cricetidae

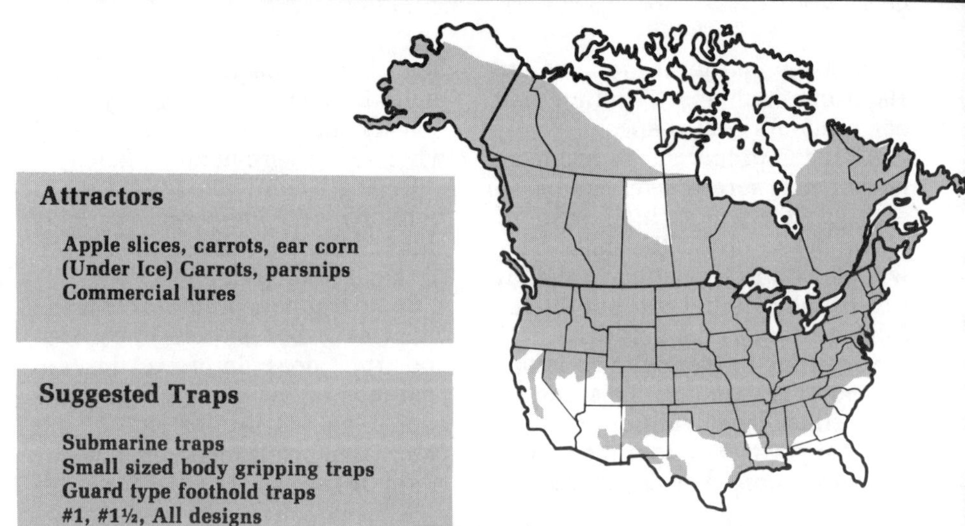

Attractors

Apple slices, carrots, ear corn
(Under Ice) Carrots, parsnips
Commercial lures

Suggested Traps

Submarine traps
Small sized body gripping traps
Guard type foothold traps
#1, #1½, All designs

The Muskrat

THE muskrat is a common and valuable furbearer. "Musquash" is a name give this species by the Algonquin Indians. The Huron Indian name of "Ondatra" was incorporated into the muskrat's scientific name. Commonly referred to as "Rats" or "Mushrats" by trappers in different areas, this furbearing rodent is not a rat. This species is recommended for novice trappers because muskrats are easily caught, and the furs can be properly handled for sale with a minimum of special equipment.

Description

The muskrat is classified as a rodent because of its four incisor teeth in the front of the mouth. The two upper and two lower incisors overlap, allowing them to self-sharpen as they are used. Folds of skin behind the incisors allow a submerged muskrat to cut vegetation without getting water into its mouth.

The size and weight of muskrats varies with regions, and the quality of available food. Southern muskrats average around two pounds in weight, and weights of three and a half or four pounds are common for muskrats in New York, New Jersey and Maryland.

Most adult muskrats attain a length of 22-25 inches, including the nearly hairless tail. A 13½ inch body length, with a 9½ inch tail length is common.

The muskrat has relatively small front feet, with four major toes and small thumbs. Hind feet are much larger, and partially webbed.

The tail of a muskrat is deeper than it is wide, and it tapers to a blunt point at the end. The species use their tails as an aid to swimming.

Muskrat fur is short and dense. Colors are mostly browns with lighter shades of greys or blondes on chest and stomach areas. The underfur traps air, and prevents the skin of the muskrat from becoming wet while it is in the water.

Musk glands are predominant beneath the skin on the lower abdomen of male muskrats. These two glands become swollen during the spring, and produce a yellowish, musky smelling fluid.

Distribution

Muskrats are widely distributed throughout North America. This species can adapt to a wide variety of climates. Muskrats are depen-

Muskrat den entrances are usually below the water level in streams.

dent upon habitats including water. This species thrive in many lakes, rivers, creeks, ponds, and fresh or salt water marshes. Muskrats can tolerate a certain amount of pollution in water, and this important furbearer is often found living within large cities.

The muskrat is managed as a furbearer in most states, and 48 states currently have muskrat trapping seasons.

Sign

Muskrats are dependent upon water, and the edges of streams, lakes and ponds often show evidence of muskrat activity. Tracks are commonly found in muddy areas, and a distinctive tail dragging mark is often seen separating the tracks of the right and left feet. Cuttings of plants can sometimes be found when a current is not present, and trappers refer to these piles of vegetation as "feed beds", because they are regular feeding places. Narrow trails can often be found leading from the water's edge up on dry land, and these regularly used trails are commonly referred to by trappers as "slides". Trails underwater in shallow streams or marshes are also evidence of muskrat activity, and these underwater trails are referred to as "runs". Droppings are another sure sign of muskrats. Muskrat droppings can usually be found on rocks or logs exposed above the water level, or selected toilet areas along the bank of the waterway. In many marshy areas, muskrats build dome shaped lodges of vegetation in the water, similar to beaver lodges, but smaller in size. These lodges have one or more underwater entrances, and commonly house an entire family group of muskrats. Smaller but similar structures are known as "push ups". These push ups usually serve a muskrat as a protected feeding and resting area, especially after ice forms on the water surface. Bank dens are common, and these usually have underwater entrances leading upwards to hollowed out chambers in the bank above the waterline. Trails of air bubbles can often be seen through thin ice. These bubble trails are made by muskrats exhaling air as they swim beneath the frozen surface.

Muskrats often build lodges and smaller sized "push-ups" in marshes.

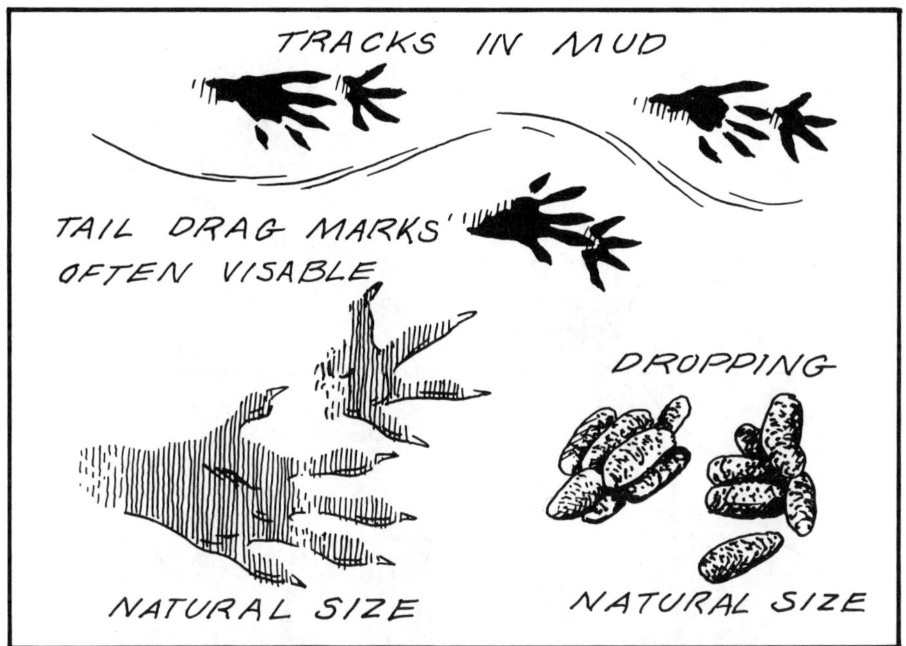

Reproduction

Muskrats are one of our most prolific species. Adult muskrats can have up to five litters in a year's time. Muskrats in northern states seem to average about 2½ litters a year. Muskrats in southern states often average 3 litters. Litter sizes vary, and 5 or 6 kits per litter is common. There is evidence that muskrat populations may be somewhat cyclic. Muskrats produce fewer litters when populations are dense, and more litters when populations are sparse. The quality and abundance of food also affects the numbers of litters as well as litter sizes. Female muskrats born in the spring are sometimes capable of raising their own litter by late summer or early autumn. An average female will raise about 15 or 16 young in a good year. One female muskrat has been known to produce 46 young in one year. The gestation period for muskrats is 29 days. Muskrats are thought to have one mate during rearing seasons. Few muskrats attain four years of age. Populations can be estimated in the fall by counting lodges, and multiplying by five.

Habits

Muskrats are somewhat sociable with others of the same species, but will often fight to the death as populations become dense. Preferred foods include a variety of vegetation, including roots, stems, and buds. Muskrats often seek out undercut banks for protection while feeding. Food is usually carried by this furbearer by mouth, and eating takes place above the water level. Muskrats are often active during the day, as well as night, with peak activities near dawn and dusk. Muskrats commonly stay underwater for five minutes while searching for food, and they are capable for holding their breath underwater for 10-12 minutes. Territory sizes vary according to population densities and

A lured stick for an attractor, and a tangle stake illustrate a popular set.

the quality of the habitat. These territories average about 200 feet in diameter in marsh habitats, and slightly longer along streams. Dispersals occur when the young are encouraged to leave the dens. Most of the young muskrats do not move further away than 200 feet in good habitats. Adult muskrats sometimes disburse further distances, particularly in the early spring before mating season begins.

Trapping

Muskrats have fragile bones in their front legs. Both trap and site selection are important considerations for the species. Foothold traps in sizes #1 and #1½ are commonly used. Guard type foothold traps make good selections because the guards prevent the trapped muskrat from twisting in the traps and injuring themselves. Small sizes of single spring body gripping traps are also used to trap muskrats. Submarine traps are

A submarine trap in a shallow run.

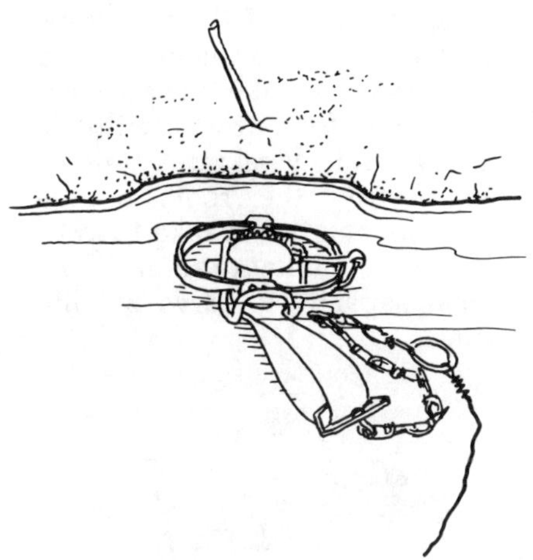

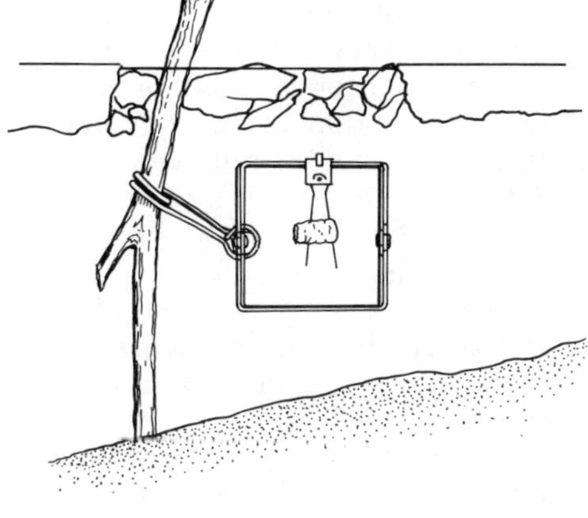

useful when suitable underwater locations can be found.

Foothold traps should only be set for muskrats where the trapped muskrat will have opportunity to drown quickly. A trapped muskrat will instinctively dive for deep water when trapped, and the weight of the trap will help to drown the muskrat in depths of more than 14 inches. Trap chain lengths on traps as they come from the factories are not long enough for muskrat traps, so many trappers use a piece of wire to extend the distance between the trap and deep water. The trapped muskrat should be prevented from climbing up on the bank, or upon any object. The wire extension and trap stake should be strong enough to hold an occasional raccoon catch.

Small body gripping traps make better trap selections where the water is shallow, and these traps can also be used in under ice conditions with a convenient sized bait impaled on the trap trigger wires. Generally, the small body gripping traps can be held in position with a stake placed through the coil of the spring.

A dry stick or weed stem dipped into muskrat lure makes a fine attractor. Muskrats are attracted to a wide variety of lures. The use of lures as muskrat attractors helps to prevent the capture of waterfowl which might be attracted to a visible bait. If a piece of bait, such as an apple slice, or a piece of carrot is used, it should be placed inside a hole at the water's edge, or under an overhanging bank.

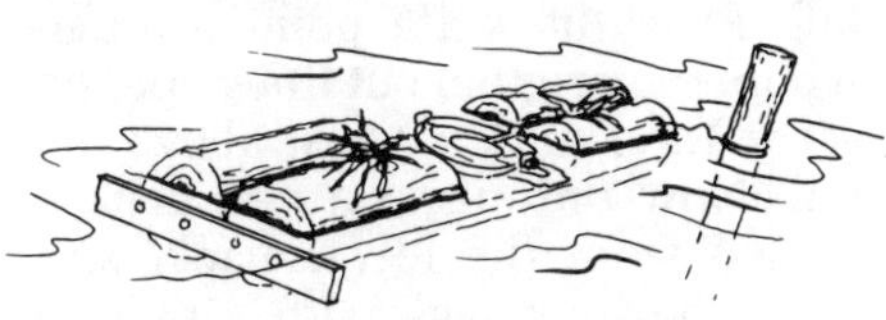

Floating sets fluctuate with water levels.

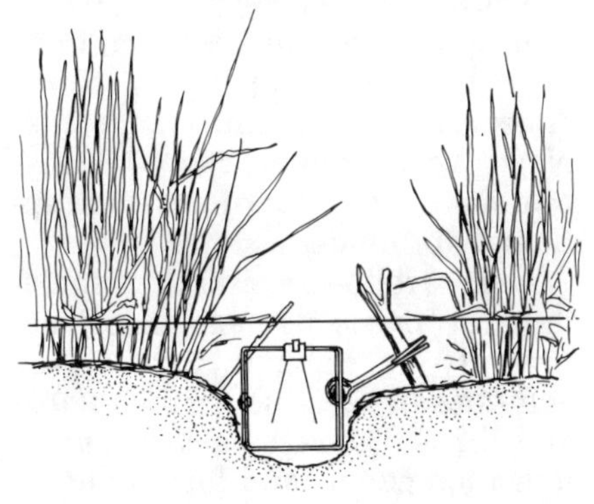

Mink are also caught in this type of set.

Due to the large reproductive capacity of muskrats, significant numbers should be trapped. In order to curtail disease problems and destruction of habitat, many managers hope to remove at least 75% of the available muskrats annually under normal conditions.

Dispatch

When trapped properly, muskrats are almost always dead when the trapper checks his or her traps. Occasionally, a trapped muskrat will entangle in vegetation and not drown. These furbearers should be dispatched with a stunning blow from a stick or trap stake, and then held under water for drowning to occur.

Controls

Muskrats are an important prey species for a variety of wildlife, including mink, foxes, coyotes, hawks and owls.

One major disease is Errington's disease. This serious virus can live in mud and infect muskrats in areas that have been unihabited by other muskrats for as long as 5 years. Epidemics can and do occur with this devastating disease. Muskrats are also vulnerable to tularemia, and a variety of internal and external parasites.

Values

The annual harvest of this important species brings 35-45 millions of dollars to trappers in North America. Wisconsin, Louisiana, New York, Ohio, New Jersey, Maryland and Illinois are exceptionally productive states.

Uncontrolled muskrat populations do cause damage to private property and habitat. Hole digging activities undermine earthen dams and dikes. Damages also occur to irrigation canals and farm ponds.

Large populations of muskrats also cause "eat-outs". These areas are simply overcropped by the feeding activities of the muskrats, and the loss of vegetation and resulting silting makes the area less productive for other wildlife species as well. Muskrat "eat-outs" often destroy the roots of the vegetation, and it may take 15 to 20 years for the habitat to return to its original capacity to serve wildlife species.

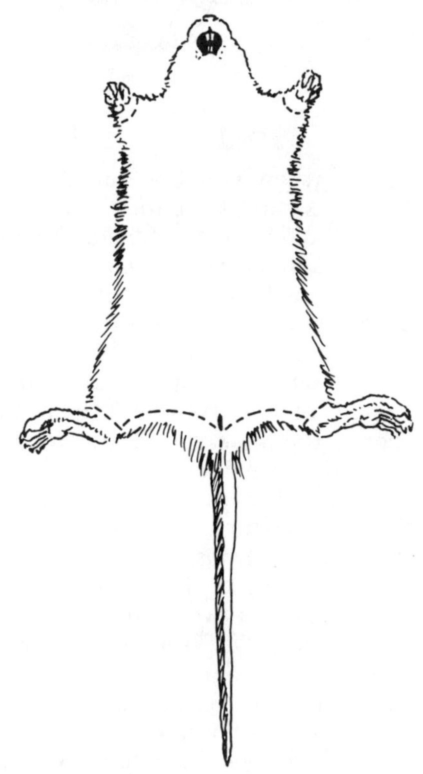

Fur Handling

Muskrats are handled cased, and the opening knife cut is made from the inside of one hind leg to the other. With the muskrat laid on its belly, pinch the fur just above the tail. Push the knife point through where the original cut lines up, and sever the skin from just above the tail. Now the muskrat pelt can be peeled from the lower back, and from the hind legs with a pulling action. At this point, set the muskrat on its haunches, and

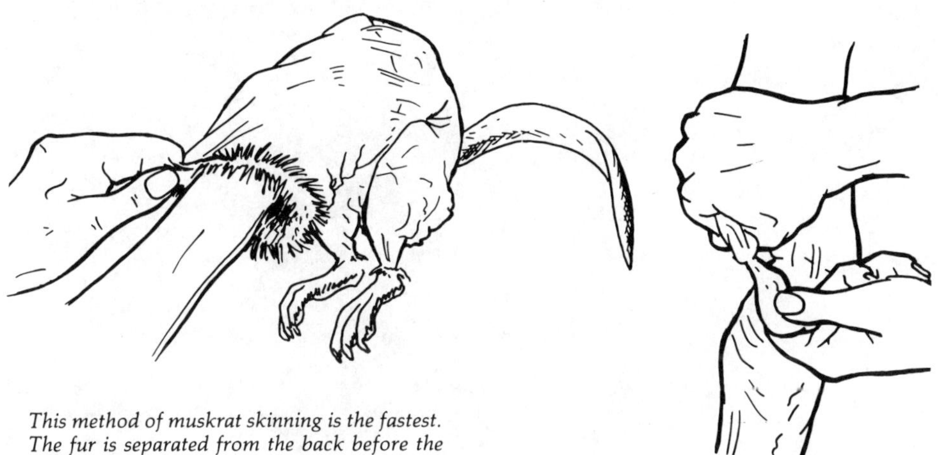

This method of muskrat skinning is the fastest. The fur is separated from the back before the belly.

Knife cuts are not necessary around the front ankles as the fur can be pulled off of the feet.

holding the lower back of the pelt, use the other hand to push the muskrat's head until the fur is separated along the back all the way to the shoulders. The skin can be freed in the chest area with thumb or finger pressure and pulled free all the way down the stomach area. The fur can now be freed from the front shoulder and front leg, and pulled right off of the front feet. Further hand pressure will allow you to pull the pelt down to the ear area, where a knife cut will be necessary. Another cut will be needed in the eye area, and the final cut will allow the nose to remain attached to the pelt.

Fleshing is accomplished with a single handled pelt scraping tool, or a dulled paint scraper. The hide is placed over a small stretcher, or even a large mink stretcher during the fleshing process, to allow an occasional turning of the pelt. All glands and fat should be scraped off of the pelt from the head area downward, or these deposits will taint and cause damage to the pelt.

Muskrats are usually stretched on wire stretchers, but properly shaped boards will also do a nice job. Importantly, a wedge must be used on all solid stretching boards to prevent the fur from shrinking tightly to the stretcher as it dries.

The pelt should always be placed on the stretcher with the fur to the inside. Drying times vary, and most pelts are ready to remove from the stretchers after several days.

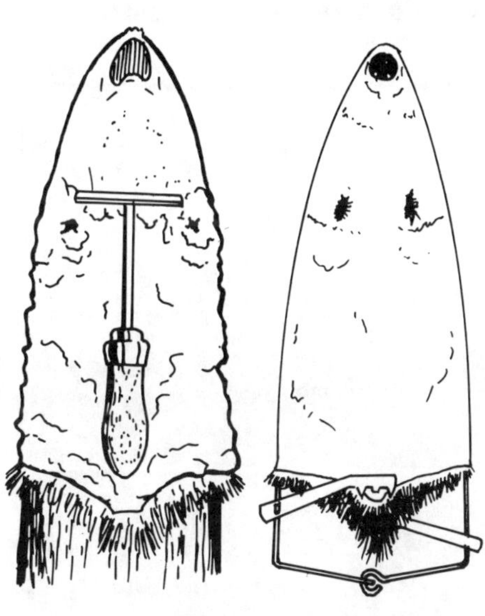

Loose fat must be separated from skins before they are placed on stretchers.

NUTRIA — Myocastor Coypus

Order — Rodentia
Family — Myocastor

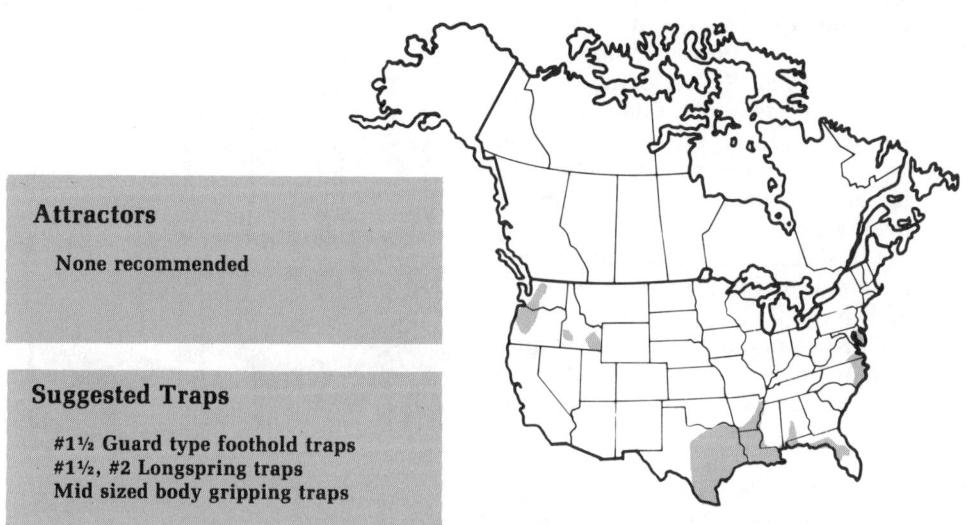

Attractors

None recommended

Suggested Traps

#1½ Guard type foothold traps
#1½, #2 Longspring traps
Mid sized body gripping traps

The Nutria

THIS member of the rodent family is native to South America, and it was introduced both accidentally and purposely into the waterways in several American states. The species has proven to be overly destructive of habitat in some areas, creating problems for muskrats and waterfowl. This species can tolerate winters in temperate areas only. An important furbearer in Louisiana and Texas coastal areas, nutria are viewed as detrimental in most other areas.

Description

Adult nutria are about 24 inches long from the nose to the base of the tail. The tail itself is 12 to 17 inches long, round, and hairless. Coloration is brownish, and both sexes are similar in appearance and weight.

The nutria is unique in that it has 3 sets or lengths of fur. Primary guard hairs are about 3 inches in length. Beneath this layer is the secondary guard hairs, which are more numerous and give the species its overall coloration. The underfur is short, and less dense than either a muskrat or beaver underfur.

Nutria average 16 to 18 pounds in weight. Occasional individuals may weigh 25 pounds or more.

The whiskers on a nutria are obvious. These whiskers are about 4 inches in length, and very numerous.

Teeth number 20, and include 4 large incisors in the front of the mouth. The skin closes behind these incisors, and allows the nutria to cut off underwater plants without getting water into its mouth.

The mouth also has glands located near the corners which produce oils that the nutria uses to comb and waterproof its fur with.

Also unique is the location of the mammary glands on the females. The teats are located high on the sides of the nutria, which allows young nutria to nurse as the mother swims in the water.

Front feet have five toes, including a small toe corresponding to our thumb. Hind feet are much larger, and unique in that all toes are connected by a skin web except for the toe corresponding to our little toe.

Distribution

The largest concentrations of nutria are in the coastal areas of Louisiana, Texas, Mississippi and Florida. Excellent populations also occur in areas of Alabama, Georgia, North Carolina and Virginia. This species is also abundant in the waterways of coastal areas in Oregon and Washington.

Sign

Nutria are active mostly at night, in the late evening, and in the early morning. A shy and retiring species, nutria are not usually seen unless there is a deliberate attempt to find them.

Nutria burrow into banks of ponds and lakes, and these holes are usually larger and more destructive than muskrat burrows. These burrows will often have tracks nearby which are easily identifiable.

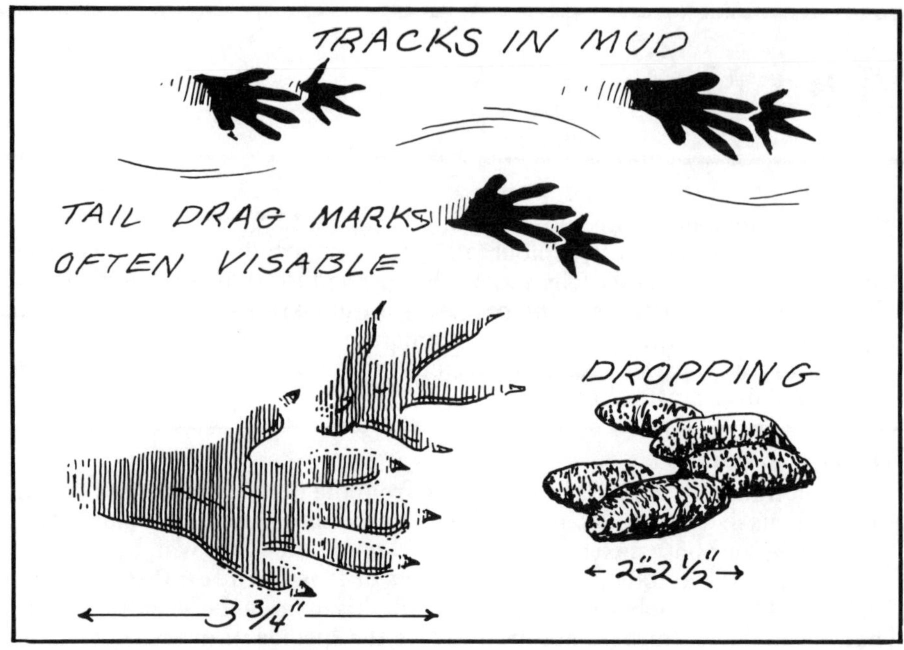

Trails through marshy areas are often visible, and these trails are used regularly by the nutria. These trails, or runs, are wider than those made by muskrats.

Another positive sign of nutria are their feeding platforms. These large sized feeding beds or platforms are constructed of cut vegetation that was not eaten. These areas are often hidden in thick vegetation.

Nutria droppings are similar in appearance to muskrat droppings, but much larger.

Reproduction

Nutria are apt to breed in any month of the year in North America. One male usually has 2 or 3 mates which share the same burrow.

Female nutria mature at about 5½ months of age, and female nutria usually have two litters per year. Many females breed within two days after giving birth to a litter.

Litter sizes vary according to a cycle. The first litter is small, with 2 to 4 being born. The second litter is larger with 4 to 6 offspring. The third litter is smaller than the second, and the fourth again increases in size. For one reason or another, each litter is either larger or smaller than the litter preceeding it, and according to a pattern.

If nutria litter sizes were averaged, five would probably be the average size.

Female nutria are capable of producing only 6 litters as a rule. Females who produce seven litters in their lifetime are rare.

A nutria is considered as old at four years of age.

Habits

Nutria spend most of their time in or near the water. Although they are awkward and vulnerable on land, the species will travel inland to feed upon preferred foods, including crops.

Nutria are thought of as colonial because the same den is shared by the dominant male with two or three females and their offspring.

Den entrances are often a foot or two beneath the water's surface, and the den entrance is often as much as two feet in diameter. The inner chamber of the den is above the waterline, and lined with grasses brought in to serve for bedding.

Nutria are vegetarians and they do have large appetites. Primarily a surface feeder, nutria often overharvest favored foods, causing the production of less favored foods for themselves and other wildlife species.

This species is territorial and tolerant of others of its kind. Four or five colonies of nutria to the mile of levees or dikes indicates a high population as a family or colony territory is about 1,000 feet in length.

Nutria do not remain underwater for long periods of time. Research shows that they are capable of holding their breath while submerged for about five minutes.

Nutria commonly cut off a preferred food near the waterline and swim or carry it to a feeding platform for eating. These platforms are used most often during trapping seasons, possibly because they are warmer on the nutria's hairless feet.

Favored foods include rushes, reeds, cattails, arrowhead, square-stem spike rush and sawgrass. Sugarcane, alfalfa, corn and rice are also eaten if available.

Trapping

Good traps for nutria include size 1½ longspring guard traps, number 2 longspring traps, and mid sized body gripping traps. The selection of the trap should depend upon whether or not the nutria are to be harvested for

Traps need not be covered on feeding platforms.

Trail sets can be made in existing trails in shallow water or on dry land.

fur only or whether or not there is an effort to reduce populations. Because only large sized pelts are wanted by the fur trade, many fur trappers use only foothold traps so that the smaller and worthless animals can be released.

Coilspring traps are usually not used by nutria trappers because the brackish waters inhabited by nutria often weaken the springs quickly. The 1½ longspring guard trap is favored by many trappers as this trap will also be effective on muskrats which often get caught in nutria sets.

The most common method of fastening a nutria trap is to use a long stake of cane or bamboo. These long stakes are usually pushed through the ring on the end of the trap chain. Their long length makes them visible to a trapper making his trap check rounds in the swamps and marshes.

Where there is an effort to control nutria populations, many trappers use mid sized body gripping traps, which are usually set in trails. Mid sized body gripping traps with a single spring are used by some trappers. These traps are usually fastened with long stakes as well.

Nutria are almost always caught in trails, or on their feeding platforms.

The species is not thought to be trap shy at all, and traps are usually not covered or disguised.

Lures or baits are not used to trap nutria. Many experiments with different lures or baits indicate little value in trapping this species.

Whether or not the species should be trapped conservatively depends upon the area, the nutria population, and the capacity of the habitat. Nutria do compete for the same foods as muskrats, and muskrat populations can be increased by harvesting significant numbers of nutria.

Nutria are always trapped conservatively when they are harvested for fur with foothold traps. Significant numbers of nutria are juveniles at all seasons of the year. Animals smaller than 12 pounds have no value and are released.

Dispatch

Nutria trappers carry a stick with them in their boats, or they use a stick as a wading staff while wading the marshes. These sticks are used to both release or kill nutria in traps. Animals to be released are simply pinned down with the stick as the trap is removed. Animals to be killed are killed with a sharp rap to the top of the head. This species is easily killed by a blow to the top of the head. A second blow to the top of the skull insures a stress free death.

Controls

Nutria are preyed upon by alligators, cottonmouth moccasins, hawks, owls and eagles. Juveniles are usually most vulnerable to predation.

Parasites include flatworms, roundworms, fleas and lice. The seeds of beggarstick also plague nutria as the barbed seeds entangle in the fur and puncture the skin, resulting in infections.

Values

The sale of nutria furs is an important source of income for many trappers in regions where nutria are numerous. Most pelts are harvested in Louisiana, and the 2 million pelts harvested annually bring about 11 million dollars to trappers.

Nutria usually have a negative impact on other wildlife species. Because they are colonial in habit, nutria often overharvest edible plants within their small range, resulting in the killing of the desirable plant species. These "eat-outs" destroy productivity as often less desirable plants replace the more desirable ones. Large populations of nutria definitely have a negative impact on the ability of the habitat to support both muskrats and waterfowl.

The burrowing habits of nutria cause problems with dams, dikes and levees. The holes dug can be numerous, and the size of the holes are significant, oftentimes causing damage.

The roundworms infesting nutria can cause health problems for man. The roundworm larvae is present in the water where nutria are found, and this larvae can penetrate human skin. Known as "nutria itch", severe inflammation can result, which requires medical attention.

Fur Handling

Nutria furs are handled cased, with the fur on the inside. Pelts which stretch less than 23 inches on a straight sided 7 or 7½ inch stretcher are not wanted in the fur trade. Pelts measuring more than 26 inches have full value.

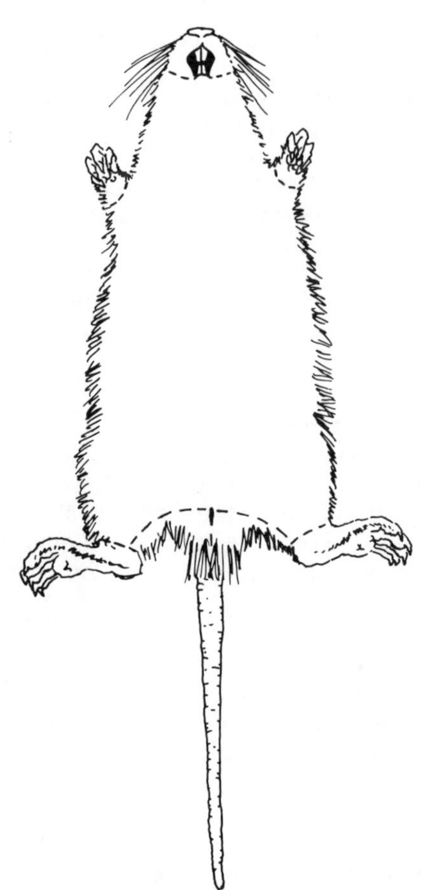
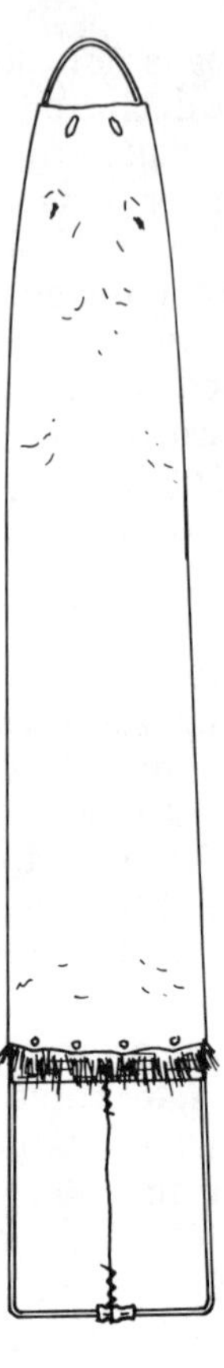

Nutria are skinned like muskrats. The first cut is made from the inside of one hind leg to the other. The fur is then pulled from the hind legs, and severed from around the tail. A strong man can place one hand on a nutria's head and pull the fur all of the way off of the back down to the shoulder area. An alternative method is to pull the pelt with the animal carcass suspended from a skinning gambrel. The fur can then be pulled from the belly and the front feet pulled through the leg area. A knife cut will be needed to separate the ear canals and the eyes. As soon as the eye holes are separated the nutria pelt is severed leaving the entire nose on the carcass. (Nutria noses are fatty, have no value and can cause pelts to spoil.)

Nutria pelts are usually only lightly fleshed. There is loose fat on the shoulder, belly and side area on the pelts. This can be removed with a single handled fleshing tool.

Special wire stretchers are usually used to stretch the pelts. These stretchers are 7 or 7½ inches wide with straight sides. A sliding wooden block is used on the stretcher to get a square bottom to the pelt as tacks or nails are used to hold the fur on the wood.

Commercial trapping camps usually speed dry nutria pelts overnight with high temperatures and fans for air circulation. When nutria pelts are allowed to dry naturally, they are usually dry enough to remove from the stretchers in several days.

COYOTE — Canis Latrans

Order — Carnivora
Family — Canidae

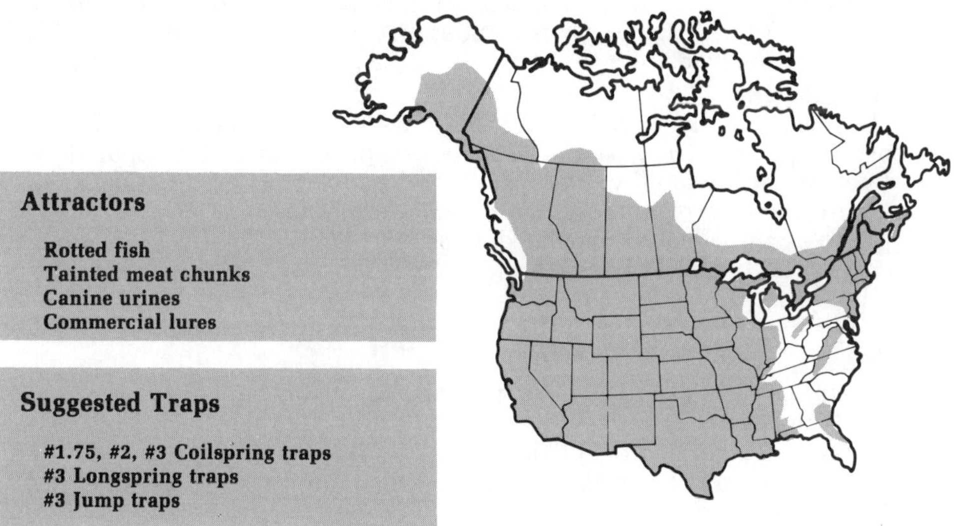

Attractors

Rotted fish
Tainted meat chunks
Canine urines
Commercial lures

Suggested Traps

#1.75, #2, #3 Coilspring traps
#3 Longspring traps
#3 Jump traps

The Coyote

COYOTES are widely dispursed throughout the United States, and they are an important predator of sheep and many wild species. Efforts to contain wild populations of coyotes have only been temporarily successful in spite of bounties, poisons and a total lack of protection in many states. This species is very adaptable and they can thrive in forests, farmlands, prairies, mountains, deserts and swamplands. Coyotes are clever, possess keen senses, and thrive in wilderness and suburban localities. Hated and loved, coyotes are a challenging species to trap.

Description

Coyotes are wild canines, with dog or wolf-like features. Weights are slightly heavier for males, with average weights in the western states of about 30 pounds for males versus 25 pounds for females.

A coyote immigration has impacted eastern states since the early 1950's, and the eastern coyote is now recognized as a true breeding subspecies of coyote. The eastern coyotes do attain larger body weights than western coyotes, and this may reflect hereditary traits as a result of cross breeding between northern coyotes and eastern timber wolves. Weights of over 60 pounds have been recorded for some eastern coyote males, although the majority of the males weigh between 30 - 35 pounds.

Coyotes have 42 teeth including four long incisor teeth. Eyes are yellow or amber, with round, black pupils which indicate that coyotes were probably daytime hunters before man began persecuting the species in earnest. earnest.

Guard hairs on a coyote pelt are about 3 inches long on the back, and 5 inches long in a patch between the shoulders known as the "mane" or "hackles".

Coloration varies with individuals and sections, with most coyotes being mottled greys with lighter colored bellies. Brownish and reddish colors also occur commonly in areas, and melanism or black colors occur more rarely.

Distribution

Coyote populations are known to exist in 46 states, and it is possible that coyotes will soon be present in all states except Hawaii. Dense populations of coyotes occur in all western states and populations are least dense in eastern farmland regions and the southeastern states.

Coyotes can adapt to populated areas, and thousands of coyotes living within the city limits of Los Angeles have led to severe management problems.

Coyotes are managed as furbearers, predators and varmints.

Sign

Tracks of coyotes are dog-like, with the coyote having a narrower footprint. Coyote tracks usually display nail prints, and the track pattern is more in a straight line than a dog's track pattern.

Coyotes often follow trails and old roads in their travels. These are good places to search for tracks.

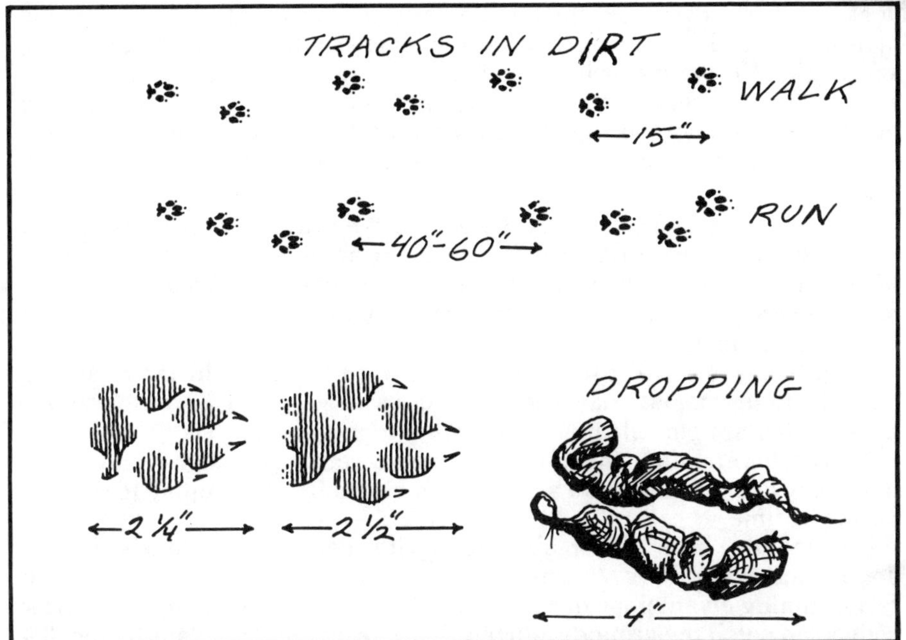

Droppings are also narrower than those left by dogs, and they usually evidence fur particles and crushed pieces of bone. Coyotes are prone to leaving droppings in obvious places, possibly as a communication to other coyotes.

Coyotes frequently howl at night where they are not heavily persecuted. Some fur harvesters locate coyotes by blowing a siren to encourage them to howl and reveal their location.

Sheep and calves are also killed by coyotes in some areas. Attacks are usually to the throat areas, but some coyotes attack both sheep and calves at the hind quarters. Typical feeding patterns are at the rib cages, flanks and noses of calves.

Reproduction

There is evidence to suggest that coyotes mate for life, and that new mates are accepted after the removal of one of the pair.

Mated male coyotes attend the females who give birth to the annual litter in an underground den. A regular den is often used year after year, unless the coyotes feel threatened at the den site.

Breeding occurs in February in southern states, and March in northern states. The gestation period is 63 days, and the female coyote will stay underground with her young until their eyes open 11 or 12 days later. During this time the male will bring food for the female and then help bring food to the den for the coyote pups.

Litter sizes average 5 to 7 pups in many areas. Litter sizes seem to be dependent upon coyote population densities, and litters may average 8 or 9 pups where coyote populations are sparse. Too, this phenomenon may reflect healthier coyotes due to an abundance of food.

Crosses between coyotes and dogs do occur rarely, and these crosses are known as "coy-dogs". Coy-dog reproduction is very poor because the coy-dogs breed in November which culminates in mid-winter births. Also, the male coy-dogs do not bring food for the females after the birthing process, and neither do the males help the female feed or raise the young.

Some juvenile female coyotes accept mates at 9 or 10 months of age, but most coyotes do not pair up with mates until they are 20-22 months of age.

Coyotes are considered to be old at 10 to 12 years of age.

Habits

Coyotes are territorial during the bulk of the year. Territory sizes vary a great deal, and territories are far larger in areas where food is sparce. Males range much farther than females. It appears that female territories do not overlap, but a male coyote territory may overlap the territories of several other male and female coyotes.

Female coyotes will usually stay within 5 to 8 miles in their ranging habits. Mature males may have territories as large as 30 to 40 square miles which are patrolled on a somewhat regular basis.

Territories are often abandoned during shortages of food. Several family units may concentrate in an area with an abundant food supply for a short period of time.

Coyotes do have a social order, with certain individuals having dominance over others. At times, coyotes will hunt in packs, or teams, to relay running an antelope or jack rabbit. Coyotes are even known to follow badgers to catch the ground squirrels that are chased from dens by the digging activity of the badger.

Juvenile coyotes usually disperse in November or December to seek their own territories and mates. Dispersal distances vary a great deal, and the young may be required to travel further when coyote populations are dense. In areas where coyotes are uncommon, the young may only have to travel a dozen miles or so to find an unoccupied and suitable territory. Male coyotes usually have to travel further to find the larger territories that they need, and a number of young male coyotes have been known to relocate further than 100 miles away from their birth places.

Coyotes are skilled hunters. Vision, sense of smell, and hearing are all extremely good, and enable the coyote to feed itself easily during most of the year. In the extreme weather of mid-winter, coyotes frequently eat carrion.

Significant numbers of deer and antelope are killed by coyotes. Deer are particularly vulnerable during deep snow conditions when coyotes often pack up to hunt. Although healthy adult deer and antelope are sometimes killed by coyotes, the fawns of both species are particularly vulnerable to coyotes.

Sheep on rangelands are a particular temptation to coyotes, and it seems likely that some coyotes develop a taste for lamb after natural mortalities of sheep occur on the range. Nevertheless, coyotes soon learn to kill sheep when they are available, and it is virtually impossible to discourage them after they develop a taste for sheep.

Coyotes also kill calves, and sometimes these calves are eaten as they are being born. Bob-tailed calves are frequently seen on western rangelands and usually the result of an attack by one or more coyotes.

Coyote depredation upon livestock depends a great deal on the coyote population in the area as well as the availability of other foods. Fertile farmlands usually contain an abundance of small game, and livestock predation is less likely to occur under these circumstances.

This flat set has a lure application under the chaff in front of the dry bone. Double staking may be necessary in some soils with short chained traps.

Important coyote foods vary with the area, and include jackrabbits, cottontails, prairie dogs, mice and rats. Game birds, muskrats, squirrels and domestic fowl are also taken when available. Fruits such as watermelons, grapefruits, apples and persimmons are also eaten seasonally if available.

Trapping

Foothold traps are needed to catch coyotes as the species will avoid both cage traps and large body gripping traps. Longspring traps in size 3 are favored by some western trappers. Many others prefer coilspring traps in sizes of 1.75, 2, 3 or 4.

Coyotes are strong animals, and it is important to be sure that trap stakes will hold coyotes. Many coyotes will jump after being caught in traps, and an effort should be made to insure that the coyote will not be able to pump the trap stake out of the ground.

Cross staking, also known as cross pegging, uses two stakes driven at different angles under the trap. This method is preferred by many trappers who stake coyote traps in sandy or porous soils. Other trappers prefer long chains on the traps to prevent a coyote leverage when jumping in a staked trap.

As a general rule, most coyotes will be held in traps that have relatively short trap chains of 10 to 18 inches, as longer trap chains permit the coyote to gain speed before the trap is tested.

In forested or brushy areas, many trappers prefer to use traps with longer chains attached to grapples. This fastening technique allows the

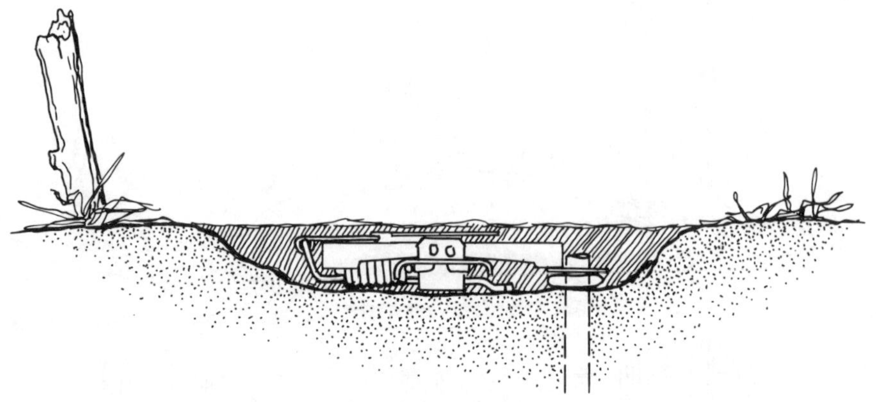

A scent post set uses an application of coyote urine on the stick. The trap must be covered well.

coyote limited progress from the trap set before it tangles the grapple and trap chain around brush. Grappled traps should have chain lengths of 4 to 6 feet. The addition of a swivel in the chain near the trap is responsible.

When grappled traps are set, a deeper trap bed is dug beneath the trap, and the grapple is buried first. Be sure to pack dirt over the tines of the grapple before coiling the chain in the trap bed, or the tines might catch in the trap chain allowing the grapple to be pulled backwards. This can prevent the grapple from hooking on brush, and allow the trapped coyote to travel a considerable distance before it entangles.

Basic coyote sets include the dirt hole set, the flat set, and the scent post set.

Coyotes are curious animals, and they are attracted to all types of holes in the ground where there is a promise of food.

Flat sets are favored in many areas for coyotes, and these sets rely on the use of a lure to attract the coyote to the concealed trap. Usually, a small amount of lure is applied on the ground next to a clump of grass, cow chip or stone, and the trap is carefully concealed 12 to 14 inches in front of the lured spot.

Scent posts can be either natural locations already in use or imitations. This set requires an application of coyote urine on the scent post object, and capitalizes on the coyote's habit of investigating where another coyote has deposited urine.

Most coyote trappers prefer to use odor free traps that have been cleansed by boiling in a trap dye solution. This appears to be especially important in eastern states.

Coyote lures and coyote urine are attractive to free ranging dogs. A somewhat selective bait for coyotes is a tainted meat bait. Baits are more effective for coyotes when they are lightly covered with dirt or debris, as this will cause many coyotes to hunt for the bait whether they would eat it or not. Covered baits also help to avoid accidental captures of predatory birds.

Set locations are important in coyote trapping. Favored locations include logging roads in woodlands, and fringes of woods and open areas. Good locations in farmlands include fence corners, ridges and valleys. Low spots or saddles between elevations are excellent mountain locations. Traps set 30 to 50 feet away from dead carcasses are effective in all habitat types.

Although coyotes may be feeding on dead carcasses, trap sets are more productive when they are set some distance from the dead animal. Scent post or flat sets made nearby are not only more efficient, but they are more selective as well, and prevent the accidental capture of eagles and hawks. Too, many trappers prefer to miss the skunks and opossums that might be feeding upon the carcass, and a reasonable distance between the trap and the carcass helps to miss some of these furbearers.

Coyotes have sharp senses. Better coyote trappers take pains to stabilize or bed their traps as steadily as possible, leave as little human scent as is practical around the set, and try to leave the set with a natural, undisturbed look.

Adequate breeding numbers of coyotes seem to avoid traps, and the species can withstand intense harvesting pressures.

Dispatch

Some coyotes are rather timid in traps, but most will bite in self defense. Keep a safe distance from a trapped coyote at all times.

Coyotes are normally dispatched with a shot from a .22 rifle or handgun. A brain shot is quick and effective, but some trappers prefer to shoot the coyote through the heart as it is standing broadside. If the heart is missed, both lungs will still be pierced by the bullet, and the coyote will still die within a minute or so.

If you are not an adult and catch a coyote, get some adult help to dispatch the coyote if you are not allowed to use a gun.

Controls

Adult coyotes are very rarely killed by other wild species. Juvenile animals are sometimes killed by eagles, mountain lions and dogs.

Coyotes are vulnerable to a variety of diseases, including parvo enteritis, mange, distemper and rabies.

Heartworms afflict coyotes in areas, as do other internal parasites. External parasites include lice, mites, fleas and ticks.

Values

Coyotes contribute to the health of many prey species by keeping the populations in check.

The carrion eating habits of coyotes help to reduce the population of injurious insects which afflict livestock.

Coyote pelts yield a total of more than 30 million dollars annually to fur harvesters in many American communities.

Coyotes do cause a significant loss to livestock producers in some areas. These losses amount to millions of dollars, and cause hardships for many western and southern livestock producers.

In western states coyotes serve as a host for fleas and ticks which carry bubonic plague. This disease can be fatal to man. Western coyotes should be placed in large garbage bags after they are killed, and then sprayed with an insecticide. This will kill the parasites before they abandon the cooling body of the coyote.

Fur Handling

Coyote pelts are handled cased, with the fur on the outside. The opening cut is made from the inside of one hind leg to the other. Two more cuts are then made from the base of the tail around the vent, to the opening cut. The fur can then be separated from the hind legs, and cut off just above the hind feet. A gambrel can be used to suspend the coyote at this time. A cut can

then be made ⅓ of the way down the underside of the tail, and the tail can be stripped from the tailbone with the aid of a tail stripper or a pliers. After the tail has been freed, the pelt must be pulled down past the shoulders, and a little light cutting with a knife may be necessary. A bluntly pointed tool, such as an old sharpening steel or a large Phillips screwdriver can be forced between the pelt and the flesh in the armpit area, and used as an aid to free the pelt down to the front elbow area. The pelt can be severed at the front elbows, and some trappers prefer to cut the front feet off prior to this time with a hacksaw. After the legs are separated, the pelt must be pulled down to the ears, eyes and nose which are all separated with deep knife cuts. Many trappers leave the fur on the lower jaw of the coyote on the carcass, as this fur has no value on the pelt.

The amount of fat on coyote pelts varies with individuals and areas. Most coyotes do need to be scraped free of fat, and a fleshing beam with a two handled fleshing knife does the job best.

Some trappers prefer to wash coyote pelts. If you elect to wash the pelt, use cold water only and a mild soap. Never use warm water or a detergent, as either of these can cause a pelt to shed its fur. Excess water should be stripped from the pelt by pulling it through your hand with a stripping action.

Coyote pelts must be placed on stretchers with the fur to the inside to begin the drying process, whether you wash the pelt or not. Be sure to use a wedge shaped belly board if you use a wooden stretcher. If the fur is wet, it is a good idea to direct a fan at the fur overnight. Some trappers insert a mink stretcher inside of the stretched skin to separate the pelt enough to allow air circulation to the wet fur.

Most coyote furs will be ready to turn fur side out in a day or two, but they should not be turned until the skin side of the pelt is dry to the touch. The pelt is removed from the stretcher, and the nose inserted back through the hole where the mouth was to begin the turning process, and continued until the pelt is completely turned with the fur to the outside. The drying process is completed with the skin side back over the stretcher. It usually takes a week or so to completely dry the pelt.

If holes are cut in the pelt at any time, they should be sewn together before stretching. A curved upholstery or taxidermy needle is handy for this. Hard or brittle leathers may be softened by wetting with a damp rug.

A fur comb or curry comb will improve the appearance of the finished pelt.

RED FOX — Vulpes Vulpes
Order — Carnivora
Family — Canidae

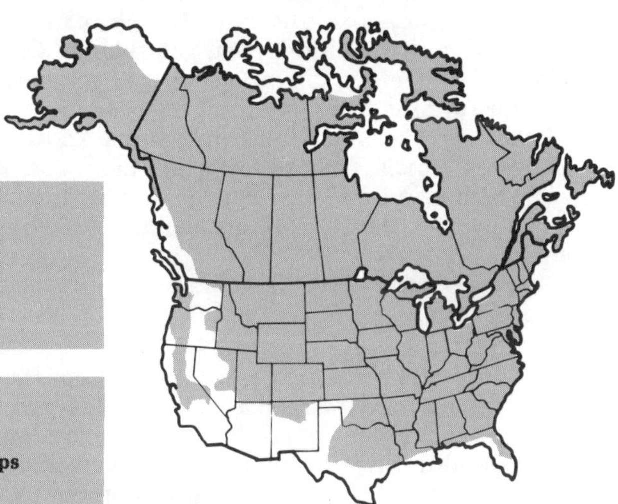

Attractors

- Rotted fish
- Tainted meat chunks
- Canine urines
- Commercial lures

Suggested Traps

- #1½, #1.75, #2 Coilspring traps
- #2 Longspring traps

The Red Fox

THE red fox is easily recognized by its color. This species is native to North America, and red foxes are widely distributed in the United States and Canada. Red foxes are suspicious by nature. Many foxes have earned reputations as being clever. This species can adapt to many climates, habitat types, and human population densities. An important farmland predator, red foxes are considered by many trappers as being one of the more difficult to trap species.

Description

The long fur of red foxes gives them an appearance of being larger than they really are. Red foxes commonly weigh 10 to 12 pounds in many areas, with occasional large specimens weighing up to 14 pounds. Red fox are slightly heavier in the northern parts of their ranges, and slightly lighter in far southern locations.

Distinctive marks on red fox include feet that are usually black, with black fur also on the backs of the ears. A white tipped tail is common, and the red colors of the fur mute with grayish or whitish fur on the throat, bottom of the neck and belly areas.

Colors vary in sections, and with individuals. Many southern red fox are blondish, and darker reddish colors are usually found in northern farmlands and forests. Red foxes on the western high plains are somewhat pale in color.

Color phases do occur with red foxes, even in the same litters. Color phases are much more apt to occur in northern or colder regions, and almost never occur in southern regions. Other than the most common color of red, red foxes can be black, silver or a cross between red and silver known as "cross fox". Black fox have black tipped guard hairs, and silver fox are black with white tipped guard hairs. Cross fox often have reddish sides and dark along the middle of the back area, with a cross of dark colored fur running from one front leg over the back to the other front leg.

Relatively uncommon are red foxes known as "bastard" foxes and "Sampson" foxes. Bastard foxes lack color and are brownish or greyish in color. Sampson foxes have few or no guard hairs in their fur.

The eyes of the red fox are yellow or amber in color, with elliptical pupils.

Red foxes have 42 teeth, including 4 canine teeth to help them catch and kill prey species.

Distribution

Red foxes are present in every state except Hawaii. Southern California, parts of Nevada and Arizona have very few red fox.

Larger populations of red foxes usually are found in farmland areas, but red foxes also thrive in forested areas as well as treeless plains.

Coyote populations have an impact on red fox populations, and red fox are usually not abundant where coyotes are also abundant.

Red foxes are presently harvested by trapping in 35 states.

Sign

Indications that red fox are present include tracks and droppings. Red fox tracks are distinctive by relatively small pads on the feet, and a track pattern habit that causes the prints to fall in a relatively straight line. A red fox track resembles a house cat track, except more elliptical and the toenail prints will be seen in the red fox tracks.

Good places to look for red fox tracks are at the edges of fields, haystacks, inactive roads and trails.

Droppings are dark in color when fresh, slender and usually pointed. Fur and bone fragments are often obvious in red fox droppings.

Fox droppings are sometimes deposited in obvious places where another red fox will notice them, such as around old burrows, or near a dead animal.

Reproduction

Male and female red foxes begin to pair up in December or January, and mating is usually accomplished in January. Evidence suggests that red foxes do pair up with the same mates of the past year, if both are still alive.

The litter is born 52 or 53 days later, usually about mid-March, in an underground den. These dens are often located on slopes with good visibility in all directions, and several entrances and connecting tunnels are typical. Oftentimes, these dens are abandoned woodchuck or badger diggings, which were renovated by the foxes.

Average litter size for red fox is 6 to 8 pups.

During the first week after birthing, the female stays in the den with the newborn pups, and the mate brings food to the female at the den opening. Later, both mates hunt to provide food for the litter.

Red foxes usually have an alternate den selection. The female will not

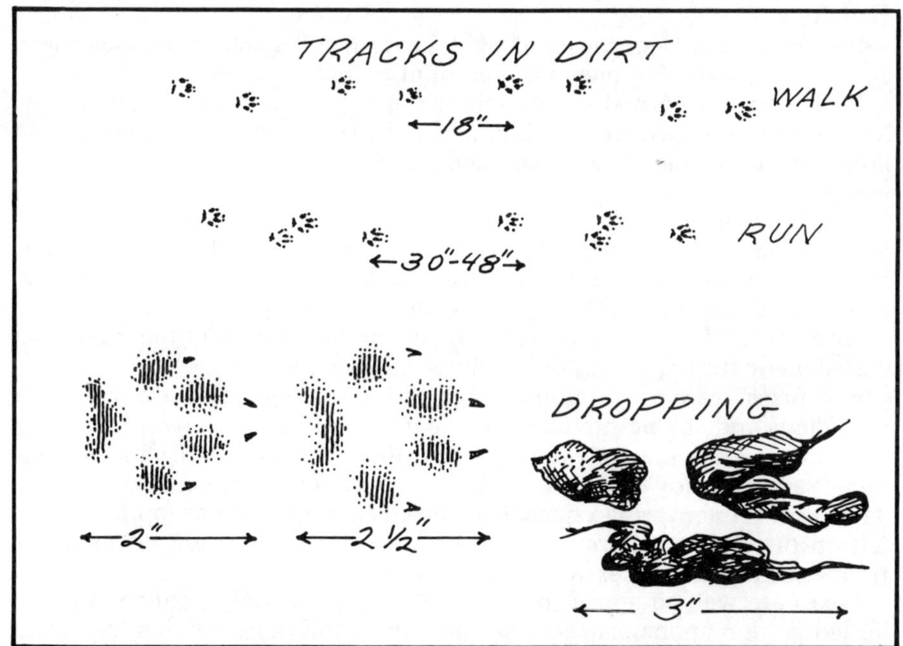

A good location for red fox near a fence corner. The vegetation should be low where the set is made.

hesitate to move the litter if she feels that the den is threatened.

Red foxes have one litter per year. 12 years of age is considered old for red fox.

Habits

Red foxes have keen senses of sight, hearing and smell which they use to advantage in avoiding enemies, and hunting prey species.

Red foxes are normally shy, nervous or flighty and they startle easily. Enemies are escaped by running, and red foxes have been clocked at 45 miles per hour. Red foxes have good endurance. They can run for miles when they are pursued.

Red foxes prefer open areas where visibility is good, and often seek out open places in the forests when hunting or resting for the day. Daytime resting areas are usually on elevated spots, such as knolls or haystacks and usually in sunny places during the winter.

Underground dens are used mostly during the rearing of the litters and occasionally during windy or stormy weather conditions.

Red foxes are curious animals, indicating intelligence. However, their suspicious and shy nature compels them to avoid obvious dangers.

Red foxes are playful, another indication of intelligence in animals. Some seem to enjoy being chased by dogs, and some red foxes will make a game out of uncovering concealed traps. Many times, a dropping will be left on the uncovered trap, or nearby, as a communication either to the trapper or to other foxes who might happen by.

Foxes are well equipped to hunt, and they commonly pounce in a stiff legged fashion upon unsuspecting voles, mice and rabbits. Other important

A dirt hole set showing trap placement.

foods include fruits and berries, grasshoppers, snakes, ground nesting birds, muskrats and domestic fowl if available. White footed mice are an important food source during snow conditions, as these mice travel on top of the snow while most other mice and voles tunnel under the snow.

Red foxes do not chew their food, but swallow small species whole. They cut pieces from larger species which are also swallowed whole. This accounts for the abundance of fur and crushed bones found in fox droppings.

Red foxes commonly kill more food than they eat at a time, and they bury the extra food in caches. These caches are made by the fox digging shallow depressions with its front feet. The excess food is then placed in the depression, and dirt is pushed over the food with the fox's nose.

Red foxes are territorial throughout most of the year, and the choice territories are usually occupied by the more dominant foxes. Territory sizes vary according to fox population densities, and the abundance of food. Where red foxes are abundant, it appears that territories overlap. Some areas seem to be shared by two or even three different family units. In rare instances, communal denning does occur, with more than one female with her litter sharing the same den.

Red foxes are thought to mark territorial boundaries by urinating on objects at regular places. These objects are known as scent stations, and these scent stations seem to be visited by every fox in the area.

Under good habitat conditions, most fox territories will be about 2 or 3 square miles. However, if hunting conditions are good, most fox stay within one square mile daily, especially in mild weather.

Coyotes persecute red foxes. Coyotes dominate the better territories where the two species are both found. Red fox move when coyotes are pre-

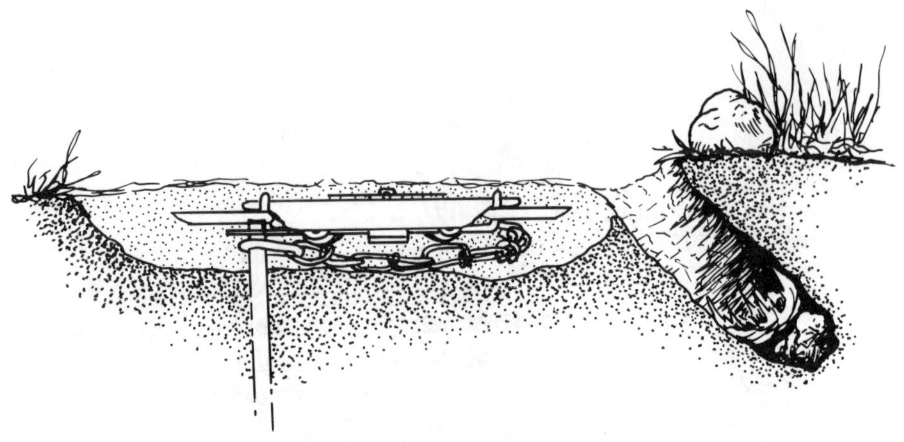

A light covering over the bait in the bottom of the hole is an advantage.

sent. Red fox territories seem to be in territories not claimed or used regularly by coyotes.

Juvenile red fox begin to wander from family units during August and September. Significant dispersals occur during the months of November, December and January as young foxes seek their own territories and mates. Many older red fox who have lost mates also seek new mates. Males seem to travel further than females. Many female red fox prefer to stay in the same territory, even if they have lost their mate.

Dispersal distances vary a great deal and are unpredictable. Two Wisconsin red foxes were tagged in August of 1962, and one of the juvenile male foxes was killed the following March 245 miles away in Indiana. The litter mate was killed in June, just 300 yards away from the original den site.

Red foxes like to climb upon things in order to get a better view, but they are poor tree climbers. Foxes usually avoid getting wet, but red fox can and do swim when they are forced to.

Trapping

Good traps for red foxes include sizes #1½ through #2. Number 2 longsprings, #1½ coilsprings and #2 coilsprings are favored by many fox trappers.

Where raccoons or gray foxes may also be caught in the same sets, many trappers feel that the #1½ coilspring trap is the best compromise trap.

In areas where coyotes may also be caught in fox sets, many trappers prefer to use slightly larger traps. Trap sizes #1.75 and #2 coilsprings have greater jaw spreads for the larger footed coyotes.

Most red fox trappers prefer to stake traps solidly at the set, and short chains of 8 to 10 inches keep the trapped animals from making long lunges while in the traps. Swiveling is important with shorter chained traps. Many trappers use metal stakes to allow the trap to swivel freely around the stake top.

In timbered or brushy areas, many fox trappers also use grapples on long chains to allow the trapped fox limited freedom away from the set. A chain length of 4 or 5 feet is recommended between the trap and the grapple, and many trappers add a swivel in the trap chain near the trap.

Fox traps should be dyed for best results. Some fox trappers also wax their fox traps. Rusty or oily traps can be smelled by red foxes, even when concealed beneath the dirt and these traps are usually avoided.

Set locations are important in the trapping of red foxes, and sets should be made close to the expected line of travel. The presence of tracks or droppings usually indicates a good location. Good locations can often be found near the edges of open fields, fringes of woods, fencelines, or old roads and trails.

Fox often shy from sets where they cannot get a clear view, and red fox sets are usually most productive when they are located some distance from large objects that they cannot see around or over.

Traps set for red foxes must be covered with dirt, snow or whatever is natural at the site. Some trappers prefer to use a pan cover of some type to prevent dirt from filling under the trap pan, yet some trappers prefer not to use pan covers at all.

One of the most important things to consider is the stabilization of the set trap, known as "bedding" the trap. This is important in fox trapping, and a trap that is tippy as a fox steps on a jaw or spring is apt to be discovered by the fox. Commonly, red foxes carefully scratch the dirt off of the trap, and continue the "game" with other trap sets as well.

To stabilize or bed fox traps, pack dirt around the outside of the trap jaws and over the springs to make it as solid as possible.

The vast majority of red foxes are caught in dirt hole sets, which resemble a small mammal's burrow or a place where another fox cached some extra food.

Scent posts are attractive to all wild canines.

There are many variations of dirt hole sets. Many fox trappers prefer to make their dirt hole sets against a small clump of grass, or a stick, which acts as "backing" for the set, and serves to guide the fox toward the hidden trap. Hole sizes are often 2 to 4 inches in diameter, and 6 or 8 inches deep. A bait is usually placed in the bottom of the hole, and most fox trappers use fox lure as an addition to the set, or in place of the bait. Most trappers complete the set with an application of fox urine to the set backing, to indicate that another fox had visited the set.

A trowel and a dirt sifter are aids in the construction of dirt hole sets for red foxes, and many trappers wear gloves when handling clean traps to prevent contaminating them with their own scent.

If you use the same gloves to handle lures, baits and traps, you may find that the contaminated gloves will contaminate the traps too. For this reason, many trappers keep their lures, baits and dirty gloves away from the clean traps, and use only clean gloves when handling the traps.

To prepare for winter trapping, many fox trappers store up dry dirt in the summer and use it later in the winter to cover the traps. Dry dirt cannot freeze over the traps until it becomes wet.

The lures and baits commonly used to attract red foxes also have an attraction to roaming dogs. A percentage of roaming dogs can be avoided with the use of tainted, or partially rotten baits, which are still very attractive to red foxes. Also, when the trap is placed as close to the bait hole as is possible, the trap will catch the majority of foxes and miss many dogs who are built larger, and stand somewhat further from the trap while investigating the lure or bait.

Red foxes have demonstrated that they can withstand heavy harvest without detriment. The greatest threat to the species is underharvesting, and increasing coyote population densities.

Dispatch

Foxes can be shot in the head with a .22. Care should be taken so that the bullet does not exit along the fox's back or sides.

A more common method of dispatching red fox is to stun the animal with a sharp blow with a trowel or trap stake to the head or bridge of the nose. With the unconscious fox laying on its side, the trapper places one foot over the fox's neck and takes his other heel, places it over the fox's rib cage right behind the shoulder, and places his weight on the fox's lung and diaphragm area. Most foxes do not regain consciousness before death occurs within a minute. Always check for any eye reflexes before removing a fox from a trap and touch an eyeball with a finger to see if there is any reaction at all.

Controls

Red foxes are vulnerable to several diseases, and severe devastation can and does occur when populations are high enough for easy transmission of the disease between individuals.

Most serious of fox diseases at present are mange and parvo enteritis. Mange in red fox is caused by mites which tunnel in the fox's skin, causing irritation and loss of fur. Infections occur as a result of the growing eggs and excrement in the fox's skin, and caking or crusting of the skin occurs, particularly around the eyes and nose of the infected fox. Nearly naked tails are observed in mange infected foxes, and it appears that virtually all red foxes infected with mange die slow and painful deaths.

Parvo is a virus that appears to be a mutation of feline distemper. It is probably spread by contact between infected individuals, and symptoms include fever, diarrhea and nervous disorders. Juvenile animals appear to have less resistance to this disease, and large population reductions can occur when fox populations are high.

Values

Red foxes contribute to the overall health of prey species by keeping the prey species controlled.

The red fox provides sport hunting for many Americans, and this species is an important furbearer for fur harvesters in many areas. Annual yields of foxes are about 400 thousand pelts, which bring more than 25 million dollars annually.

Red fox can and do take domestic fowl when the opportunity presents itself, particularly during the spring when there is a need to provide foods for growing litters. Due to modern farming practices in many areas, this problem is lesser than it has been in the past.

Red foxes are also vulnerable to rabies, and rabid animals can infect pets, or even man.

Fur Handling

Red foxes are handled cased, with the fur on the outside of the pelt. The opening cut is made from the inside of one hind leg to the other. Two more cuts are then made from the base of the tail, around the vent, to the opening cut. The fur can then be separated from the hind legs and cut off just above the hind feet. A gambrel can be used to suspend the fox at this time. A cut should be made ⅓ of the way down the underside of the tail, and the tail can be pulled off of the tailbone with the aid of a tail stripper, pliers, or even two sticks pinched together. After the tail has been freed, pull the pelt down past the shoulders, and work the skin free in the armpit area with thumb pressure. The skin should be pulled ½ way down the length of the front legs, and separated with a knife cut. Further pulling of the pelt will strip it down to the ear area, where knife cuts will be needed to free the ears, and again at the eyes, and the final cut will leave the nose attached to the pelt.

Scraping of red fox pelts is usually not necessary. Meat or fat adhering to the skin can usually be removed easily by hand.

Foxes **must** be stretched with the fur to the inside to partially dry, whether wire stretchers or wooden stretchers are used. If you use a solid wooden stretcher, be sure to use a wedge shaped belly board on the stomach side of the pelt. Drying times with the fur to the inside are usually about 24 hours or so, or until the flesh side of the pelt is dry to the touch.

At this time, remove the pelt from the stretcher, and turn it fur side out starting at the head by pushing the nose through the hole left by the mouth. Take care when turning fox pelts, as the leather is thin and vulnerable to tearing with too much pressure. If the leather appears to be too brittle to turn without damage, a softening can be accomplished by wiping the skin side with a damp rag.

When the pelt is turned with the fur to the outside, it must be placed back on the stretcher for the final drying process. Be sure the back and belly of the pelt lines up in the center of the stretcher for the final drying process, which might take several days to a week.

Red fox furs can be enhanced with a combing or brushing before they are sold. If you grab the pelt by the nose, you can fluff the fur by a gentle shaking of the pelt.

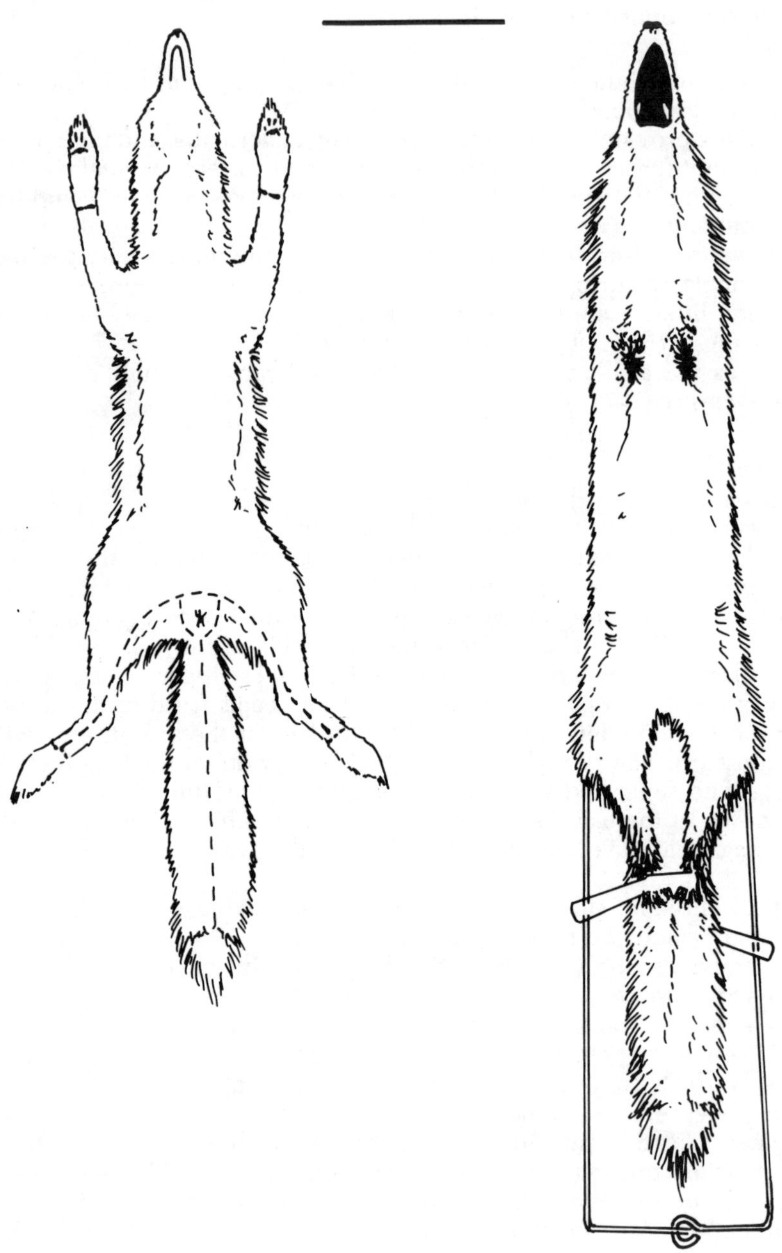

GRAY FOX — Urocyon Cinereoargenteus

Order — Carnivora
Family — Canidae

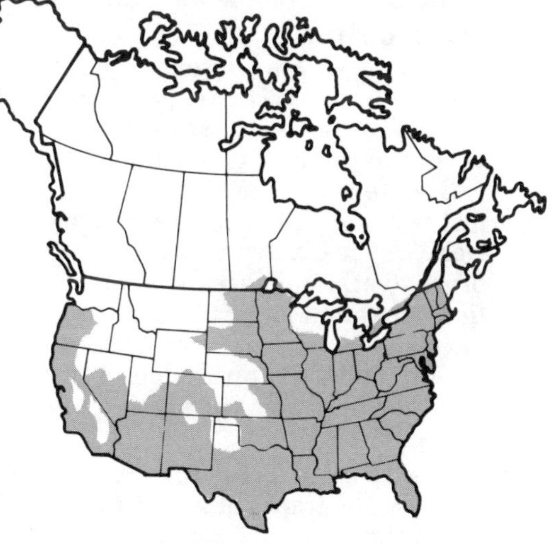

Attractors

Fermented persimmons
Fresh & tainted meat chunks
Rotted eggs, rotted fish
Canine urines, commercial lures

Suggested Traps

#1½, #2 Double jawed traps
#1½ Coilspring traps
#1½, #2 Longspring traps

The Gray Fox

GRAY foxes are widely distributed in the United States. This species prefers brushy or forested habitats, and is unique in that this fox is a skilled tree climber. Gray foxes have small ranges, and they commonly take advantage of whatever type of food is available at the time. Gray foxes are often more aggressive than red foxes, and an abundance of gray foxes will prevent an abundance of red foxes in the same habitat. Grays are usually easier to trap than red foxes, but experienced or trap-wise gray foxes can be quite difficult to catch.

Description

The gray fox is often confused with the red fox because the gray has rusty-red fur on its ears, ruffs and neck. Overall coloration is gray, and the darkest color extends in a suggested stripe along the top of the back down to the end of the tail. The belly, throat and chest areas are whitish in color.

Gray foxes appear to be smaller than red foxes. The shorter leg length and stockier body are deceptive. Many gray foxes weigh about the same as red foxes in the same habitat types. Males and females both weigh 8 to 11 pounds on the average. Weights are often around 8 pounds in southern states, and nearer 11 pounds in northern states.

Compared to red foxes, grays have shorter muzzles, and shorter ears which are usually held erect and pointed forward.

Many gray foxes stand about 15 inches tall at the shoulders, and overall lengths are around 40 to 44 inches including tails of 12 to 15 inches.

The claws on a gray fox foot are strong. They are not retractable.

Gray foxes have dark eyes with elliptical pupils. Teeth number 42, including 4 canine teeth. Both male and female gray foxes have a scent gland under the skin on the top of the tail.

Distribution

Gray foxes are present in all states except the northern and western mountain states. The range of gray foxes has been expanding for a number of years, as this species was found only in southern and mid-western states when this country was settled.

Gray foxes prefer habitat types of brush. This fox is not afraid to get its feet wet, and they commonly inhabit swamps. Arid conditions are no barrier. Gray foxes also thrive in deserts as long as sagebrush or other types of brushy vegetation are available. Gray foxes also thrive in forests. Populations are often largest in second growth forests or mixtures of forests and farmlands.

Gray foxes are rarely found in grasslands or prairies, which indicates that they need trees or brush to climb to escape predation by coyotes.

Sign

The tracks of a gray fox are an obvious indication of the presence of the species. The tracks of a gray fox show larger pad sizes than the red fox. At times, the prints are side by side as the gray fox does not usually place its back foot in the same track made by a front foot as is the case with the red fox.

Tracks can often be seen in the dust or sand on lightly traveled roads. Grays rarely follow these old roads far, and many times only a set of tracks crossing the road will be found.

Droppings resemble red fox droppings, but they are usually darker in color. There is apt to be more vegetation in the gray fox droppings, which like the red fox, are often deposited near a large rock, stump or other conspicuous place.

In areas where persimmon trees are found, gray foxes leave scats with the large seeds in evidence.

In some southern areas, gray fox droppings are not firm during trapping seasons. The almost constant diarrhea does not seem to affect the animals adversely, and may reflect diet or an abundance of internal parasites.

It is difficult to predict where gray fox tracks will be found due to the erratic habits of the animals.

Reproduction

Gray foxes are thought to mate for life. The breeding season extends from January to May, with peak periods around the first of March. Gestation varies from 51 to 63 days.

Most gray foxes breed and raise litters during their first year of life. There is one annual litter and 3 or 4 pups are a common litter size.

Male gray foxes bring food to the denned up female and assist in teaching the pups to hunt.

Gray foxes are considered as old in the wild at 12 years.

Habits

Gray foxes are seldom seen because they are normally active only during the night and because of the brushy habitat they inhabit.

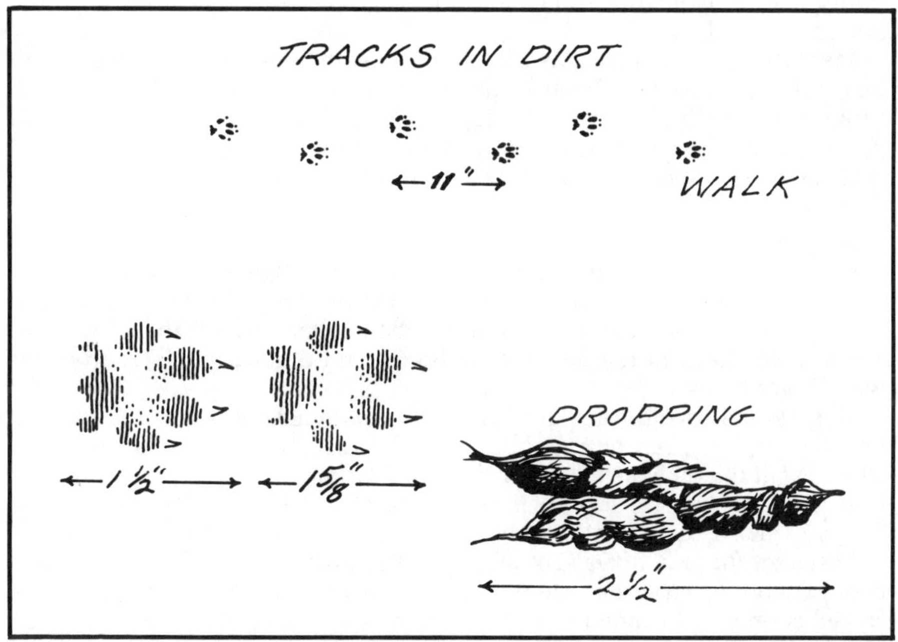

Gray foxes are very territorial. These home ranges are usually one square mile or even less. Because a gray fox might spend years or even its entire life in this small range they soon learn to know their ranges very well.

Traveling habits are erratic as the gray fox seems to wander within its territory seeking food. This species will eat a variety of foods, including fruits and other vegetations. This ability allows the gray fox to capitalize on whatever food is available at the time. If food is abundant, gray foxes will become fatter and heavier than usual.

The tree climbing ability of gray foxes is unique. Grays can climb trees that are straight up and they do not require leaning trees to climb. These foxes will climb trees at times to escape predators and they also climb because they want to. At times, gray foxes will climb trees to take a nap in a sunny location, and they have been known to hide or sleep in hawk and owl nests. Rarely, gray foxes will also raise their litter twenty or more feet above ground in a hollow tree.

Gray foxes climb trees head first, and they have the ability to descend a tree either tail first or head first.

Gray foxes use dens more frequently than do red foxes. These dens are usually underground cavities, and the same dens are often used year after year. Dens seem to be used more frequently by gray foxes in northern locations, as compared to southern locations. Cold weather and deep snow hamper gray foxes, so a likely explanation is that the dens provide more warmth for the northern grays.

Dispersal distances of young gray foxes are short. Most young grays relocate and select new home ranges within a mile of their birthplace. For that reason, high densities of gray foxes can sometimes be found in suitable habitats.

Although gray foxes have keen sense of smell, they seldom track prey species. The preferred method of hunting is to wander this way and that until a victim is heard or smelled. Then the gray fox will often stalk and pounce upon the prey.

Meat items frequently eaten by gray foxes include rabbits, mice, squirrels, rats and insects. Game birds are frequently eaten, including quail, turkeys and ruffed grouse. Nesting adults are frequently killed, and all ground nests are vulnerable within the territory of a gray fox.

Gray foxes will eat carrion. Vegetation eaten includes virtually all fruits, nuts and berries.

Trapping

Gray foxes are sometimes bold enough to enter cage traps. Still, foothold traps are more effective and preferred by the majority of gray fox trappers.

Traps larger than size 1½ should not be deliberately set for gray foxes. These foxes have rather slender leg bones and damage is likely to occur with larger traps.

Size 1½ coilspring traps are favored by many trappers for this species, and this type of trap is a good choice if a raccoon, red fox or opossum should visit the set before the gray fox does. Other good choices for gray fox traps include size 1½ longsprings and number 1 traps with two springs. Traps in size 1 or 1½ with double jaws are also excellent choices.

Traps set for gray foxes should always be attached strongly in case a raccoon, coyote or stray dog should happen to get caught. The traps can be staked solidly or fastened to grapples with 4 or 5 feet of chain.

Dirt hole sets in the woods are effective gray fox sets.

Set locations can be hard to determine when trapping gray foxes. The better locations are usually wherever gray fox signs are found. The small territory size suggests that the gray fox will return to wherever its tracks are found within a short time and traps set outside of a gray fox territory are usually doomed to failure. Although the gray fox may not return to the same locations every night, the chances of a catch are greatly multiplied wherever tracks or droppings are found.

Some trappers locate gray foxes before trapping seasons by pre-baiting, or leaving baits without traps. This is one way to locate gray foxes. But, be sure to use a bait that the gray fox will eat or it may not investigate your trap set later on to investigate the same bait. For this reason, it is an advantage to use fresh meat baits.

Gray foxes have a good sense of curiosity and they do respond well to a wide variety of lures and baits.

Dirt hole sets are favored by many gray fox trappers. They can be made nearly anywhere and baits, lures or a combination of both can be very effective with this set. The trap should be set close to the hole where it will be very effective on gray foxes while reducing the chance of catching a larger and longer animal, such as a stray dog.

Urine post or scent post sets are also effective on gray foxes. In this set construction, fox urine is applied to a dry stick, clump of grass, or a rock with the trap set and concealed several inches away.

Traps set for gray foxes should be well hidden. Most trappers scrape out a depressed trap bed to hide the trap in. Experienced trappers pack dirt around the set trap to stabilize it, and then use a sifter to sift dirt completely over the trap. A proper dirt covering over the trap should be ¼ to ½ of an inch.

When sets are made for gray foxes, the urine, lure or bait should be placed where the fox can't roll in it. Gray foxes will roll in putrid smells and the object is to catch the fox while it is trying to investigate the attractor. For this reason, it is best to not apply any attractive smell over the top of the trap.

Traps set for gray foxes work best when they are clean and dyed, waxed or both.

Under most conditions, gray foxes are conservatively harvested due to their relatively small ranges. Many landowners who do not allow harvesting protect this species due to the small ranging habits of the species.

It is an advantage to use tainted meat baits or fruit baits for gray fox. This will minimize the chance of catching a stray dog.

Dispatch

Gray foxes can be shot in the head with a .22. Care should be taken so that the bullet does not exit along the fox's back or side.

The most commonly used method of dispatching a gray fox is to stun the animal with a sharp blow to the head. With the unconscious animal lying on its side, the trapper places one foot over the fox's neck and takes his other heel, places it over the fox's rib cage right behind the shoulder, and shifts his weight on the fox's lung and diaphragm area. Most foxes do not regain consciousness before death occurs within a minute. Death can be determined by touching the fox's open eye and any reflexes or blinking indicates that the animal is not dead.

Controls

Other than man, the worst enemy of gray foxes are dogs. Significant numbers of gray foxes, particularly juveniles, are killed by dogs before they escape to a hole or are able to climb a tree for safety.

Gray foxes are able to resist mange. A more important disease of gray foxes is distemper, which is oftentimes fatal. This disease can decimate gray fox populations whenever there is opportunity for contact between individual animals.

Gray foxes are also susceptible to parvo enteritis, rabies, roundworms, tapeworms, lice and mites.

Mountain lions kill gray foxes, as do golden eagles. Coyotes are a serious predator wherever the two species share the same habitat.

Values

Gray foxes contribute to the overall health of prey species by keeping the prey species controlled.

Gray foxes are usually very beneficial to man because of their preference for wild foods. The number of rodents eaten outweigh a very rare visit to a farmyard where a chicken might be vulnerable.

In southern states, goodly numbers of cotton rats are eaten. These rats do prey upon quail nests, so the net effect might be that the grey fox also serves the quail in spite of the fact that they also eat quail and rob nests as well.

Gray foxes serve man for sport. The species is sought by hunters with hounds, and gray foxes respond well to predator calls, especially at night.

Trappers enjoy the resource in many states. Harvests by hunting and trapping yield about 300 thousand pelts annually, bringing 8 to 10 million dollars to many families in many American communities.

Fur Handling

In many states gray fox pelts are handled cased, with the fur on the outside. However, pelts taken from the southeastern states are wanted cased, with the fur on the inside by some buyers. Check with your local fur buyers if you are in doubt as to how your furs are wanted.

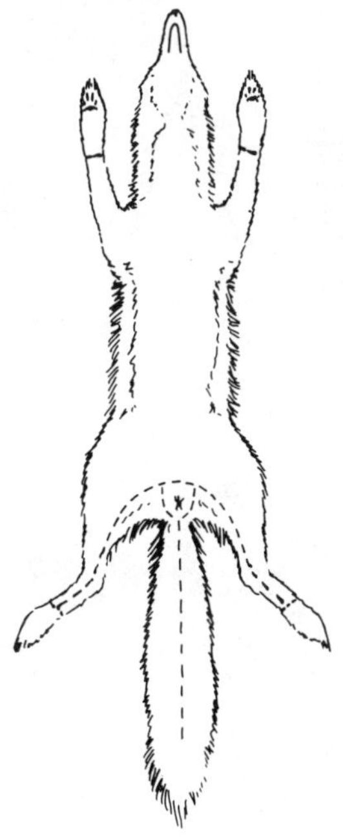

The opening cut is made from the inside of one hind leg to the other. Two more cuts are then made from the base of the tail, around the vent, to the opening cut. The fur can then be separated from the hind legs, and cut off just above the hind feet. A gambrel can be used at this time to suspend the fox, and the tail can be pulled off of the tailbone with the aid of a tail stripper or a clothespin. After the tail has been freed, pull the pelt down past the shoulders and work the skin free in the armpit area with thumb and finger pressure. The skin should be pulled ½ way down the front legs and separated with a knife cut. Further pulling of the pelt will strip it down to the ear area where knife cuts will be needed to free the ears and again at the eyes, and the final cut will leave the nose attached to the pelt.

Most gray foxes can be fleshed over a wooden stretcher with a single handled fleshing tool. Foxes that are exceptionally fat can be best handled on a fleshing beam with a two handled fleshing knife.

Either a wooden stretcher or wire stretcher can be used to stretch the pelt. If a wooden one piece stretcher is used, a wedge shaped belly board must be used to prevent the pelt from shrinking too tightly to the stretcher.

The fur should be placed over the stretcher with the fur on the inside. After one or two days, the fur can be removed from the stretcher and turned with the fur to the outside before it is replaced on the stretcher for the final drying process, which usually takes a week or less.

Gray fox furs can be enhanced with a combing or brushing before they are sold.

RACCOON — Procyon Lotor

Order — Carnivora
Family — Procyonidae

Attractors

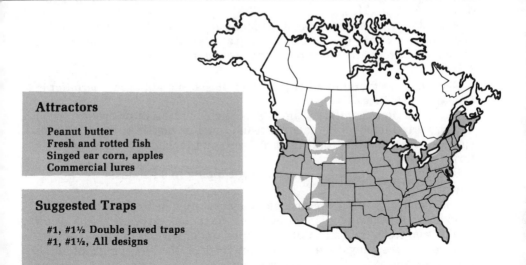

Peanut butter
Fresh and rotted fish
Singed ear corn, apples
Commercial lures

Suggested Traps

#1, #1½ Double jawed traps
#1, #1½, All designs

The Raccoon

THE raccoon is one of the easily recognizable furbearers with a ringed tail and patches of dark fur over the eye areas resembling a mask. Known to many as "coon", the raccoon is managed by some states both as a game animal and as a furbearer. This important and well distributed species is adaptable to a variety of habitat types and the species thrive in both wilderness and urban areas.

Description

Raccoon weights vary from region to region. Generally, raccoons attain larger weights in northern states and lighter weights in southern states. Most adult male raccoons in northern states weigh 15-18 pounds during fall harvest seasons, with females averaging 2-3 pounds less. In some southern areas, mature males weigh about 9-10 pounds with females from the same areas weighing 8-9 pounds.

Occasional specimens in northern states may weigh 30 pounds. Several individual raccoons have been taken from the wild weighing more than 50 pounds, but whether these animals may have been fed as captives is unknown.

Raccoons have 40 teeth, including 4 elongated and sharp canine teeth.

The hind legs of the raccoon are longer than the front legs, giving them a hunched appearance as they walk or run. Toes number five on each foot and the front feet are dexterous, allowing the raccoon to grasp and clutch items.

The fur of raccoons has guard hair of 2-2¼ inches long on the back areas, and underfur is 1½ or 1¾ inches long and dense. Depending upon market demands, raccoon fur is used both as a long haired fur and as a sheared and dyed, short haired fur.

Fur colors vary in areas. Most raccoons are a dirty blondish with darker colors of guard hairs mottling the overall appearance. Reddish colors occur regularly in areas and some raccoons are darker colors.

Distribution

Raccoons are found in all of the lower 48 states and the southern tier of Canadian provinces.

Raccoons do a significant amount of their hunting in or around water and preferred habitats include a stream, pond or marsh in the area. This species does roam far from water at times and raccoons do not appear to thrive in arid or desert areas.

Raccoons are presently harvested by trapping in 44 states.

Sign

Raccoon tracks are distinctive and they can often be found in the mud or sand along streams, ponds and marshes. Raccoons do wade in the water readily and fresh tracks can often be seen under several inches of water.

Raccoon droppings are usually larger than the droppings of other furbearers and indicate what the raccoon had been feeding upon. Regular

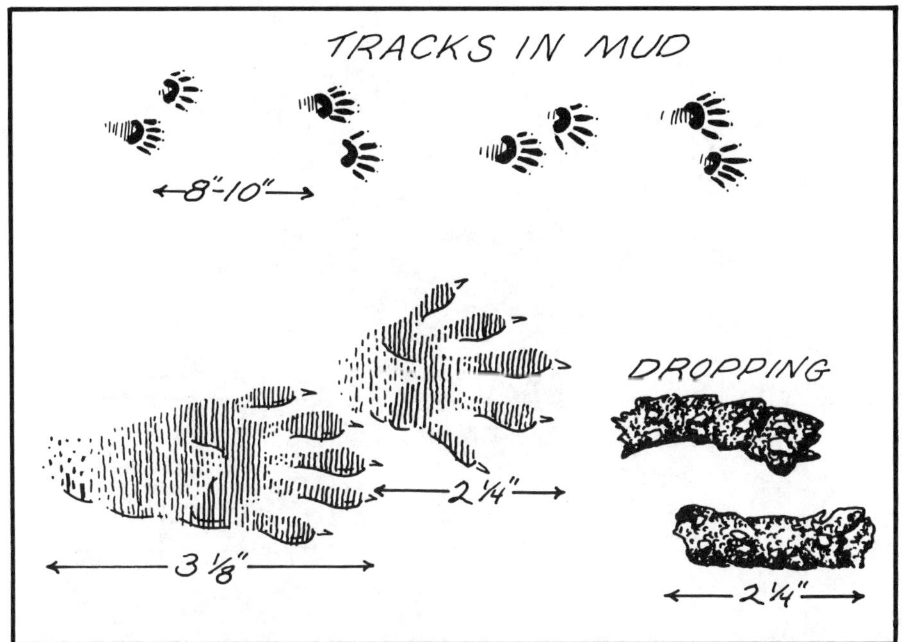

toilet areas are favored and fallen logs are sometimes used as a toilet area by more than one raccoon. In farmland areas corn is often obvious in raccoon droppings during harvest season.

Hollow trees are known by every raccoon in the area. Many times scratches can be seen on the tree trunks indicating that raccoons are climbing the tree regularly.

Good places to look for raccoon sign include old abandoned buildings, garbage dumps, orchards and along stream banks and ponds.

Reproduction

Breeding seasons for raccoons are usually in January in southern states, and February in the middle and northern states. Young males are evicted from the dens at this time and mature male raccoons search out all available females at this time.

Female raccoons are capable of breeding at 10 months of age, but males do not breed until their second year of life.

Gestation is usually 63 days, and 2-4 young are common in southern states. Litters of 4-6 are more common in northern states. The young raccoons are cared for solely by the mothers and mother raccoons are aggressive in the protection of young.

Ten years of age is considered old for a wild raccoon.

Habits

Raccoons eat a wide variety of foods and store up layers of fat during the fall to prepare for winter. Contrary to common beliefs, raccoons do not hibernate during extreme weather, but they do stay in dens for weeks at a time using up stored body fats. In southern states, raccoons may stay active all winter.

This species does exhibit a curiosity which is an indication of intelligence.

A bait lodged under a rock can be productive at the water's edge. Note the tangle stake which will prevent the raccoon from returning to shore.

Raccoons are both good swimmers and good tree climbers. When climbing a tree, a raccoon will usually climb in a hand over hand fashion, but they are capable of bounding up a tree.

Raccoon descend trees either by backing down or turning around and coming down head first. They do not hesitate to jump from heights of 30 feet when they feel threatened.

The front paws of raccoons are very dexterous and the species commonly hunt in shallow water by turning over stones in search of crayfish and other foods. Washing of foods before eating is not normally done by wild raccoons and this activity by some penned raccoons may reflect boredom or curiosity.

Raccoons are opportunists, commonly eating whatever is available. Important foods include crayfish, mussels, clams, frogs, salamanders, earthworms, fruits, nuts, grains, carrion, eggs and any available warm blooded small mammals or birds. Preferred foods may include fish and sweet corn.

Territory sizes vary with individual raccoons and most home ranges seem to cover 2-4 square miles. The shapes of the territories are irregular and usually include the waterways within the area.

A raccoon may cover as much as 3-5 miles on mild fall nights and eat as much as 5 pounds of foods while storing up body fat for winter. Usually, the raccoon will den up for the day at a convenient den.

Attempts to transplant raccoons are rarely successful because the species does not stay where they are relocated. In one South Carolina attempt, 789 raccoons were released and only 14 were ever recovered. Two were recovered within 20 miles of the release sites, and a dozen were found at distances of 20-180 miles. The rest could not be located.

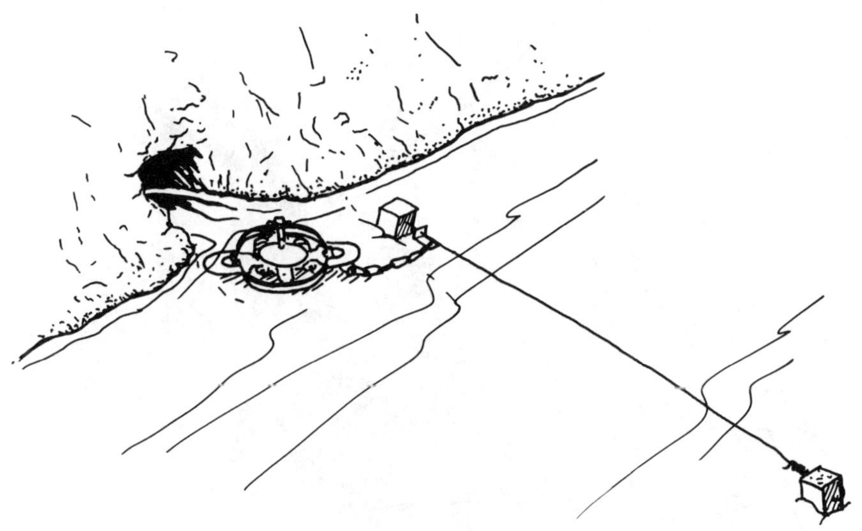

A slide wire set construction can be made where the water is deep enough to drown the raccoon.

Trapping

Raccoons are strong animals, yet traps larger than #2 should not be deliberately set for this species. Number 1 and 1½ traps make good trap selections and the double jawed traps in these sizes are excellent choices for raccoon trapping.

The method of fastening the trap, as well as the site selection, are as important as the trap selection in raccoon trapping.

Sets made along the water's edge are usually staked solidly in deep water. Care should be taken to not put the trap set where a trapped raccoon can reach something solid to grasp and help it pull from the trap. An extension wire can be an advantage in these sets and many trappers place another submerged stake where the trapped raccoon is sure to entangle and drown.

Another alternative for water sets is to construct a one way slide wire between two stakes to drown the raccoon. A slide lock must be applied to the trap. It takes a little more time to drive two trap stakes, but raccoons rarely escape these set constructions when properly made.

When traps are staked solidly on dry land for raccoons, a short chain length, of 8-10 inches, is an advantage with an extra swivel.

Many trappers prefer to use either grapples or clogs when trapping this species on dry land. A chain length or wire extension length of 4-5 feet is recommended between the trap and the clog. The clog should be hardwood and firm enough to prevent the raccoon from chewing through it. If wire is used for this purpose it must be strong.

Sets for raccoons can be either natural sets without attractors or sets with attractors. Raccoons do respond to a wide variety of baits and lures, and attractors that have a fishy, sweet or fruity smell are very efficient and somewhat selective towards raccoons.

Many trappers use a piece of fish to attract raccoons to water sets.

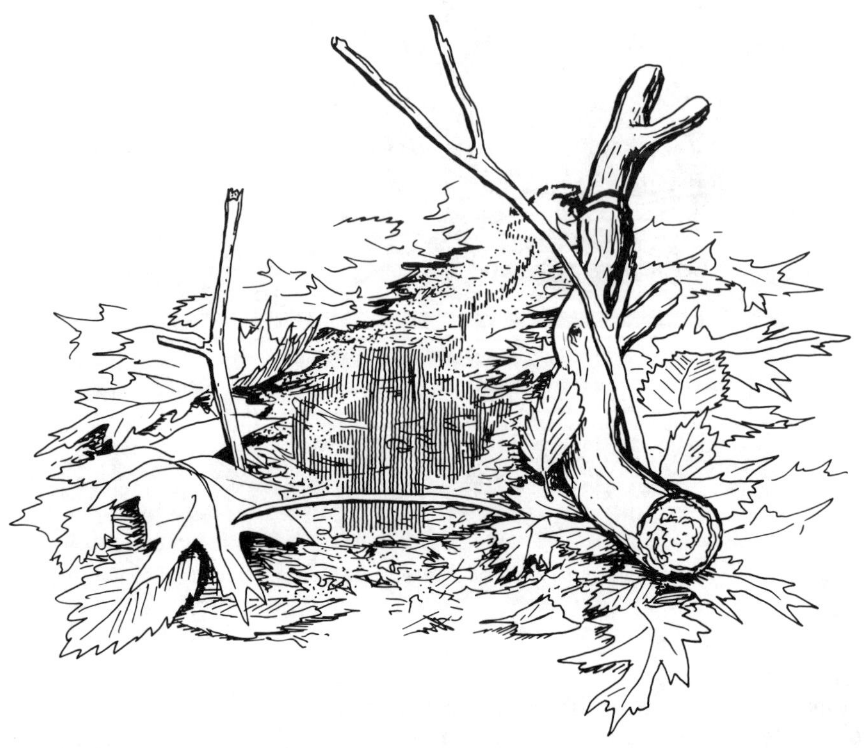

A trail set. Be sure to use a strong wire and hardwood clog.

Dryland raccoon sets can be baited with partially burnt ear corn, apples, jam or honey to prevent accidental catches of stray dogs or cats.

Raccoons follow trails regularly and traps set in trails can be made more selective for raccoon by placing brush or a log over the trap at heights of 10-12 inches. This will cause deer, dogs and many other non-target animals to go over the set, or around it, without having opportunity to step into the set trap. If brush is used, be sure that there is a convenient opening for the raccoon to go under or through the brush.

Don't be discouraged as raccoons begin to den up during cold snaps. Raccoons do hunt and travel on moderate nights.

In many areas, raccoons can sustain a large harvest along waterways without detriment. These areas are preferred habitat types and an influx of new raccoons will fill in the gaps during the late winter and early spring migration times.

Dispatch

Raccoons can be difficult to kill and many trappers dispatch their raccoons by shooting with a .22 bullet into the brain area. Whenever you shoot a raccoon in a trap, direct your shot so that the bullet will not exit the skin along the entire back of the animal, damaging the value of the pelt. Wait for a side shot to the head or direct the path of the bullet so that it will lodge inside of the animal after passing through the brain area.

Raccoons can be killed with a sharp blow to the top of the head area with a metal trap stake or a hard club. Be sure to make the first blow properly to stun the animal and a second blow is recommended to the unconscious animal to insure death. Always test for any eye reflex before taking a raccoon out of a trap. Raccoons do get rabies and you must avoid any situation where a raccoon might be able to bite you.

Controls

Adult raccoons are sometimes preyed upon by coyotes, bobcats and mountain lions where ranges overlap. Juvenile raccoons are also killed at times by large owls, eagles and fishers.

Several diseases afflict the species, including both canine and feline distemper. Raccoons occasionally carry leptospirosis, which can be transmitted to man via biting. Rabies is also a problem in raccoons and this species is the leading carrier of this dreaded disease in some eastern and southeastern states.

Parasites affecting raccoons include roundworms, flatworms, tapeworms, mange causing mites, lice and fleas.

Values

The raccoon does not compete severely with other species in the demands upon the habitat. Many species can and do share the same areas with raccoons with a minimum of friction.

The raccoon resource has a huge value for man and raccoon hunting with hounds is popular in many states. The actual harvest of raccoons is dominated by hunters who harvest between eighty and ninety percent of the total annual take, with the balance mostly taken by trapping.

Fur prices for raccoons have brought over 100 million dollars a year to American hunters and trappers in virtually every community. North American harvests yield 4 million pelts during a typical year.

Raccoons also serve man as a food source.

Raccoons can and do cause damage at times, especially when they are abundant. Waterfowl nests are raided regularly for eggs and raccoons sometimes raid farmyards for chickens or other fowl. Corn in the milk stage is vulnerable to raccoons and they find sweet corn particularly attractive. The damage to sweet corn by raccoons can be extensive, as this species commonly wastes more sweet corn than it eats.

Fur Handling

Raccoon pelts are handled cased, with the fur to the inside. The opening cut is made from the inside of one hind leg to the other. Two more cuts are then made from the base of the tail, around the vent, to the opening cut. The fur can then be separated from the hind legs and cut off at the hind ankle area. A gambrel can be used to suspend the raccoon for the rest of the skinning at this time. A cut should be made ⅓ of the way down the underside of the tail and the tail can be pulled off of the tailbone with the aid of a tail stripper, pliers or similar tool. After the tail has been freed, pull the pelt down past the shoulders, making light knife cuts behind the skin as is necessary. A bluntly pointed and strong instrument, such as an old sharpening steel or a trap stake, can often be forced between the skin and flesh in the armpit area and used for leverage to pull the skin down past the elbow area, where the separating cuts can be made for the front legs. Further pulling of the pelt will strip it down to the base of the skull, where two cuts will be necessary to free the ears and again at the eyes, and the final cut will leave the nose attached to the pelt.

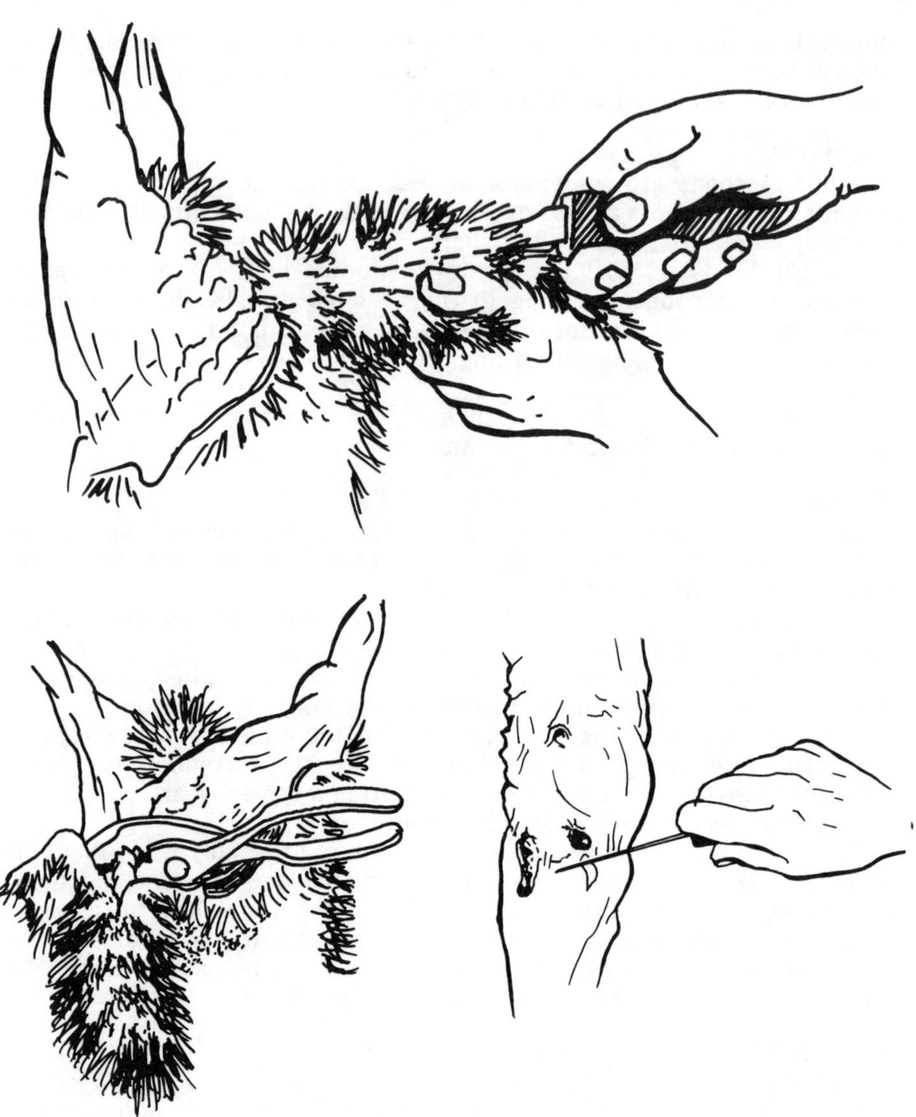

It is an advantage to open the tail part way before stripping. The skin must also be cut at the ear canals and eyes.

Raccoon fleshing requires proper tools, including a two handled fleshing knife and a fleshing beam. If you do not have the equipment, you should consider freezing the pelt for a later sale or selling it at once.

Raccoon fleshing is usually accomplished by beginning scraping on the throat area of the pelt down the middle of the belly and then rotated for scraping of both sides and the back. The scraping process is somewhat more difficult on the back of the neck and some fur handlers begin this area using the sharp side of the two handled fleshing knife to separate gristle from the skin. Importantly, all fat and flesh must be removed from raccoon pelts, including the fat along the entire length of the tail.

A fleshing beam and two handled fleshing knife are essential to prepare raccoon hides easily.

Wood or wire stretchers are used for raccoon pelts. Stretching for width is not as important as stretching for length. Don't overstretch and just pull the pelt as far as it will go comfortably.

Some trappers enlarge the "inspection window" on the lower belly of the fur by removing a small strip of worthless belly fur to help expose the color and density of the back fur.

Raccoon furs dry in a week or so under normal conditions.

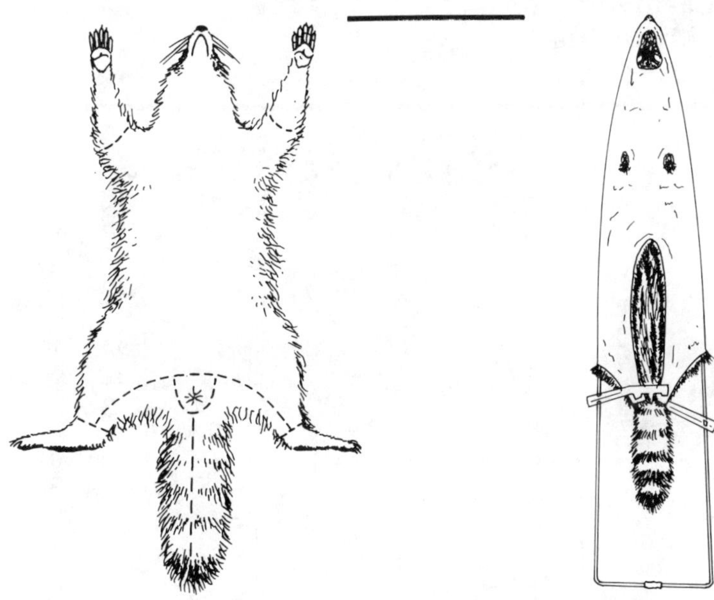

MARTEN — Martes Americana

Order — Carnivora
Family — Mustelidae

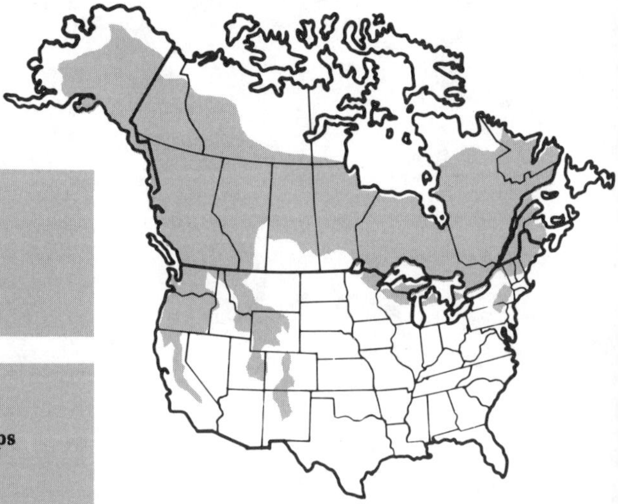

Attractors

- Strawberry jam
- Fresh meat chunks
- Fresh or rotted fish
- Skunky commercial lures

Suggested Traps

- Small sized body gripping traps
- #0, #1, #1½ Longspring traps

The Marten

MARTEN are woodland animals. American marten are sometimes confused with the European pine marten and the Russian sable, both of which are different species of martens. Uncontrolled fires, clear cutting lumbering practices and trapping pressures caused a significant decline in marten populations from the late 1800's to the 1940's when trapping seasons for martens were closed in most states and Canadian provinces. Since that time protection and the reintroduction of martens into acceptable habitats has proven to be a great success. Martens are currently present in 17 states and harvested by trapping in 10 states.

Description

Marten have silky fur with guard hairs of about 1½ inches in length. Colors vary from lighter buffs to darker browns and many marten exhibit throat patches that are orange in color or sometimes creamy white.

Males are consistently larger than females. Average males are 2 to 3 pounds in weight, with overall lengths of 25 to 30 inches including a furred tail of 9 to 12 inches. Tails are usually the darkest color on the individual animals.

Females are about ⅓ smaller than males in all sections.

Martens have 38 teeth, including 4 sharp canine teeth and flattened molars to allow chewing of foods.

The marten has five toes on each foot, however, the toe that is similar to our thumb is reduced in size and usually does not appear in tracks left by the marten.

Like other mustelids, martens have a pair of scent glands located near the anus. The musk is released from these glands when the marten is excited and the odor is not as objectionable or as powerful as mink, weasel or skunk musk.

Martens also have a large gland on their stomachs which give off odors during the mating seasons.

Semi-retractable claws on each foot are extended to aid the marten in climbing and killing prey species and the ability to retract the claws while running keeps the claws sharp at all times.

Distribution

Marten are habitat dependent and the species only thrives in coniferous forests or mixed forests of conifers and hardwood trees. Young forests and open areas are avoided during winter, although martens will frequently hunt pikas above timberline during the short summers in high altitudes.

Marten are abundant in the Rocky Mountains as far south as New Mexico and the species also thrives in the Sierras, Cascades and the frontal ranges of California, Oregon and Washington.

Reintroductions have established excellent populations of martens in the boreal forests of northern states, including Minnesota, Wisconsin, Michigan, New York, New Hampshire and Maine.

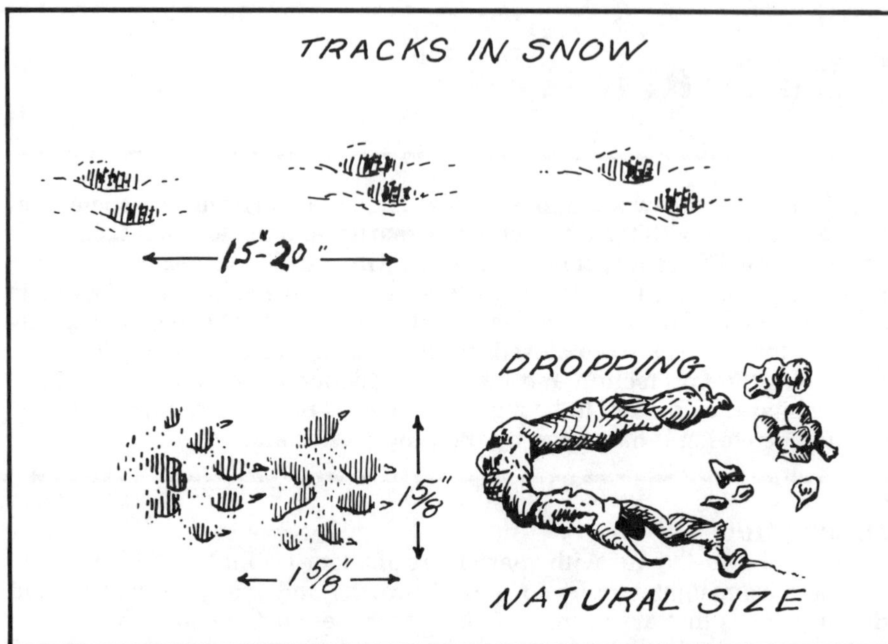

Sign

Tracks are similar to mink although the marten has a slightly larger foot. Marten tracks frequently lead to trees and martens are prone to running on downed logs. Martens travel with a loping gait spanning a distance of 15 to 20 inches, with male marten tracks averaging slightly longer lopes than female tracks.

Marten do not seem to use trails with any regularity and their overland traveling habits often follow dense evergreen thickets. Marten also seem to follow along mountain streams a great deal, but the species seldom enters the water.

Droppings are also similar to mink droppings and they are usually deposited on a prominent rock or log as a possible communication to other martens.

Red squirrels or other prey species are usually not found after they are killed by martens as the species usually retreats to a hiding place to eat, and stores or caches surplus foods.

Reproduction

Marten mate in July in most regions and the gestation period varies from 220 to 275 days because implantation is delayed. The length of daylight seems to trigger the final development of the offspring, which usually number 1 to 4. Litter sizes of 3 seem to be most common.

Males may breed with more than one female and the females are solely responsible in the raising of the young.

Although juvenile martens reach adult sizes at 4 to 5 months of age, they usually do not breed until their second year of life, which allows their first litter at three years of age.

A marten is considered to be old at 9 years of age.

A bait should be placed inside the box to attract martens.

Habits

Martens are active primarily at night. An extremely alert animal, martens move quickly through trees and over land as a normal activity. A high metabolic rate requires regular feeding and martens seem to be always hunting.

Except for breeding seasons, martens are not sociable with others of the same species and the animals lead mostly solitary lives.

Although martens seem to prefer not to get wet, they can swim and the species frequently hunt around mountain streams. Spawning fish are occasionally killed in shallow water streams when the temptation to kill is greater than the fear of getting wet.

This species is territorial during the bulk of the year, and male territory sizes are larger than female territories. The amount of cover and the availability of foods probably influence the size of the territory, with territories being larger when cover and prey species are sparse. A female territory can be as small as one square mile in good habitats, and several times that in poorer habitats. Males often cover 5 to 10 miles regularly, and male territories usually overlap the ranges of both other males and female martens.

Coverage of territories is irregular as martens do not seem to have regular circuits and established trails are seldom followed far. However, generation after generation of martens will usually cross and recross trails at nearly the same places for one reason or another.

Traveling is interrupted by rain, strong winds and strong snowstorms.

Dens in cavities in trees are used irregularly. Martens often seek out a temporary den to rest after feeding.

Martens are highly skilled tree climbers and they can literally gallop up a tree and run over the branches in pursuit of prey. At times, marten will travel from tree to tree, and available trees are used as refuge from pursuit.

Martens use the same type of habitat required by red squirrels and red squirrels appear to be an important part of the winter diet of martens in many areas. The most commonly eaten food is the redbacked vole, meadow mice and white footed mice. Aggressive predators, marten will attack and kill the much larger snowshoe hares and marmots.

Diet varies according to season and insects may be the favored food in the summer months. Berries and seeds are eaten when available and martens often scavenge carcasses of deer and moose, returning regularly to feed. Ground and tree nesting birds and their eggs are another important marten food.

Trapping

Marten are one of the easiest species to trap as they will step into uncovered traps without hesitation. Too, they require food regularly and the sharp senses of smell and sight enable a marten to find and investigate a variety of baits placed by trappers.

Small traps are adequate for marten trapping and number 0 or number one foothold traps are used by many trappers for this species. Small body gripping traps are also effective and preferred for tree sets where the marten may be suspended after it is captured.

Artificial or natural cubby sets on the ground are probably the most effective marten sets if made where the marten will find them. Locations should be chosen under dense evergreens or logs for these sets, to keep them operative as long as possible as snow levels deepen.

Tree sets are often used as snow begins to deepen and usually a pole is leaned against a tree trunk to encourage a marten to investigate the set. Sets are constructed under the protection of heavy branches or a trapper may elect to construct a "roof" of branches over the top of the set to catch the snow before it covers the set.

A simple cubby set is effective before deep snows.

When small body gripping traps are set on slanted poles, known as "running poles", a branch or two is often nailed over the top of the trap to encourage the marten to attempt to go through the trap to reach the bait. These traps can be set with baited trigger wires as well. Small boxes designed to hold the traps and the bait are very effective.

Meat baits are commonly used for marten trapping, and baits should be placed where they are not easily seen from above to discourage the accidental capture of birds. For this reason, baits should be placed on the underside of branches, or lightly covered from view.

Lures are sometimes used to attract marten and this species will respond to a wide variety of lure smells. Some trappers use lures with skunk essence added for effectiveness during extremely cold temperatures.

Selective baits include strawberry or raspberry jams. High sugar contents in jams prevent freezing in moderate temperatures.

Because marten have a low reproductive rate and they are easily caught, they should be trapped conservatively. Due to ranging habits, more males than females are normally caught and tree sets are also selective for male martens. Female tracks in the snow can usually be identified due to the shorter distance in the loping gait and many wilderness trappers move their traplines after a week or ten days to new areas to prevent overharvest while keeping production acceptable.

In rugged mountainous areas, martens can be trapped harder as large tracts of inaccessible land serve as reservoirs for numerous martens. Dispersals of juvenile martens and relocations of adults takes place in summer months.

Dispatch

Martens trapped in tree sets are almost always dead when the traps are checked. However, the animals caught on land sets in foothold traps are frequently alive when the trapper arrives.

Live marten are usually killed with a stunning blow from a stick. Then the unconscious animal can be stood upon with the heel of one foot over the chest area. Trappers wearing snowshoes often stun the animal, and then squeeze the heart area between the thumb and fingers with gloved hands. Death occurs quickly with either method.

Controls

Marten frequently escape predators with their quickness and tree climbing abilities. Fisher occasionally kill marten and they have the ability to catch a marten on the ground or in trees. Large owls also kill martens occasionally and most other predators don't have much of a chance because martens seldom venture far from protective cover.

The solitary nature of martens coupled with the infrequent use of the same dens keeps martens relatively free of internal and external parasites. Mange occurs rarely.

Values

Martens serve a variety of prey species by helping to keep populations in check. In many mountainous locations marten are the only major predator remaining in the high altitudes during winter conditions.

Marten populations do not have an impact upon man's crops or livestock. The species prefers wilderness or semi-wilderness habitats where contact with man is rare.

Pelt values are important to Alaskan and Canadian trappers, but have a lesser importance to most American trappers. Although the pelts of martens are soft and luxurious, pelt prices in recent years have discouraged harvesting. Twenty-five to thirty thousand are harvested in the United States during normal harvest years, resulting in cash values of about $400,000.

Fur Handling

Marten pelts are handled cased with the fur to the outside. Skinning is accomplished easily and little or no scraping is necessary with marten pelts.

To skin a marten, a cut must be made from the inside of one hind leg to the other, and another cut is made from the base of the tail around the vent to the opening cut. The fur can be separated from the hind legs and a knife cut should be made to leave the feet on the carcass. Both hind legs can be supported by the same hook on a skinning gambrel and the tail must be stripped from the tailbone. The tail should be opened the entire length with a cut along the underside of the boneless tail. The fur can then be pulled down to the shoulder area which is normally separated with thumb pressure. The front feet too can be left on the carcass with a knife cut, and deeper cuts will be necessary to free the ears, eyes and nose.

The skinned pelt should be placed on a mink or marten stretcher with the fur on the inside. Most marten are skinned in cabins, and if the pelt is placed near the stove it will be dry enough to turn with the fur to the outside in about an hour. The skins are thin and prone to tearing, so care should be taken to not let the pelt dry too thoroughly before it is turned. The turned fur should be tacked to prevent shrinking during the final drying process, and most marten pelts will dry completely in two or three days.

Always use a belly board with a wedge shape when using a solid wooden stretcher to prevent the pelts from sticking too tightly to the stretchers as they dry and shrink.

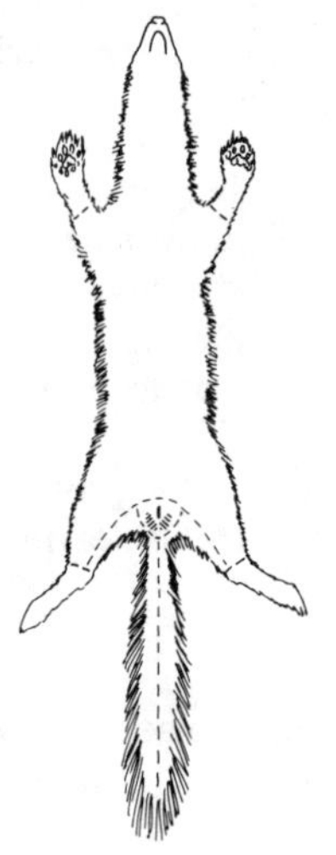

FISHER — Martes Pennanti

Order — Carnivora
Family — Mustelidae

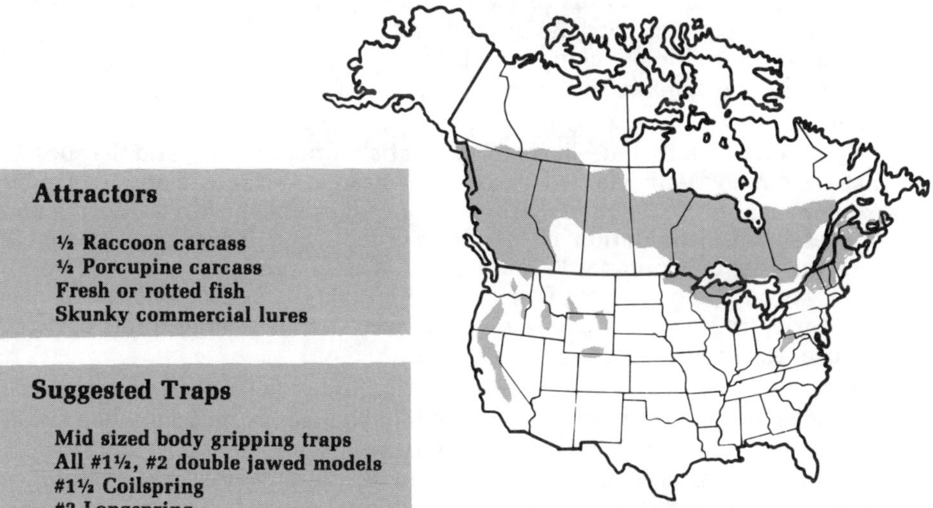

Attractors

½ Raccoon carcass
½ Porcupine carcass
Fresh or rotted fish
Skunky commercial lures

Suggested Traps

Mid sized body gripping traps
All #1½, #2 double jawed models
#1½ Coilspring
#2 Longspring

The Fisher

FISHERS are woodland animals, and among the most effective predators on land. They are also the fastest American animal in trees. Females are less than half as big as males, yet command higher fur prices due to an extremely soft and silky fur. Also known in areas as fisher cat, black cat, tree fox or pekan, fishers have been known to follow traplines, destroying the catches before the trapper arrives. Destruction of woodlands and high fur prices caused population declines up until the 1940's, but protection and reintroductions have encouraged good fisher populations in many suitable habitat types.

Description

Fishers are usually dark brown in color. Males oftentimes have a lighter, grizzled coloration on the face, head and over the shoulders. The longer guard hairs in the fur are 1½ to 2 inches in length on the body and a ½ inch longer on the tail. The fur on males is much coarser than on the females, and both are darkest on tail and legs. Two small, white patches of fur are found in the front armpit areas.

Males may measure 36 inches or longer and adult males often weight 10 to 12 pounds. Males rarely weigh more than 14 pounds.

Females weigh about ⅓ of the average weight of males and most females are about the size of large mink, although their longer fur makes them appear to be larger. Typical females weigh between 4 and 5 pounds.

Fishers have 38 teeth, including four sharp canine teeth and flat topped molars to aid in chewing.

Five toes register in fisher tracks and the inside toes are smaller and placed behind the other four.

The fisher cannot retract its claws and they are usually dulled somewhat by constant contact with the ground and rocks.

A pair of anal musk glands are present on both males and females and this musk is often released when the fisher is frightened or angry.

Distribution

The northeastern states have excellent fisher populations and the species has reclaimed many wooded areas in Minnesota, Wisconsin and the Upper Penninsula of Michigan. Fishers are also well established in California and successful reintroduction efforts have established fisher populations in Oregon, Idaho, Montana, Wyoming and West Virginia.

It was once thought that fishers required mature forests, but the species can thrive in newer second growth forests, favoring large tracts of pine, spruce, aspen, birch and cedar swamps.

Sign

Tracks in the snow are usually the only sign easily noticed when fisher are present in an area, as the species is not usually observed in the wild. Tracks in shallow snow are usually in a loping pattern, resembling a marten track, but the tracks are larger and consistently farther apart.

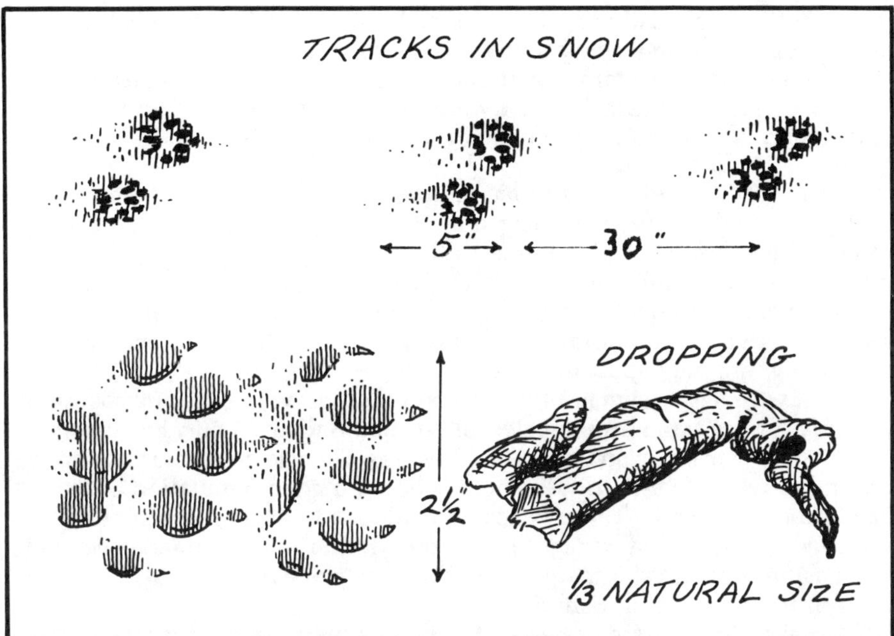

Marten seldom lope farther than 2 feet in one jump. Fisher are capable of spanning as much as 8 feet while running at top speed, although a 2-3 foot loping span is typical.

Female fisher and marten tracks can be difficult to separate in the snow, but the presence of 5 toes on each foot identifies the female fisher track, which will be somewhat larger.

During deep snow conditions, martens continue to travel in a loping fashion, while fishers may walk taking advantage of their larger feet which act as snowshoes.

Reproduction

Female fishers mate 6 to 8 days after giving birth to their litters and delayed implantation causes a gestation period averaging 352 days or nearly a year. Breeding normally occurs during late March or early April, and the fertilized eggs do not become attached to the female's uterus until the following January, after which the growth of the litter begins.

One to four young are born in March or April and 2.7 is an average litter size. More females than males are usually born, contrary to most other furbearing species.

The young are cared for strictly by the mother fisher and the natal den is usually in a hollow tree although a fisher will use an underground den if a better location is not available.

Females usually breed when they are one year of age and males do not breed until they are two years of age.

Ten years of age is considered old in fishers.

Habits

Fishers are solitary animals throughout most of the year, although snow tracking often indicates that two or more fishers will hunt in parallel patterns. Activity is mostly at night, although it appears that fishers hunt frequently during daylight hours in wilderness habitats.

Male territories are larger than female territories and the sizes of these regularly patrolled areas vary according to the availability of prey species. A 10 square mile territory is typical for a female fisher and males commonly hunt a 30 square mile area.

Circuits are irregularly patrolled although fishers travel pretty much in a straight line when they have determined to go to a certain location. Males usually pass through a given area in their territory about once every two weeks. Female circuits in winter usually vary from 3 days to a week.

Both male and female fishers are highly skilled predators and territory relocations are sometimes necessary as fishers are capable of overharvesting prey species.

Fishers are aggressive hunters and competition with other furbearers is not only for the same prey species, but direct. Raccoons may be killed by a large fisher in trees or on the ground. Fishers can also catch martens on the ground or in trees, and usually there is either a good population of fishers or martens, not both. There is strong evidence to suggest that fishers kill significant numbers of bobcat kittens too. Mother bobcats must leave their kittens unattended to hunt and there is no safe place in which to hide a bobcat den from a hunting fisher.

Snowshoe hares are a preferred food and a main reason that fishers like to frequent the dense cedar swamps. With keen senses of sight and smell, fishers often stalk the snowshoe rabbits, but they will trail them as well by scent alone. Red squirrels are a common prey species and fishers also eat mice, rats, voles and shrews, which are avoided by most predators due to a musky odor. Grouse and ptarmigan are eaten regularly and there are records of fishers killing foxes, mink and otters.

Fishers are skilled at killing porcupines. Attacks are to the face of the porcupine as the fisher circles and circles the porcupine who attempts to keep it's back toward the fisher. After repeated attacks to the quill free facial area, the porcupine becomes vulnerable to a throat attack.

Porcupines are not safe when climbing trees, as fishers simply attack from the top side. Porcupines may be safe from fisher attacks when they are on branches and facing away from the fisher, or when they are in a position to hide their faces in a crevice or hole.

Fishers often clean these skins as clean as if they had been skinned by a man. Fisher droppings often include quills, which seem to pass through the digestive system without ill effects.

Uneaten foods are usually cached for later use by fishers and the species will sometimes deposit their musk on the uneaten portions to discourage other animals.

Fishers also eat carrion and substantial amounts of wild berries in season.

Trapping

Fishers are usually trapped with medium sized body gripping traps and size 1½ foothold traps. Larger sized foothold traps are not needed to hold them, and the larger jaw spreads may encourage a trapped fisher to chew on its own foot beneath the trap jaws. For that reason, many trappers prefer to use coilspring traps in the 1½ size.

Traps should be staked or attached with strong wire for fishers at all sets.

Fishers don't seem to go over the trap when the bait is close to the trap.

They are strong animals and active after being caught.

Although exposed foothold traps will often catch fishers, concealment is an advantage and may result in a fox catch too. A relatively few fishers learn to avoid traps, but most are caught easily when they are intent upon a meat bait.

Cubby sets are commonly used on land with foothold traps for fishers, and the cubbies can be either natural or artificial. Cubby sets hide the baits from above and prevent the capture of birds which might be attracted to the bait.

Many trappers use lures to attract fishers from greater ranges. Lures with skunk essence work well in extremely cold weather conditions when fishers are normally trapped.

Medium sized body gripping traps are commonly used on running pole sets during periods of deep snow. Three or four nails are used to stabilize the trap on the inclining poles. They are driven into the poles part way on the inside of the trap jaws so they won't interfere with the closing of the springing trap.

Many trappers prefer sizable baits, such as ½ of a porcupine, or ½ of a skinned raccoon. On running pole sets with body gripping traps, these baits are placed as close to the trap as possible, with just enough space to allow the trap to close without hitting the bait. Baits may not be covered as this set construction is very selective for furbearers able to climb the running pole and birds are not apt to spring the body gripping trap.

The bait should be wired tightly to the running pole and guiding branches over or around the trap are not needed when the bait is close to the trap.

Good fisher populations are considered to be one fisher per 10 square miles. Populations of one fisher per 1½ or 2 square miles do occur at times in preferred habitat. These high populations are very hard on other furbearers and other wildlife species due to the efficiency of fishers as predators.

Sets are not selective for either male or female fishers. Deliberately trapping the females is a good conservation practice with this species because significantly more females than males are born annually. Due to the smaller territories of females, adequate numbers usually remain in inaccessible places during trapping seasons.

Dispatch

Fishers usually expire rapidly when caught in medium sized body gripping traps and foothold traps during cold weather. Live fishers in traps are to be respected. They are very quick and inclined to protect themselves by biting.

Live fishers should be shot in the brain with a .22 rifle or hand gun. Trying to stun a live fisher with a blow from a club can be risky. When shooting a furbearer, always consider where the bullet might exit and wait for a side angle to prevent the possibility of any fur damage by the bullet.

Controls

Predation upon fishers by other predators is not thought to be serious. A lynx or bobcat will rarely kill a fisher and wolves have been known to kill fishers caught out on frozen lakes. Young fishers are killed at times by large owls, eagles and coyotes.

The solitary nature and infrequent use of the same dens keeps fishers relatively free of most diseases and parasites. Mange can occur and fishers are also vulnerable to distemper, fleas, tapeworms and nematodes.

Values

As the only consistent predator of porcupines, fishers provide a service by controlling this species, as well as the damage that the porcupines inflict upon forests.

Fishers contribute to the overall health of prey species when their densities are light or moderate.

Dense populations of fishers create problems for a variety of other species, including other furbearers. Fishers do have to abandon territories as food sources become depleted and less mobile furbearers can become malnourished when competing for the same prey species as fishers.

Fisher pelts, particularly female pelts, have a considerable value most years and this value is appreciated by many trappers when they are abundant.

Four to five thousand fishers are harvested in the U.S., and fifteen or sixteen thousand fishers are also harvested annually in Canada, bringing annual values to trappers of 1½ to 2 million dollars.

Fur Handling

Fisher pelts are handled cased, with the fur on the outside. If you are not an experienced fur handler, it would be wise to seek help rather than take a chance of ruining a valuable pelt.

To skin a fisher, an opening cut is made from the inside of one hind leg to the other and another cut is made from the base of the tail around the vent to the opening cut. The fur can then be separated from the hind legs and a knife cut should leave the feet on the carcass. The fisher can then be suspended from a gambrel and the tail stripped off of the tailbone with the aid of a tail stripping tool or pliers. As soon as the tail is stripped is a good time to open the tail with a cut on the underside all the way to the tip of the tail.

With the hind legs and tail freed, the skin can be pulled down to the shoulder area, where prying thumb pressure will separate the fur from the shoulder area and allow the further skinning of the front legs down to the ankle area where the fur should be severed. Further cuts will be necessary at the ear canals, eyes and nose.

Fleshing can be accomplished on a wooden stretcher with a single handled fleshing tool or similar dull device. Much scraping is not needed or desired, but all fat should be removed from tho belly area and anywhere else.

A wedge shaped belly board should be used with a solid wooden stretcher as the pelt is allowed to dry overnight with the fur on the inside. As the leather becomes dry to the touch, the pelt must be removed from the stretcher, and turned with the fur to the outside before it is replaced on the stretcher for the final drying process.

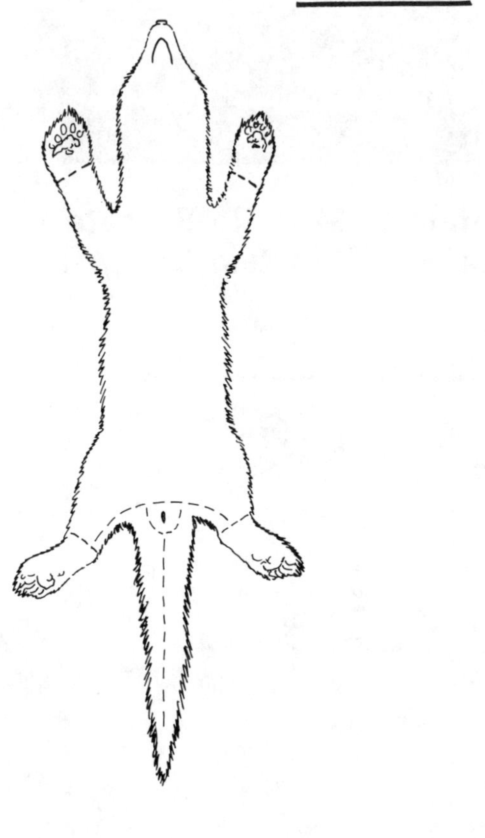

WEASEL — Long-Tailed — Mustela Frenata
Short-Tailed — Mustela Erminea

Order — Carnivora
Family — Mustelidae

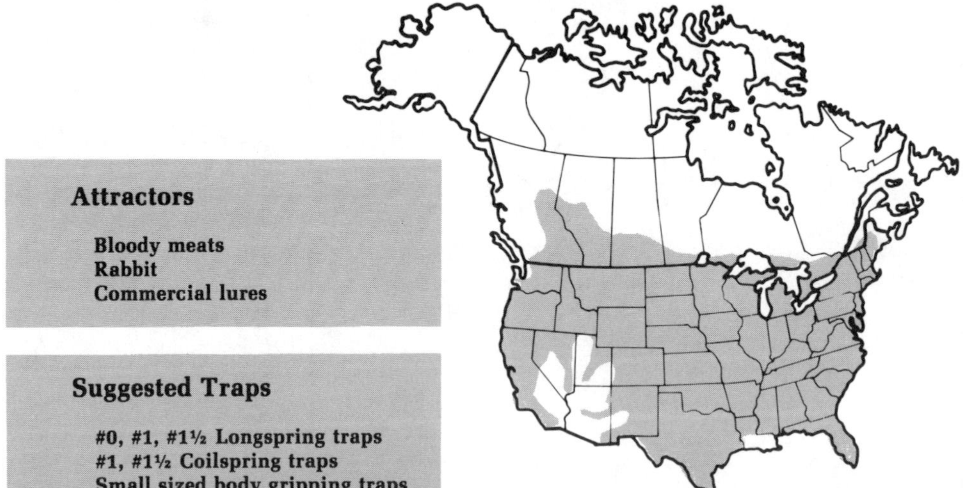

Attractors

Bloody meats
Rabbit
Commercial lures

Suggested Traps

#0, #1, #1½ Longspring traps
#1, #1½ Coilspring traps
Small sized body gripping traps

The Long-Tailed Weasel

BOTH the long-tailed weasel and the short-tailed weasel are widely distributed throughout North America. Both species turn white in the winter in northern and high altitude areas during winter seasons, and both species are marked with black tipped tails. Weasels can enter any hole that they can get their head into, and they frequently enter the dens of rodents to kill the occupants. White weasel pelts are known as ermine.

Description

Weasels have short fur. The longer guard hair lengths are ½ inch or shorter over most of the body, with lengths of 1½ inches on the black tipped tail ends.

Summer coloration is light brown over the backs and sides of weasels, with a lighter creamy colored throat and belly. In northern areas, weasels molt twice a year to change the color of the fur by growing either white or brown hairs to replace the other color being shed.

Male weasels are larger than females. Most adult long-tail weasels measure between 13 and 17 inches in total length including a tail of 4½ to 6½ inches long. Females are usually between 11 and 13 inches in total length, including a tail measuring 3½ to 5 inches.

Short-tailed weasels, "Mustela erminea", are slightly smaller than the long-tailed weasels. Tails seldom exceed 4 inches in total length. This species shares the same habitat with long-tailed weasels in northern and western states, but the range of the short-tailed weasel extends throughout all of Alaska and Canada.

Both weasels have beady eyes and relatively long and lithe bodies. There are five toes on each foot with sharp, nonretractable claws. Both also have 34 teeth, including four canine teeth which often extend below the upper lips.

White weasels are often stained a yellowish color on the hind legs and bellies in late winter. Weasels changing from brown to white, or white to brown are known as "greybacks" in the fur trade, and these pelts have little or no fur value.

All weasels have a pair of musk glands located beneath the skin near the anus, and an angry or frightened weasel expels this powerful musk as a defense mechanism.

Distribution

Long-tailed weasels are widely distributed throughout the United States. These weasels are found in all of the lower 48 states in areas of suitable habitat in mountains, farmlands, forests and prairies.

Weasels require drinking water, and they are rarely found far from a source of water. Mice and voles make up an important part of a weasel's diet, and weasels are more abundant where there is an ample and constant supply of these small rodents.

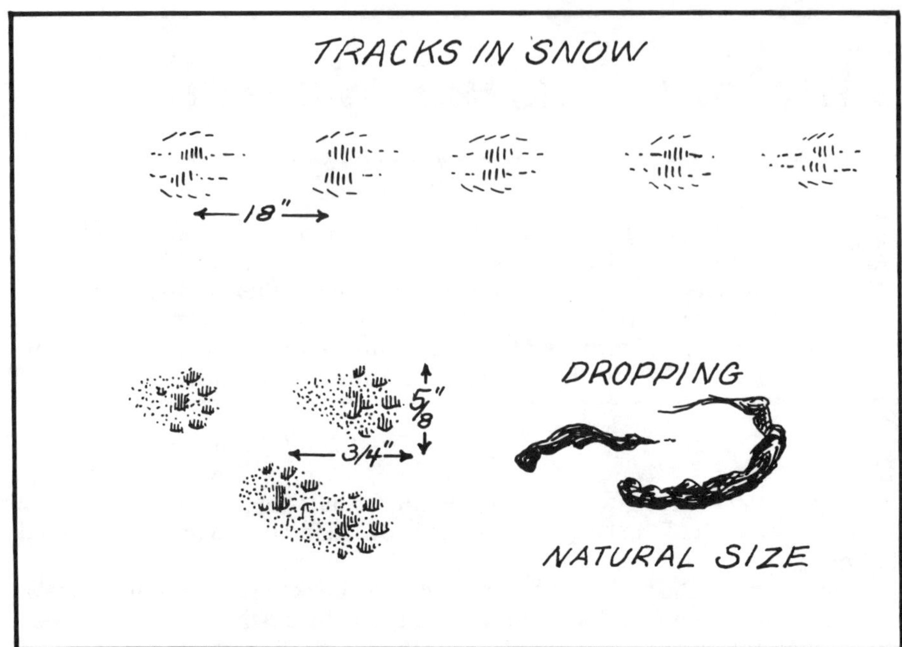

Sign

Weasel tracks are rarely identified, except in snow. The track pattern in snow is easily identified by the loping pattern, and small footprints. The hind feet land almost exactly where the front feet were, and the trail in the snow is apt to lead in an erratic pattern as the weasel investigates any area where a mouse might be found.

Scats are usually not noticed. At times, they will be evident near active weasel dens, and weasels often leave a dropping on a prominent log or rock. The scats resemble minature mink droppings, and contain bits of fur and bones.

Reproduction

There appears to be significantly more male weasels in the wild than females. For this reason, males probably do not mate with more than one female.

Most weasels mate during July, and delayed implantation occurs. This allows a gestation period of 270 to 280 days before the litter is born. Litter sizes average 6 for both species.

Female weasels mature at 3 or 4 months of age, and they usually breed at this time. Males do not mature until the following summer.

A six year old weasel is considered to be old.

Habits

Weasels have a high metabolic rate, and it seems as if they are always hungry. They are apt to hunt during daylight hours, particularly when it is snowing, to satisfy their appetite to eat half of their body weight daily.

Weasels can walk, but seldom do. They usually bound from place to place as they investigate holes, brush piles, junk piles, or anything that might harbor a prey species.

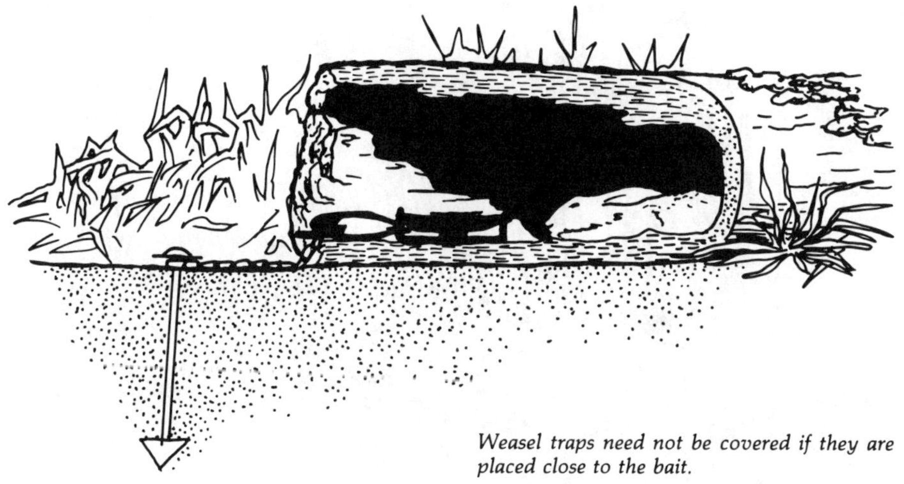

Weasel traps need not be covered if they are placed close to the bait.

Weasels have regular territories which are hunted thoroughly and irregularly. These territories are not defended from others of their kind, and these regularly used areas frequently overlap. Weasel densities vary according to the quality of the habitat, and in areas where there are a lot of slash piles or trashy areas to sustain high populations of mice, weasel populations can be as high as one to every 8 or 10 acres. In average woodlands, the habitat will support about 4 weasels per square mile.

Like many other species, males travel much further than females. A male weasel will often travel 3 miles or more in a night's hunt, yet never get farther than ½ mile away from its own den. Typically, one small area will get investigated thoroughly, and then it may be ignored for a week or longer.

Mice make up about 50% of a weasel's diet. Shrews and cottontail rabbits are another important food, and rats, birds, snakes and insects are also eaten.

Weasels commonly kill more than they can eat. Excess foods are stored. When a larger animal like a cottontail rabbit is killed, the weasel will often eat what it can, and drag the rest off to a safe hiding place. Then, the weasel will sleep for 3 hours or so, feed, and rest again until the food source is gone.

Weasels have a good sense of smell, and they commonly hunt by trailing the scent of a prey species until they locate it. Weasels will stalk a target animal or bird when they see it, and strike it with incredible speed when they are within range.

Weasels can swim, but do so infrequently. They are also good tree climbers, and do not hesitate to climb a tree after a chipmunk or bird.

Chickens can be vulnerable to predation by weasels. The little predators can go through chicken fencing, and there are many records of a single weasel killing 30 or more chickens in a single night. Sometimes, only a few chickens will be partially eaten. However, many weasels apparently do not kill chickens when given the opportunity, as they are attracted to the area by the available mice and rats which are probably easier for the weasels to kill.

A single den is used regularly by both male and female weasels. These

Old stone fences make good weasel locations. Simply place the bait in front of the trap.

are oftentimes located in a hollow stump or root, rock pile, or under an old building. Nests are lined with grasses and fur from prey species.

Trapping

Weasels can be held in the smallest of foothold traps. Cage traps are not effective for the species due to the light weight of the weasel. Body gripping traps in small sizes can be used for weasels, but the furbearers often avoid the trigger as a matter of convenience.

Many trappers prefer to use a #1½ longspring or coilspring trap for weasels. These traps are set so that the weasel will step between the jaws instead of over them, and the high catch usually kills the weasel quickly and humanely.

Weasels are bold, and not the slightest bit trap shy. Traps set for weasels need not be covered as long as they are placed where the weasel will want to step.

Weasels are easily caught in simple sets. Hunting weasels are almost always hungry, making them vulnerable to a wide variety of fresh meat baits. Their keen sense of smell enables them to find most sets as they investigate all promising locations.

Simple and crude cubby sets are very effective when made close to brush piles, old buildings, stone walls, hollow logs, weedy fencerows, haystacks, or any areas that promise a supply of mice. Traps should be placed close to the bait or any place that the weasel must step while attempting to investigate the bait.

Lures can be effective to attract weasels, and both long-tail and short-tail weasels will respond to a wide variety of predator lures.

In areas where snow is apt to be deep, some trappers construct small wooden boxes with a hinged top. A hole of 2 inches in diameter is cut into one end, and a trap is place inside of the hole. A bait of rabbit is placed beyond the trap to entice the weasel to enter the box. This set is not affected by snowfall, and is very selective for weasels due to the size of the entrance hole.

Hollow logs make good weasel sets as they are sure to investigate these logs for mice. Traps can often be set inside the hollow with a piece of bait, and these traps are protected from freezing rain or snow.

Low fur prices discourage an adequate harvest of weasels. Males are much more vulnerable to trapping because there are more of them, and they range further than the females increasing their chances of being trapped.

Dispatch

Weasels are usually dead when they are caught in #1½ traps before the trapper arrives at the set. Weasels caught in winter also expire rapidly in traps. Live weasels can be stunned with a blow to the top of the head, and killed quickly by standing over the chest area with the heel of one foot.

Controls

Weasels are preyed upon by a variety of species. Red foxes and mink kill significant numbers of weasels, and they are never abundant when either of these two species is abundant.

Other predators include coyotes, gray foxes, bobcats and housecats. Hawks and owls also kill weasels. It is thought that the black tipped tail of weasels causes a significant number of owl misses, particularly when the weasel is white and running on snow at night.

Weasels often have ticks, lice and fleas because they use the same den, and keep reinfesting themselves. Internal parasites include tapeworms, roundworms and flatworms.

Values

Weasels are significant predators of mice. The rapid metabolic rate of weasels allows them to eat 3 mice per day, and this translates to over a thousand mice annually. This directly benefits man, and helps to prevent uncontrolled population explosions of mice, benefiting the mice species as well.

Weasels can cause considerable damage in hen houses. This occurs only rarely, as most weasels seem to prefer to attack the rats and mice also attracted to the area by the supply of chicken feed.

North American weasel harvests yield approximately 100,000 pelts, with total values of $120,000.

Fur Handling

Weasel pelts are handled cased, with the fur on the inside. The initial cut is made from the inside of one hind leg to the other. Another cut will be needed from the base of the tail around the vent, to the first cut. Do keep the knife point shallow in this area to avoid cutting into the scent glands. Weasel musk is very powerful, and some people find it more offensive than skunk musk.

The skin can be loosened from the hind legs and freed with cuts in the hind ankle area. Both hind legs can be suspended over a single hook on a skinning gambrel to finish the skinning process. The tail must be stripped from the tailbone, and then the pelt can be pulled down past the front shoulder area, where thumb and finger pressure will free the front legs. The leg fur must be cut off near the front ankles, and then the pelt can be pulled down to the ears. Deeper cuts will be needed to sever the ear canals, eyes and nose.

Weasels require little or no fleshing. If any flesh appears on the pelt, it can usually be pulled off easily. The tail must be split to the end.

If a wooden stretcher to fit the pelt is not available, a wire form can be easily made by cutting and bending a heavy coat hanger. The wire ends should be placed into a soft board to keep the proper shape as the pelt is drying.

Most weasel pelts are fully dry in a few days.

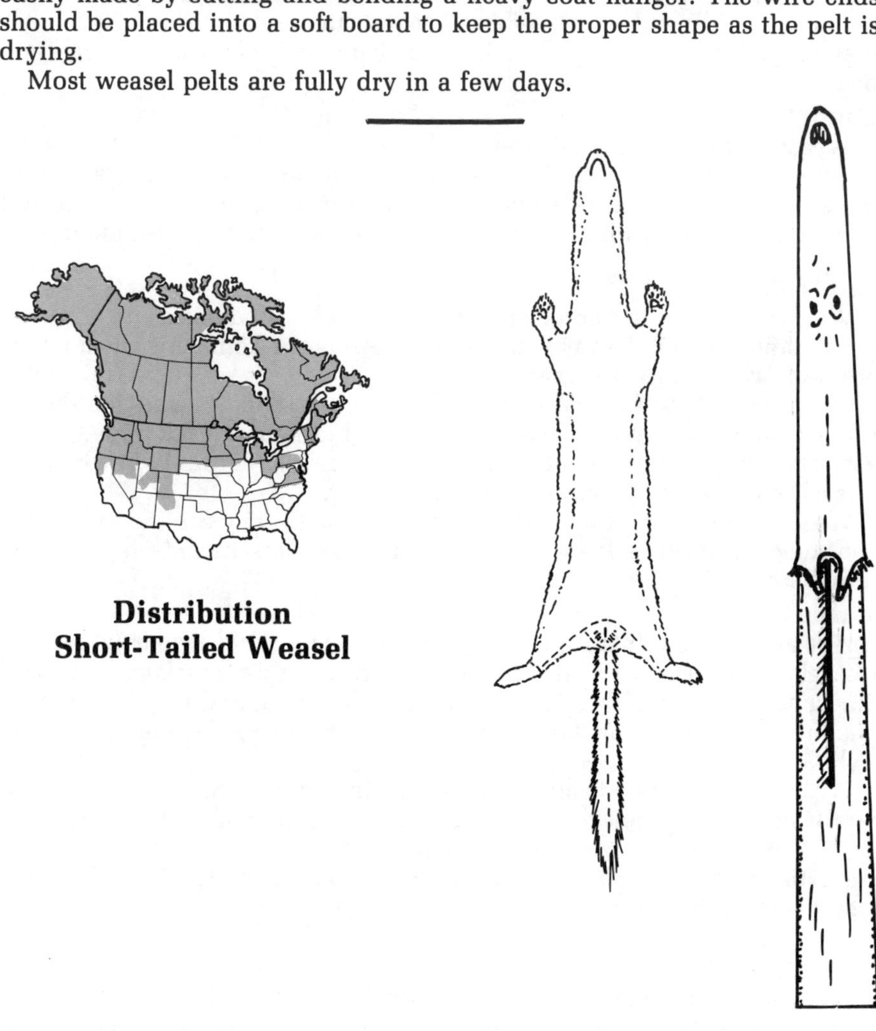

**Distribution
Short-Tailed Weasel**

MINK — Mustela Vison
Order — Carnivora
Family — Mustelidae

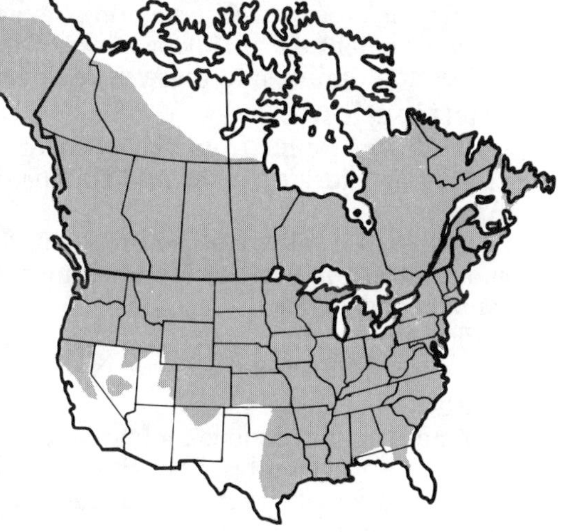

Attractors

Fresh fish
Fresh muskrat meat
Fresh rabbit
Commercial lures

Suggested Traps

Small sized body gripping traps
#1, #1½ Guard type foothold traps
#1, #1½ Coilspring traps
#1, #1½ Longspring

The Mink

WILD mink are adaptable to a wide range of climates, and this species is far more common than most people realize. Efficient predators, mink are quick on land, skilled swimmers, and capable tree climbers. They are often found in habitat types suitable for muskrats, and they are often taken in traps set for muskrats. Mink are usually shy, but they can become bold when their curiosity is aroused. Mink are not sociable with others of their kind, except during the breeding season, and avoidance or fighting between mink is common.

Description

Mink have 34 teeth, with 4 prominent canine teeth to help in the killing of prey species.

Mink have rather long and supple bodies with relatively short legs. There are 5 toes on each foot which have partial webbing between toes. Tails are fully furred.

Males are larger than females. Overall lengths of males are 20 to 30 inches, and females measure 16 to 21 inches. Male weights exceed 3 pounds in many areas, and females usually weigh 1½ to 2 pounds.

Mink fur is short and dense. Shades of color vary somewhat according to region, and individuals. Most shades of color are chocolate to almost black. Patches of white fur are typical on the chins of most mink, and many mink exhibit patches of white fur on throats, chests and bellies. These small patches are irregular in shape, and vary with the individual.

Musk glands are present near the anal area under the skin of both male and female mink. Musk is sometimes released when the mink is excited or stressed. The odor is powerful and unpleasant.

In some areas, occasional mink have a light colored and wooly underfur. This is evident on the lower backs of the mink. These pelts are referred to as "cotton" mink, and these pelts have lesser value.

Distribution

Mink are found from the edge of the tundra all across Canada and Alaska, to Florida, Texas and California. This species might be absent in Arizona.

Although mink are sometimes found traveling or living far from water, most prefer the habitats found along the shores of streams, lakes, marshes, canals, and ponds.

The mink is managed as a furbearer in most states, and 47 states provide mink trapping seasons.

Sign

Tracks are an obvious indication of mink, and the best place to search for tracks is on the mud right at shoreline edges. Experienced trappers can tell male from female tracks in the mud at a glance, judging solely by the size of the footprints.

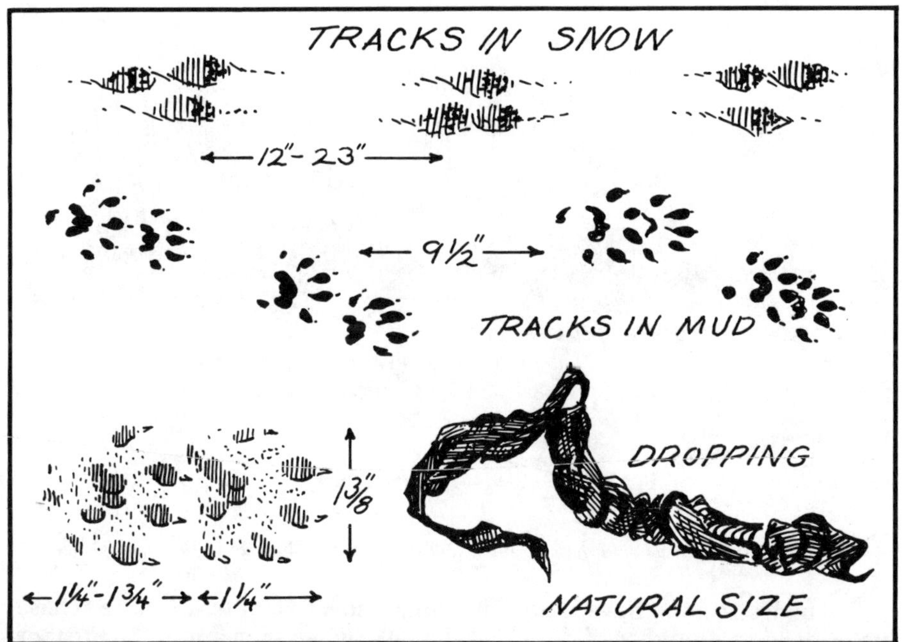

Droppings are another sure sign. These scats are about a ½ inch or less in diameter, segmented, and usually 2 or 3 inches long. These droppings are usually left in a prominent place, such as a rock or log exposed above the water level. Fresh scats are dark in color, and they turn lighter as they age. Scales, bones and fur are usually noticeable in mink scats.

Reproduction

Breeding occurs over much of the mink range during late February or early March. Males attempt to find several females during this short season. The males usually abandon the females after breeding takes place.

Females have one litter per year, usually raising about 4 young.

Gestation times vary from 40 to 75 days, due to a delayed implantation process.

Females raise the young entirely by themselves. Dens in abandoned muskrat dens, hollow logs, and rock piles are common. Mink do not usually dig their own dens, but they sometimes burrow into exposed muskrat and beaver lodges above the waterline for denning purposes. Many female mink seem to seek out secluded ponds or small streams with an abundant food supply and good protection to raise their young.

A 7 year old mink is considered old; and worn teeth are an indication of age.

Habits

Male mink have territories or ranges much larger than females. Males seem to be constantly on the move, covering miles in a single day. Females often restrict their travels at night to 20 acres or so in marsh habitats, and they seldom travel further than 100 yards up or downstream from their dens near rivers or creeks.

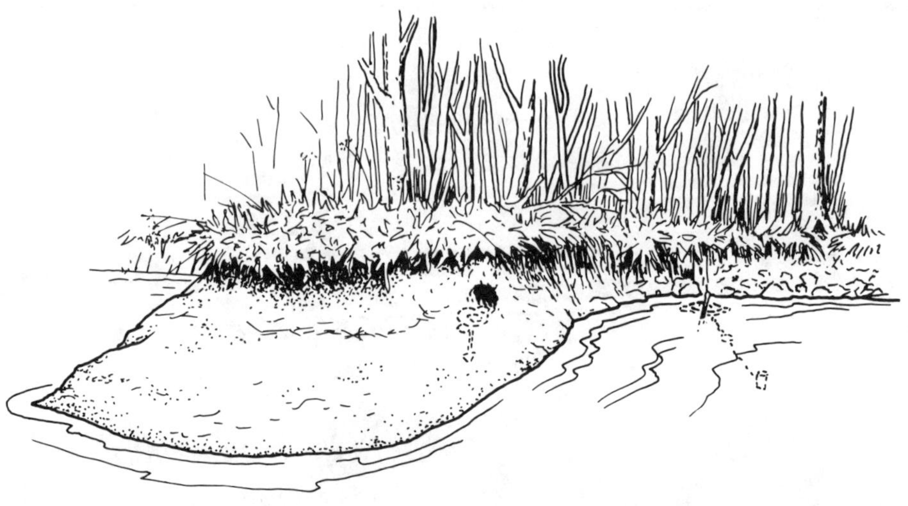

A pocket set constructed where a passing mink will see it, and a blind set at the water's edge.

The males seem to have routes that might cover 25 miles or more. These males have any number of dens that they use when they are in the area, or feel like resting. It appears that males commonly store food in some of these dens for later use.

Many trappers think that males return from their travels about once a week, and follow nearly the exact same route, crossing streams at the same places, and investigating the same brush piles or undercut banks for food.

Holes, hollow logs, rock piles, and brush piles interest many mink as protected places to hunt.

Mink are capable at trailing or stalking prey species, but it appears that they are usually opportunistic feeders who pursue prey after they surprise and startle the prey into flight.

Mink hunt and travel mostly at night, but they are occasionally active during the day, especially just before storms or when it is raining or snowing.

During periods of extreme cold or deep snow, mink seem to stay near their dens. At times, they will live in dens with underwater accesses and do the bulk of their hunting under the ice.

Mink kill a variety of prey species, including muskrats, crayfish, frogs, rabbits, fish, birds, snakes, grasshoppers and water beetles.

Some individual mink appear to kill muskrats with regularity, while other individual mink do not appear to kill muskrats at all. A mature muskrat can surely give a mink a battle in a tight place, or when cornered. Many mink seem to prefer easier and safer prey. However, muskrat seems to be a preferred food for mink, and virtually all will scavage dead muskrats if they are hungry and the meat is fresh.

Mink often catch fish. They are capable of catching a muskrat in the water because they use all four feet for propulsion, and the muskrat only uses its back feet for propulsion, with the tail acting more as a rudder.

Mink are usually shy and avoid humans, but at times, exhibit boldness when their curiosity is triggered.

A hollow log at the water's edge is sure to be investigated by mink.

Trapping

Mink are most often trapped with foothold traps set in the water along the edges of shorelines. Number 1½ traps are often used in these sets, and an extension wire to a submerged stake straight out in the lake, pond or stream will allow most trapped mink to drown quickly.

Mink traps seem to be more productive when they are set under an inch of water or less, and set so that the mink approaches the trap between the trap jaws instead of over them.

Mink can become quite cautious around the tracks of men, so many trappers prefer to wade to and from their mink sets to prevent tracking up the banks near their mink sets.

Mink are somewhat predictable in their habits. Many trappers set mink traps at culverts, drain tiles, hollow logs, and other holes located close to shorelines.

Mink usually hug the shores as they travel, and prefer staying on dry land when they have a choice. At times, an obstacle such as a protruding rock or log may cause the mink to detour into the water. These sites make excellent nautral sets. Very often, a stick or weed can be placed in a position to guide the mink into the set trap.

Small body gripping traps are also used to catch mink. These traps are usually set where a mink will attempt to go through them, and they can be effective both on dry land and submerged in the water. Because mink frequent the same areas as muskrats, goodly numbers are caught in the underwater runs where trappers place body gripping traps for muskrats.

When body gripping traps are set on dry land trails for mink, most trappers blockade the sides of the traps to prevent mink from going around

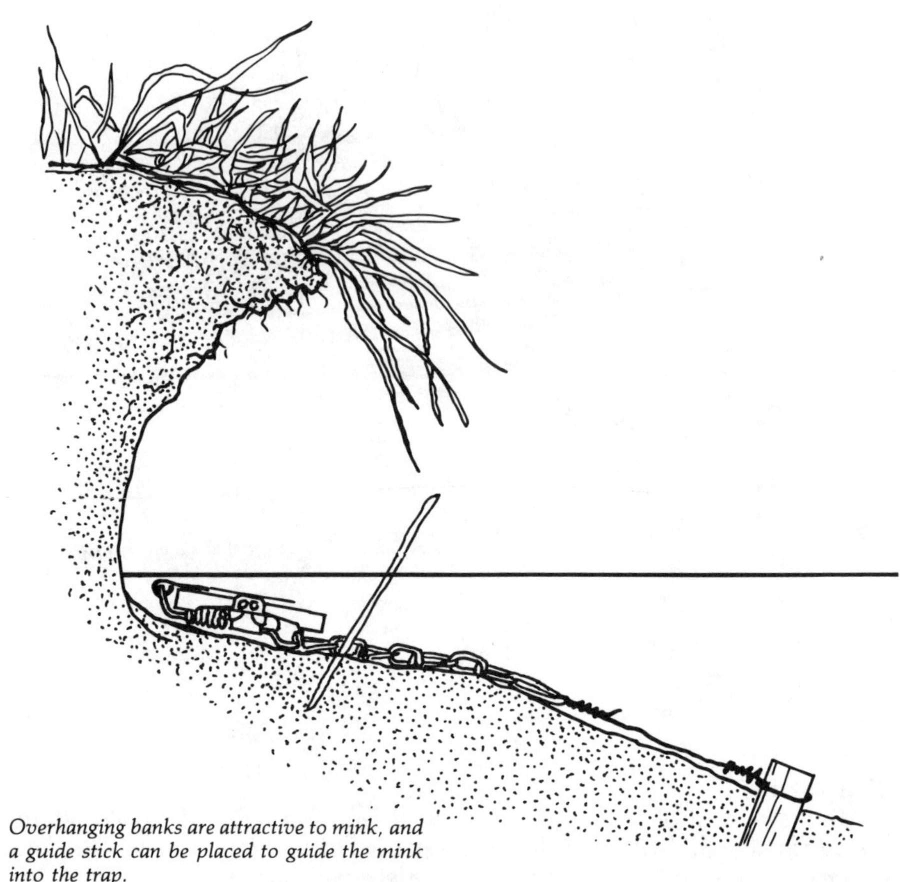

Overhanging banks are attractive to mink, and a guide stick can be placed to guide the mink into the trap.

them. Small body gripping traps should have strong springs, or a double set of springs, for mink on dry land. Larger male minks sometimes escape weaker single springed body gripping traps on dry land, and the extra power of two springs helps to stun and strangle the animals.

Foothold traps set on dry land for mink should be carefully covered with dirt, or natural debris. Traps should be dyed to remove odors, and triggers should be set light to allow the trap to spring quickly and easily.

Baits and lures can be an aid to catch mink at times, but neither is the key to making good catches. Good baits include muskrat flesh and fresh fish. These baits usually work best when they are covered lightly. Mink are usually capable of catching all of the prey that they need. A lightly covered bait will stimulate their curiosity more than a plainly visible bait which they would likely refuse. Covered baits will also help the trap set to be more selective.

Mink lures with a strong odor of mink musk can be used to advantage to selectively trap larger male mink. Females and smaller male mink exhibit fear at concentrations of musk, and commonly avoid these areas.

Many more males are trapped each year than females simply because the males travel so much further and they are therefore exposed to more traps and trappers. Also, many mink trappers avoid setting traps in the small areas that females are known to frequent.

A cubby set constructed near the stream bank can catch a variety of furbearers including mink.

Dispatch

Mink taken in water sets are usually drowned long before the trapper arrives to check the traps. Live mink are aggressive in traps, and caution should be used to prevent being bitten. Mink can be stunned with a blow to the top of the head with a stake or trowel, and usually drowned. If a mink is caught in a dry land set, it should be stunned with a sharp blow to the top of the head. It can be killed while it is unconscious by standing with your heel over the heart and chest area. For safety, place your free foot over the animal's head. Death will occur within a minute or less. Before you remove the mink from the trap, check to see if there is any reaction when the eyeball is touched.

Controls

Mink are preyed upon by owls, foxes, coyotes, bobcats and dogs.

Internal parasites include flukes, roundworms and tapeworms. External parasites include fleas, ticks and lice. Mink are vulnerable to distemper, parvo enteritis, encephalitis, and rabies.

Values

Wild mink pelts account for about 10% of the mink fur trade, with the other 90% being ranched furs. Prices flucuate according to popularity and supply. This varies some from year to year. Several hundred thousand wild mink are trapped in the U.S. most years, and total values often exceed 5 million dollars.

Mink probably service the muskrat resource more than other species by killing weakened or diseased muskrats. Evidence suggests that mink prey heavily upon muskrats when muskrats are diseased, and this may help prevent the spreading of these diseases to healthy individuals.

Mink have been known to enter chicken houses and kill chickens.

Fur Handling

Mink pelts are handled cased, with the fur to the inside. The opening cut is made from the inside of one hind leg to the other. Two more cuts can be made from the base of the tail, around the vent, to the opening cut. The fur should then be cut from around the ankles of the hind feet, and the fur can be pulled free from the leg area. At this point, hang the mink by placing a gambrel hook through both hind legs, and strip the tail with the aid of a tail stripper, pliers or similar tool. The pelt can then be pulled all the way down to the area of the ears, and finally to free the pelt with a cut leaving the nose attached to the pelt.

Fleshing can be accomplished by placing the pelt fur side in over a wooden stretcher. Scaping should be done with a single handled fleshing tool, from the head area down to the tail. A muscled area will be present from the shoulders over the back area, and this should be left on the pelt. Most mink pelts require little fleshing, but all fat, meat and attached glands should be removed.

Be sure to open the tail the full length with a knife cut, and the pelt can be stretched on a wire stretcher or a wooden stretcher. Hooks are provided on wire stretchers to attach to the foot area of the pelt, and at the base of the tail. A wedge, or belly board, will be needed if the pelt is to be stretched on a wooden stretcher to prevent the skin from shrinking on the stretcher as it dries. Tacks or pins can be used to hold the pelt as it dries. Drying times take several days to a week.

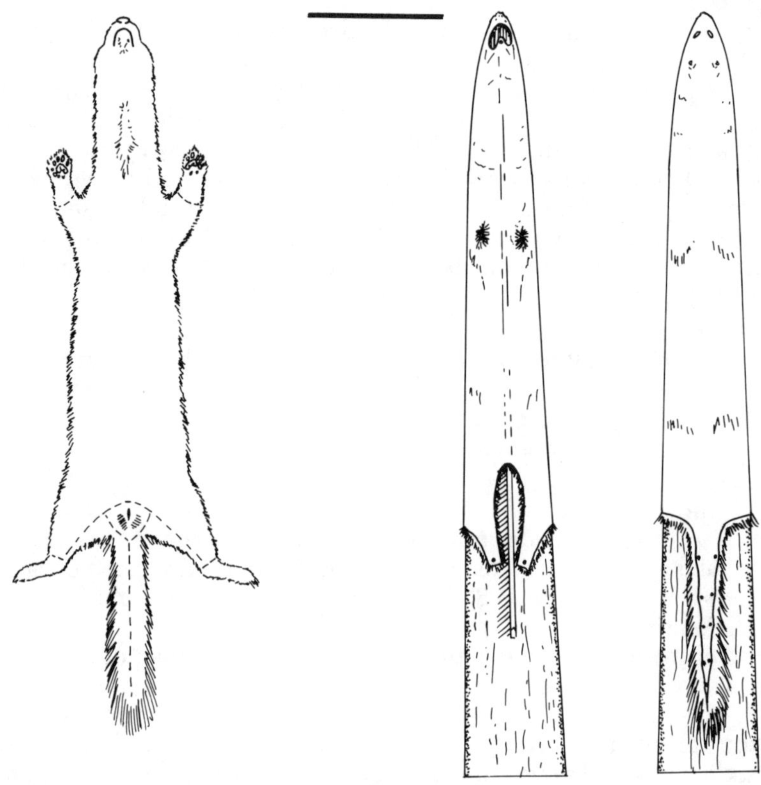

BADGER — Taxidea Taxus

Order — Carnivora
Family — Mustelidae

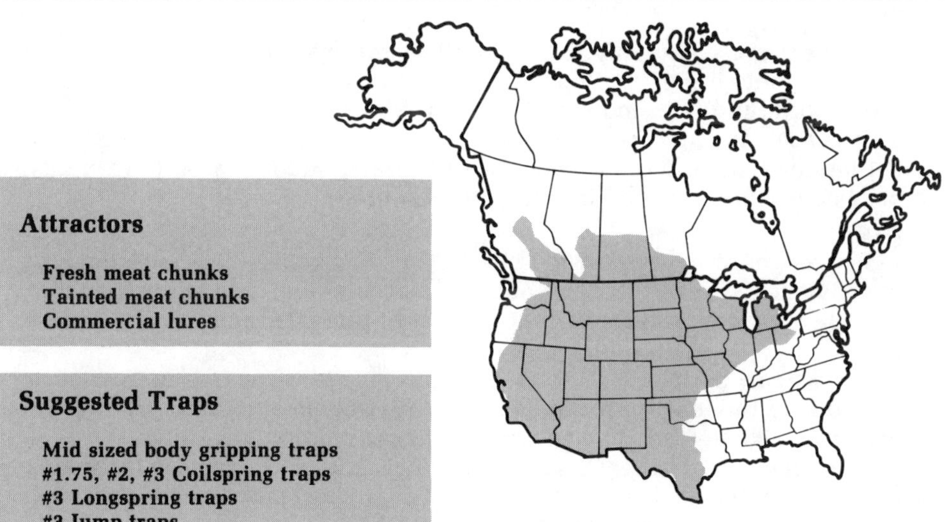

Attractors

Fresh meat chunks
Tainted meat chunks
Commercial lures

Suggested Traps

Mid sized body gripping traps
#1.75, #2, #3 Coilspring traps
#3 Longspring traps
#3 Jump traps

The Badger

BADGERS are well known for their digging habits and nasty dispositions when they are forced to defend themselves. An important predator of gophers and prairie dogs, they favor prairies, open farmlands, and deserts. Numerous excavations make badgers unpopular with some farmers and ranchers. Viewed with either affection or disgust, badgers are expanding their ranges eastwardly.

Description

Adult badgers measure 30 to 35 inches in length, including a short and well furred tail of 5 or 6 inches. Body shapes are wide, giving a flat backed appearance.

Many adult badgers weigh 12 to 16 pounds, although weights might increase to over 20 pounds in the late fall as they store up layers of fat to sustain them during periods of cold weather and deep snow.

Colors are mostly grey, with a grizzled effect due to long guard hairs that have a black band ending in a white tip. Underfur is either a light tan, or a creamy white.

A white stripe from the nose leads between the eyes and back over the head of the badger, ending between the shoulders. Ears are set low along the sides of the head.

Lower legs and feet are black in color. There are five toes on each foot, and four of the toes on the front feet have exceptionally long claws of 1½ to 1¾ inches in length.

Badgers have 34 teeth, including four sharply pointed canine teeth.

All badgers have a pair of musk producing glands near the anus as well as two skin glands located on the bellies

Distribution

Badgers are commonly found in all of the western and north central states. Although they were not found east of Indiana by settlers, badgers are being found with more and more regularity as far east as New York. This species is found rarely in the southeastern states.

Classified in different states as furbearers, predators, and varmints, badgers are harvested by trapping in 18 states.

Sign

Badgers hunt by digging rodents out of the ground. The holes they dig are obvious wherever they are found. These holes are often wider than they are tall, and there is a significant amount of dirt piled right in front of the holes.

Tracks can be found at times in many locations, and identification is easy due to the long claw marks left by the front feet. When walking, the badger is pigeon-toed, leaving tracks that are pointed inwardly.

Droppings from badgers are not usually found as the species frequently uses an underground chamber as a toilet area. Droppings contain hair and bones as the species eats animals whole.

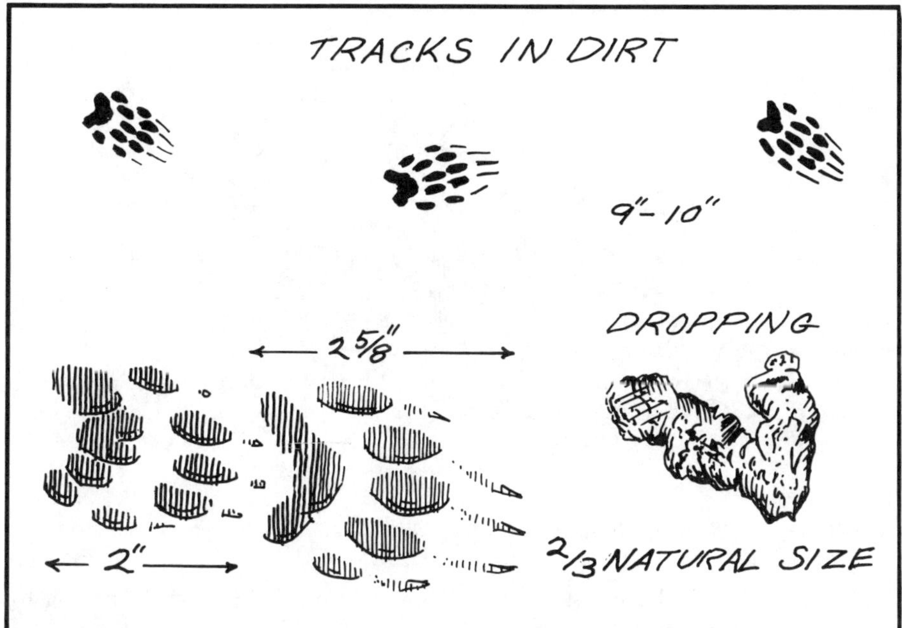

Reproduction

Badgers mate in August or September. Delayed implantation of fertilized eggs occurs, and the development of the litter begins in late February when the eggs attach to the uterus of the female. The actual development time is approximately 9 weeks before 2 to 7 young are born. Although the female has 8 teats, litter sizes tend to be small, and a litter size of 3 is common.

Females care for the litter by themselves. Juveniles disperse in late summer to begin solitary lifestyles.

Twelve years is considered as old age in a badger.

Habits

Badgers are territorial throughout most of the year. Most territories are about 3 or 4 square miles. The size of the territory might vary somewhat due to the availability of rodents, a preferred food. It seems as if territories are not defended against other badgers, or territories overlap regularly in good habitats.

Habitats with sandy or porous soils are preferred. Badgers frequent wooded areas when soils are suitable for digging.

Other than the dispersal of juveniles, badgers do not seem to migrate. Typically walking from place to place, they can trot or bound along at a gallop when they choose to.

Badgers have excellent senses of hearing and smell. Both serve in locating food species, which are usually rodents in underground dens. Vision is good, and enables a badger to recognize danger at a distance.

Badgers have been known to plug the exit holes of prey species before the badger tunnels underground to capture the prey. The long claws serve to loosen the soil and pass it backwards where the hind feet kick the soil out behind the digging animal. This dirt is often kicked backwards 6 or 8 feet in an almost continuous arc by a badger digging in earnest. Badgers close

A badger trap should always be staked away from the hole.

their eyes as they dig underground. They rely upon smell and hearing to continue digging toward the prey.

Even though badgers have relatively small territory sizes, a number of dens are used regularly over different parts of the territory. These underground dens are often quite elaborate. Most tunnels are 6 to 8 feet deep,and 20 to 30 feet long to the main den chamber which is elevated to discourage flooding. A smaller chamber is also dug underground to serve as a toilet area, and many dens have several entrances holes. Dens that have been used for generations by badgers may have as many as 30 to 40 exits, and tunnels as deep as 15 feet.

Bedding materials of grass and leaves are sometimes removed from the den chamber for airing out by a den entrance, after which it is taken back down into the chamber for reuse.

Some badgers have demonstrated that they will tolerate a fox or a coyote sharing the same den. In 1871, a lost 7-year-old Canadian boy shared a den with a badger, which at first tried to drive him away, and then appeared to adopt him by bringing him food.

Badgers are determined fighters when they are threatened. Their loose fitting skin prevents them from being held securely by another animal.

Badgers do not hibernate, but they do sleep for extended periods of time in northern states during extended periods of cold weather and deep snow. Wintering dens are sometimes found in woodlands, where the frost does not penetrate as deeply. They can stay underground for weeks at a time, but they do come out to hunt occasionally as they do not store food.

Other than rodents, badgers also eat skunks, snakes, birds and their eggs, worms, insects, berries and carrion. Rattlesnakes are eaten when available, but the badgers do not eat the rattlesnake head. Carrion is probably an important winter food when the frozen ground is difficult or impossible to dig in.

The condition of its claws are important to a badger. The species sharpens their long claws by scratching on trees or posts.

Mid sized body gripping traps are very selective at natural badger dens when no bait is used.

Trapping

Foothold traps, medium sized body gripping traps and cage traps can all be effective in catching badgers.

Number 2 or number 3 traps are usually used for badgers because the species has a large and tough foot which can be missed by a smaller trap because the foot overlaps the smaller trap jaws. Fastening is important, and metal stakes should be used whenever a badger catch is likely to prevent the trapped badger from chewing off the trap stake and escaping with the trap on its foot.

Badgers frequently dig away from the trap stake in a circle as far as the trap chain will permit after being caught. If long trap chains are used with foothold traps at den entrances, they should be staked as far as possible away from the hole to prevent the badger from being lodged deeply within the burrow because they can be difficult to get out without digging.

When foothold traps are used at badger dens, many trappers prefer to place the traps inside the entrances. A rather squat animal, it is an advantage to place the trap so that the animal steps between the jaws rather than over the jaws. Offsetting the trap to either side is an aid as a badger's feet are not normally placed under the body.

Medium sized body gripping traps are efficient at the entrances to occupied dens, and very selective when no baits or lures are used. Badger dens have strong odors, and other species are usually not tempted to enter an underground den when a badger is present.

Badgers are erratic in their traveling habits, and trails or paths are not used regularly. For that reason, sets are usually made near fresh diggings or existing dens. Badgers visit these locations whenever they are nearby.

A degree of curiosity and a well developed sense of smell makes badgers vulnerable to sets made for coyotes or foxes. They are very difficult to avoid deliberately.

Badgers are late primers, and normally are not pelt prime until late December, January or February. Badgers caught in November are very rarely prime, and most trappers prefer to release the unprime badgers. Primeness does last longer than for most other land species.

Badgers can be released with the aid of a hog catcher (choke stick, catch pole, noose-stick). Extreme care should be taken to prevent the badger from biting. Be aware that the released badger might make a false charge or two before it decides to leave. For safety, back away after releasing the animal.

Badgers are trapped conservatively when just the prime badgers are killed. Although territory sizes and reproduction rates are both small, significant numbers of badgers are not caught during winter seasons when badgers stay underground for extended lengths of time.

Dispatch

Badgers are normally killed with a brain shot from a .22 rifle or handgun.

They can also be killed with a sharp blow to the top of the skull with a metal trap stake or similar tool.

Controls

Adult badgers have few natural enemies. The species is aggressive when threatened, and they are determined fighters when cornered. Usually, a badger will escape to a hole nearby, or dig one to escape persecution.

Juvenile badgers may be vulnerable to attacks by coyotes or eagles.

Tularemia and rabies can afflict badgers, and parasites include flukes, tapeworms, roundworms, lice and fleas.

Badgers are particularly vulnerable to poisoned baits placed for coyotes. Their best protection from poisoned baits is a relatively small territory size. Poisons used against rodents are also detrimental to badgers, as the poisoned animals are eaten.

Values

Badgers serve prey species by helping to control populations. Digging habits do provide dens for a variety of other wild species.

Values to man are both positive and negative. A considerable number of damage causing rodents are eaten by badgers, but the numerous and large holes left behind can be a nuisance for farmers and ranchers. Horses have been known to break a leg by stepping in a badger hole while galloping, but this is thought to occur very rarely.

For many years, badger fur was used as paint brushes for artists, and as shaving brushes. Today, badger fur is mostly used as a trimming fur for coat collars.

Thirty to forty thousand badger pelts are marketed annually, with values exceeding one million dollars to people in many American communities.

Fur Handling

Badgers are sometimes handled cased, with the fur side out, but the preferred method is "open", with a rectangular shape longer than it is wide. Badger skins are greasy, and fleshing is best accomplished with a fleshing beam and a two handled fleshing knife.

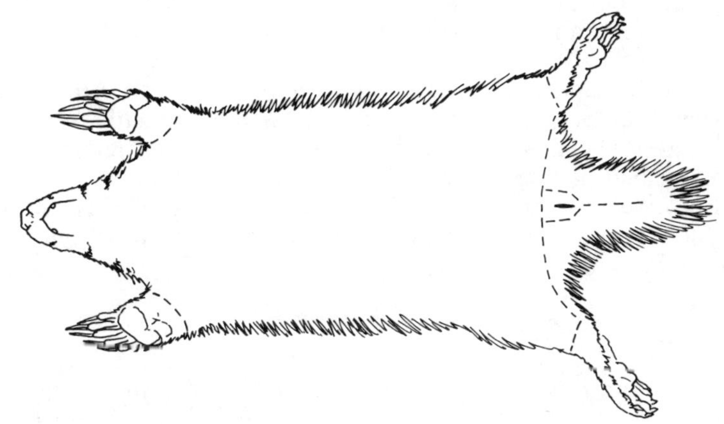

To get the best shaped pelt, the badger should first be skinned cased. A knife cut from the inside of one hind leg to the other is needed, and another cut is necessary from the base of the tail, around the vent to the first cut. The fur can then be separated from the hind legs, and the feet can be left attached to the carcass. Then the badger can be suspended from a gambrel, and a cut partway down the underside of the tail will be helpful as the tail fur is stripped from the tailbone with the aid of a tail stripping tool or pliers.

After the tail is skinned, it should be opened the entire length with a knife cut, and the fur can be pulled down over the shoulder area. The fur can be pryed from the shoulder area with finger and thumb pressure, or a blunt tool such as a large phillips screwdriver can be inserted between the skin and flesh in the armpit area, and used for leverage to pull the pelt down to each front foot, where the fur is cut.

Further pulling and light cutting may be necessary to get the pelt to the head area, where severing cuts will be needed at the ear canals, eyes, and nose.

The cased pelt should be placed over a fleshing beam for fleshing. Always be sure that there are no burs in the fur which might cause a cut as the pelt is being fleshed. Many fur handlers prefer to begin fleshing the throat and belly area first, and then flesh the sides before fleshing the more difficult back area. Badgers are more difficult to flesh than some other species, but the pelt still must be cleaned right down to the skin.

After the pelt is fleshed, a cut can be made with a sharp knife all the way down the middle of the belly to open up the skin. Do not make any cuts to the front legs, as you will get a better stretch when the front leg holes appear inside the finished pelt.

Badgers are often dirty, and the pelts will have a brighter appearance if they are washed with a mild soap in a bucket of cold water. Don't ever wash a pelt in warm or hot water, or use a detergent, or the fur is likely to shed and become worthless.

To stretch a badger pelt, drive a nail through the nose into a piece of plywood. Then measure 15 or 16 inches across the shoulder area, and drive nails in each shoulder area near the edge of the pelt. The lower legs can then be pulled downward to make the pelt as long as is possible. The lower legs should also be nailed to the stretcher 15 or 16 inches apart.

The pelt should then have a rectangular shape, except for the pointed nose area. Nails should be driven an inch apart or so all of the way around the entire pelt.

It is an advantage to lift the pelt on the nails all around. Air circulation is necessary if the pelt has been washed and is wet, and still an advantage if the pelt has not been washed because the fur will be fluffier as it drys, making the finished pelt appear as thickly furred as possible.

Drying times vary according to temperature and humidity. Most badger pelts will dry in a week or ten days, when they can be removed from the stretchers for sale.

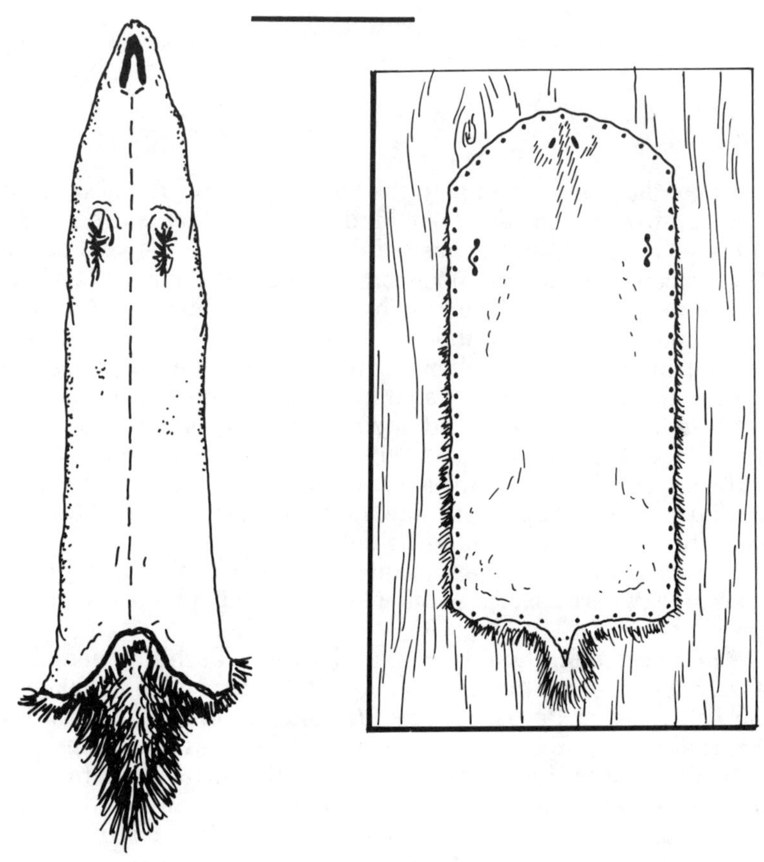

STRIPED SKUNK — Mephitis Mephitis

Order — Carnivora
Family — Mustelidae

Attractors

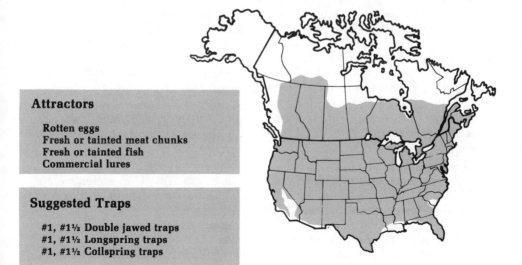

Rotten eggs
Fresh or tainted meat chunks
Fresh or tainted fish
Commercial lures

Suggested Traps

#1, #1½ Double jawed traps
#1, #1½ Longspring traps
#1, #1½ Coilspring traps

The Striped Skunk

THE Latin word "mephitis" translates to "bad odor", and many people would agree that the name "bad odor — bad odor" aptly fits the common and abundant striped skunk. Smaller spotted skunks are also distributed widely, and two species are recognized. Known as "civets" to the fur trade, the western spotted skunks experience a delayed implantation reproduction, while the eastern spotted skunks do not. All species of skunks are attracted to a wide variety of baits, and they are frequently caught in traps set for other species.

Description

Average adult striped skunks weigh 6 to 8 pounds, although body weight might be significantly heavier in late fall as the skunks attain layers of fat to sustain themselves through winter. Spotted skunks are much smaller, usually weighing 2 or 3 pounds. Males of both types are slightly heavier than females.

All striped skunks have a white stripe on the head between the nose and the forehead. A white crest, or cap, is typical on the top of the head, and a continuing white stripe usually divides over the shoulder area into two stripes that continue along the sides of the animal into the tail. The amount of white coloration varies with the individual skunk, with some having broad stripes, narrow stripes, short stripes, or even none at all.

Spotted skunks have a white patch on the forehead area, and a broken pattern of white striping that appears as blotches or spots of white in the otherwise black fur. The amount of white also varies with individuals. Some spotted skunks have mostly black tails while others can be mostly white.

The scent glands in skunks are well developed. Musk, or essence, can be sprayed repeatedly as a defense. The yellowish compound is powerful in all skunks, and contains sulfuric acid which can cause temporary blindness in both other animals and man.

Striped and spotted skunks have 5 toes on each foot. The front feet have relatively long claws to assist them in digging for grubs and other foods.

Both skunks have 34 teeth including 4 pointed and sharp canine teeth.

Skunk fur is rather long, and longer on tails than on the bodies. Underfur is white under the white guard hairs, and grayish under the black colored guard hairs.

Distribution

Striped skunks are found in all of the North American states except Alaska. Excellent populations of striped skunks also occur throughout much of the southern half of Canada.

Although spotted skunks are found in many states, populations seem to be sporadic and inconsistent in most areas.

Striped skunks seem to prefer mixtures of farmlands and woodlands.

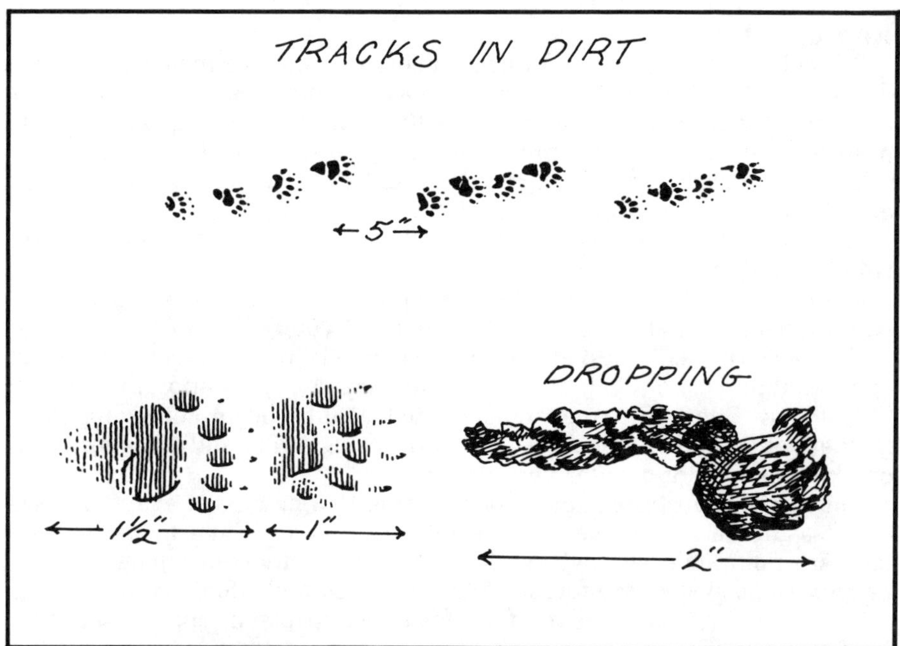

However, excellent populations are found in most habitat types where drinking water is available.

Spotted skunks seem to thrive best near unkept farms and old homesteads. Spotted skunks are commonly found in western grassland prairies, and the foothills below mountain ranges. In the south and southeast, spotted skunks are often found in rocky and wooded regions as well as farmlands.

Sign

Skunk tracks can often be noticed near old farm buildings, as these are favored locations for both striped and spotted skunks. Striped skunks leave an unmistakable diagonal pattern of tracks when they are loping. Toenail prints are usually visible in the tracks of either species.

The spotted skunk leaves a trail that is more in a straight line. Footprints of the front foot of a spotted skunk can be confused with mink, but the heel print made by a hind foot is much larger than a mink's.

Droppings are left indiscriminately by skunks, although they will occasionally be left in conspicuous places on logs or rocks. The droppings of the striped skunk often appear shiny due to the large numbers of insects eaten. Spotted skunk droppings are proportionately smaller, and often contain significant amounts of fur.

A common sign of striped skunks is the holes left behind as the furbearer digs out grubs and insects. These holes are often a few feet apart, and they are usually only a few inches deep.

Good places to find skunk tracks are around beehives. Skunks habitually visit these places to feed upon the dead bees that are expelled from the hives.

Reproduction

Striped skunks often breed during February, and the males do a great deal of traveling at this time to locate females. Many times, females will live in an underground den through the winter with only one male, who will protect the communal den from invasion by another male.

Gestation periods are usually 63 days, and all bred females seek solitary dens to raise their young by themselves.

Litter sizes of striped skunks are usually 6 to 8, except for the first litter, which usually numbers 4.

The eastern species of spotted skunk, Spilogale putorius, usually breed in April. Gestation is about 60 days before 3 to 5 young are born.

The western species, Spilogale gracilus, breeds in September or October and gestation is about 240 days due to a delayed implantation process.

The new litter of striped and spotted skunks begin following their mothers at 6 weeks of age. Travel is often single file, and the young are quick to learn to find grubs and insects.

The family units break up as the young reach 3 months of age. Dispersal is not significant, and the juvenile females may continue to share their mother's den. Males are evicted, however, by the dominant male, and the juvenile male skunks are forced to find other suitable den locations.

Six years of age is considered old for either striped or spotted skunks.

Habits

Striped skunks are mostly nocturnal, doing most of their hunting and traveling during the night. Territory sizes are somewhat small, and overlapping or sharing of territories is normal as the species does not defend its territory against others of the same species as do some other species. Home ranges are considered to be about 4 square miles, but most skunks do not travel more than a mile or so in one night's activity.

Communal dens are common during the time of year that young are not being raised, and 6 to 20 skunks might share a den with one male at a time.

Striped skunks suffer from poor vision at distances of more than 2 or 3 feet. A keen sense of smell enables them to easily locate foods, which vary with the season. Not a particularly swift animal, skunks don't need good distance vision to locate prey species which have little or no mobility. The ability to see a predator at a distance is not necessary either, as the threat of spraying its musk will usually deter all but ignorant predators, who soon receive a lesson.

Skunks usually give ample warning before they spray their musk. Spraying is a defensive mechanism, and used only when the animal feels that it is necessary to protect its own life. Warnings usually include a lifting of the tail, a turning of the back towards the danger, and sometimes, a pounding of the front feet in a drummer-like fashion.

Spotted skunks are more agile than striped skunks. Their territory sizes are similar to striped skunks. This species can climb very well, and they descend trees head first.

When threatened, spotted skunks commonly do handstands, balancing on their front feet while they lift their bodies into the air. This balancing act usually lasts for about 5 seconds at a time. The species can spray an offender from this position.

Spotted skunks are almost strictly nocturnal, usually retiring to a den before daylight, and coming out only after dark in the evening.

Spotted skunks are excellent climbers. Their activities are usually very beneficial to man.

Skunks are not true hibernators, but both species may spend weeks at a time in dens during cold temperatures and deep snow conditions.

Striped skunks usually utilize underground dens that have been made by badgers, groundhogs, or foxes. At times, they will tolerate other species in its den, even curling up and sleeping with a raccoon, or opossum.

Spotted skunks prefer dens under or in old buildings. Oftentimes, a den will be on the second floor of an old barn. Dens in haylofts are common, and the spotted skunks easily climb to the elevated dens.

Slow and poorly sighted furbearers, striped skunks are opportunistic feeders. Grubs and insects are commonly located and dug out of the ground, along with juvenile mice, rabbits, and ground nesting birds or eggs found. Fruits and grains are eaten when available, and carrion is commonly eaten during winter months when many foods are not available.

Spotted skunks are more efficient than striped skunks as predators. These smaller skunks kill and eat significantly more mice and rats. Spotted skunks also frequent the edges of streams and ponds, and they do wade shallow water in pursuit of crayfish, a preferred food.

Trapping

Striped skunks and spotted skunks can be easily caught in cage traps, small or medium sized body gripping traps, and foothold traps. With adequate defense systems, skunks are not particularly wary, and they are often caught by inexperienced trappers as well as experienced trappers.

Sets constructed near abandoned buildings often catch skunks.

If cage type traps are used where spotted skunks are abundant, a very light trigger tension may be necessary or the furbearer's light weight may not trigger the trap door. A variety of baits can be used with cage traps. It is an advantage to place some straw or hay on the floor of the trap to encourage the animal to enter it.

The small sized heads of both striped and spotted skunks make them vulnerable to small sized body gripping traps when they are placed so that the animals will attempt to stick their heads into the traps. Small body gripping traps with two springs are best. They should be set so that the trap jaws close from top to bottom, and not from side to side.

Foothold traps are used most frequently to capture skunks. Small sizes are adequate, and preferred. Many trappers use a single longspring #1 trap. The #1 coilsprings are also excellent skunk traps. Double jawed traps make the best selection, as the double set of jaws will prevent most skunks from attempting to chew below the trap jaws on the numbed foot, which is not recognized by the skunk.

Skunks are not powerful animals, but all traps should be staked or fastened with enough strength to hold the largest possible catch, such as a raccoon or dog.

A lot of skill is not necessary to capture skunks. The species will often step into uncovered traps in attempts to get the baits. Leaving foothold traps uncovered can help to make sets more selective for skunks, but the traps should be placed in shallow excavations to make it convenient for the skunk to step into the set trap.

Skunks will investigate every odor that even remotely promises food.

Eggs make excellent and somewhat selective baits. Rotten eggs are good, and fresh eggs will also work well. Generally, an egg or two is used, and broken to release its attractive odors.

Due to small ranging habits, large litter sizes, and lack of competition, striped skunks may be trapped without concern for conservation practices.

Spotted skunks are not abundant in many areas, and many of these smaller skunks can be missed by not setting traps near abandoned farm buildings.

It is wise to always respect the power of skunk musk. Exposure can be unpleasant. Care should be taken whenever dispatching a skunk to stay upwind, and out of a skunk's spraying range of 12 to 15 feet. The sprayed essence quickly dissipates in the air, forming an invisible yet powerful mist.

A few commercial products are available to help neutralize skunk essence. Washing exposed skin with tomato juice or baking soda and water can help a great deal.

Dispatch

Live skunks are most commonly killed by shooting from an upwind position with a .22 rifle or handgun. Do not shoot a skunk in the head, or spinal column. A live rabies virus might be living in the nervous tissue of the brain or spinal column, and shooting could release the live virus into the air.

Many trappers prefer to shoot skunks with .22 short ammunition, and wait for a side shot to the heart and lung area behind the front legs. Death will follow shortly if both lungs are pierced by the bullet, and goodly numbers of skunks do not spray if the trapper retreats slowly after shooting the furbearer in this location.

Due to the possibility of rabies, many trappers prefer to leave the dead skunk in the trap until the next day.

Controls

Dogs are a threat to skunks, and some dogs will kill skunks even after being sprayed by the skunk. Badgers kill skunks in western areas, particularly during winter when the skunks are slow and sleepy. Other animals that occasionally kill skunks are foxes, coyotes, bobcats, fishers, and cougars. It appears that some great horned owls kill a significant number of skunks, while other great horned owls apparently do not.

With extremely poor eyesight, skunks are very vulnerable to vehicle traffic. The erratic movements of skunks in headlights suggest extreme visual problems.

Spotted skunks have declined in numbers significantly where clean and intensive farming practices are used. Pesticides used to control grubs and other crop pests seem to either poison spotted skunks, or impair their ability to reproduce.

Diseases of skunks include distemper, tularemia, and rabies. Rabies is a particular concern in striped skunks, as this species is able to carry rabies and spread rabies without dying of the dreaded disease.

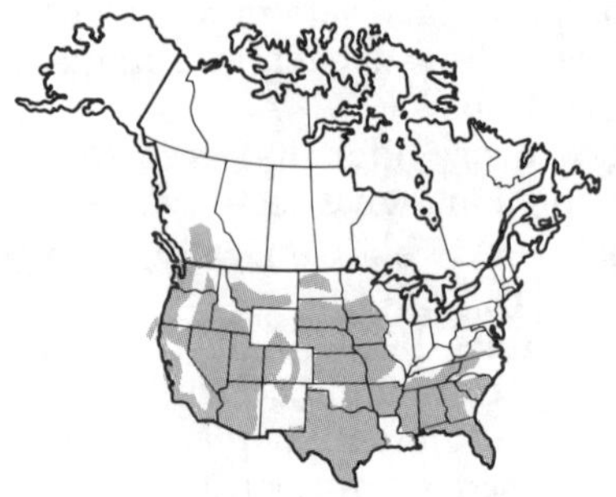

Distribution
Spotted Skunk

Values

Although skunks are not well liked by people, they do provide valuable services by controlling significant numbers of injurious insects in the larval stages. The diet of spotted skunks is almost entirely beneficial to man.

Both striped skunks and spotted skunks can raid chicken houses. The worst offender is usually the spotted skunk because it can climb easily to gain access.

Striped skunks do dig up lawns in pursuit of grubs, and this is an annoyance to those who spend time and money to groom lawns.

The concern of rabies in striped skunks is very real. More striped skunks than all other species combined are tested positive for rabies every year, and this disease is always a threat to livestock, pets and man.

Striped skunks can destroy a significant number of waterfowl nests. However, recent studies indicate that they may be beneficial to waterfowl populations because skunks are the only significant predator of a far more serious waterfowl predator, the snapping turtle. Striped skunks relish snapping turtle eggs, which are commonly found, unearthed and eaten.

In spite of relatively low fur prices, 150 - 200 thousand pelts are marketed annually, yeilding values of approximately 500 thousand dollars.

Fur Handling

To reduce any risk of rabies, many trappers prefer to handle skunks only after they have been dead for a day or two. Latex gloves that are sometimes used by housewives for washing dishes should always be worn when skinning skunks as a safety precaution.

Skunk furs are handled cased, with the fur on the inside of the pelt. The first cut should be made from the inside of one hind leg to the other. A cut will also be necessary from the base of the tail, around the vent, to the first cut, but extreme caution must be used when skinning around the vent. The powerful musk glands are located on both sides of the vent, and it is perfectly acceptable to leave a patch of fur attached to the carcass over the glands. By all means, keep the knife blade shallow in this area to avoid puncturing the glands.

After these beginning cuts have been made, the fur can be loosened around the hind legs and separated at the ankle area with a cut. The tail should be stripped from the tailbone with a tail stripping tool. The pelt is pulled with the skunk suspended by the hind feet.

Finger and thumb pressure can be used to separate the fur from the shoulder areas, and the front legs pulled down to the ankles which are also cut free.

Deep cuts will be needed at the ear canals and eyes. The final cut will sever the nose from the carcass.

Skunks are usually fleshed on a fleshing beam with a two handled fleshing knife. With more patience, skunks can be well fleshed on a wooden stretcher with a single handled fleshing tool. With either method, care should be taken to prevent tearing a hole in the pelt as skunks are somewhat more fragile than some other types of pelts.

Skunks can be stretched on either wire or wooden stretchers. If a wooden stretcher is used, a wedge shaped belly board should be used to prevent the drying pelt from shrinking too tightly on the stretcher.

Skunk pelts should be suspended in a cool place away from direct sunlight for several days to a week as the fur dries.

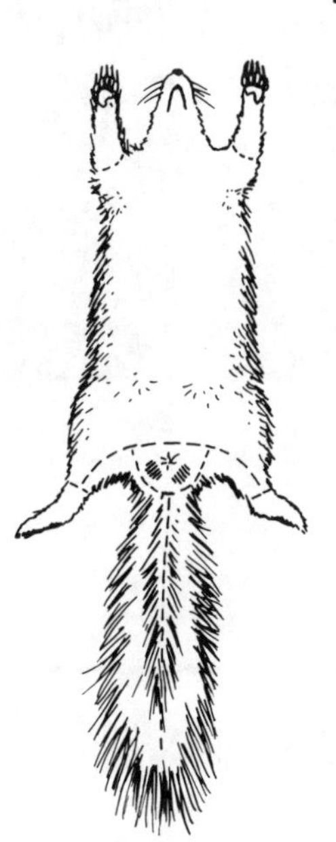

OTTER — Lutra Canadensis
Order — Carnivora
Family — Mustelidae

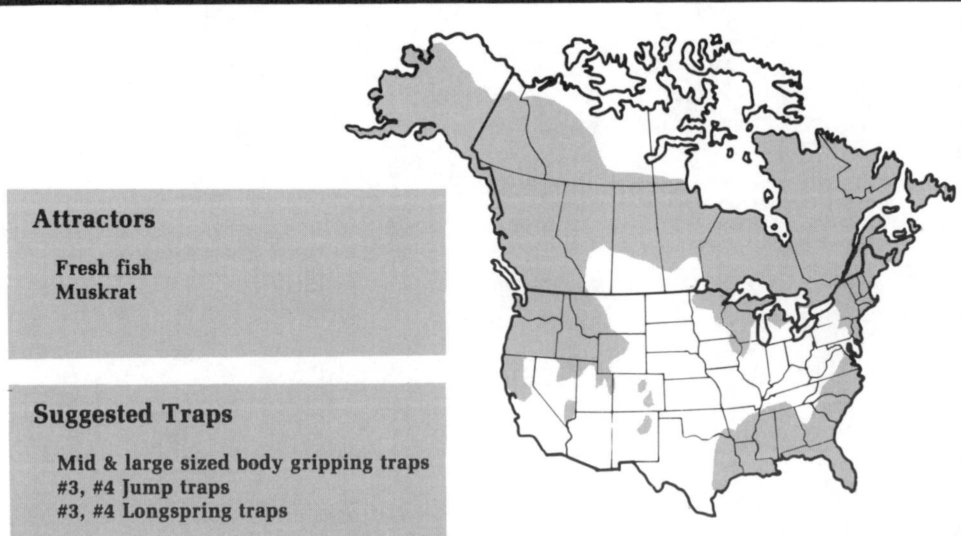

Attractors

Fresh fish
Muskrat

Suggested Traps

Mid & large sized body gripping traps
#3, #4 Jump traps
#3, #4 Longspring traps

The Otter

RIVER otters are highly skilled swimmers. Rough fish make up a substantial portion of an otter's diet, although game fish of medium size are occasionally caught and eaten. Great travelers, otter circuits may cover 60 or more miles, and take weeks to complete. This species enjoys play, and otters commonly play either alone or with others of their kind. Powerful and streamlined furbearers, otters are recognized as one of the more intelligent species.

Description

Otters have long, slender bodies with relatively short legs. The neck is long and muscular, as is the tapered tail.

Otter fur is considered as a short haired fur. Guard hair lengths are about one inch with underfur lengths of about ¾ inch. Coloration is brown, with chocolate colors common in southern states, and darker colors common in northern states. Otters from all areas are lighter in color on cheeks, throats, and bellies.

Males are larger than females. Adult males may measure 48 inches in length, and weigh up to 25 pounds. Adult females are usually 4 to 6 inches shorter, and seldom weigh more than 19 pounds.

There are 5 toes on each foot. A web of skin connects the toes on each foot. Claws are strong and nonretractable.

Otters have 36 teeth, including 4 long and sharp canine teeth.

Valves are present in an otter's nose and ears which close automatically as the otter submerges.

A pair of anal musk glands are present on both males and females. This musk can be released when the otter is frightened, but it is not as offensive as the musk of other members of the mustelid, or weasel, family.

Distribution

The heaviest concentrations of otters are currently found in the northeastern, southeastern, and northwestern states. Sparse populations occur in many other states.

Otters seem to prefer isolated habitats away from the constant activity of man. Lakes, streams and large marshes are all visited by this species as they travel and fish.

Otter populations seem to be most dense in forested regions where water is apt to be clear much of the time.

Sign

Otter tracks can be commonly seen along muddy shores, or in the snow. Five toes will show in the roundish track, including the toenails. If snow is several inches deep, drag marks can be seen that were left by the short legged furbearer's body.

Regular toilet areas can sometimes be found, and identified by an abundance of vomitted fish scales as well as droppings.

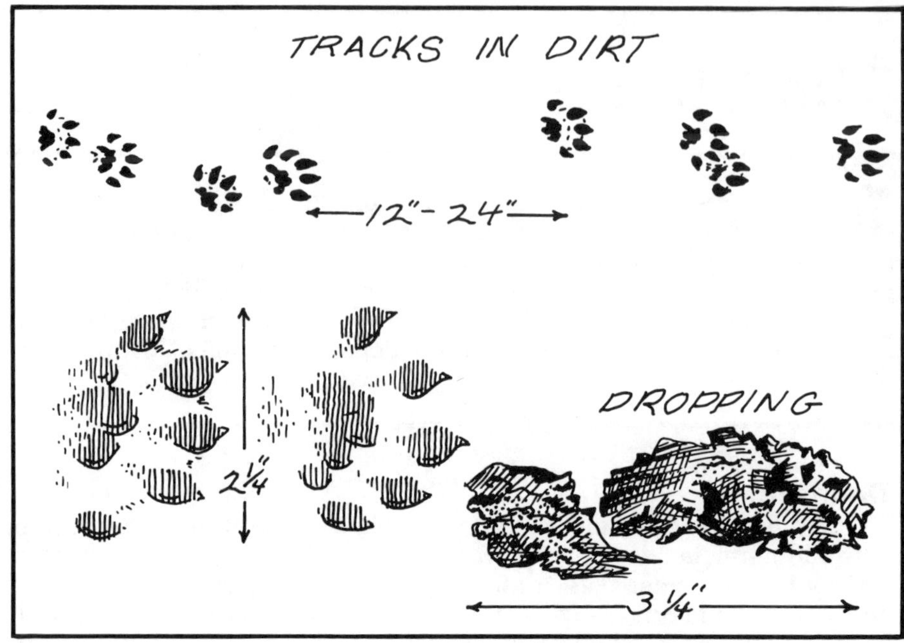

Droppings can usually be found in prominent places, such as on logs or rocks protruding from the water. These droppings are fragile and contain mostly fish scales, bones, and pieces of crayfish.

Reproduction

Breeding occurs over most of the otter range during March and April, only a few days after the litter is born. Males leave after breeding to find other females, but may return 6 to 8 weeks later to join the family.

Delayed implantation occurs, and this varies a great deal. Implantation of the fertilized eggs may take 7 to 10 months before the free-floating eggs attach themselves to the uterus walls to complete the 60 to 65 day gestation.

Litter sizes average 2 or 3, with 4 being uncommon.

Most otters do not mate until they are two years old.

Abandoned beaver dens are often selected by the female otter for the natal dens. At times, an otter will use a dryland den near the water to raise the litter. All young must be taught to swim.

Otters are considered to be old at 15 years.

Habits

Except for the raising of the litter, otters seem to be constantly on the move from place to place. They do not seem to defend their territories from other otters, and overlapping of regular territories do occur often.

The availability of food, as well as the season, determines how far the individual otter ranges. During summer months when food is easily available, otters may stay within a 20 square mile area. During winter conditions, the same otter may circulate over 60 or more square miles. Circuit times vary as well, and an otter may complete a summertime circuit in a week as compared to wintertime travels taking 3 or 4 weeks.

Otters commonly travel by swimming and loping along shorelines, but they do not hesitate to take off overland to reach a distant stream or pond.

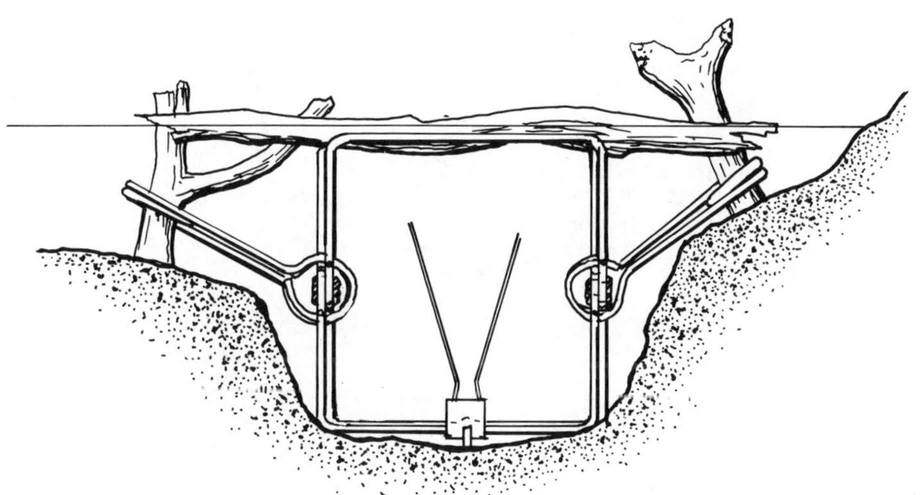

Mid and large sizes of body gripping traps are very effective when placed in shallow runs or wherever streams narrow.

These overland trails may be very distinct when otter populations are high.

Otters certainly enjoy sliding on mud or snow. Under favorable conditions, they might bound 3 or 4 times and then slide for yards before continuing to bound and slide some more. Mud slides down steep banks into the water are commonly used in many nothern areas as the otter or family of otters take turns climbing the bank to slide down the slide into the water head first.

Otters have a high metabolic rate, and food passes through the entire digestive system in about an hour. Small fishes are eaten whole. Often an otter will eat a fish while floating in the water on its back, holding the fish much like a person eating corn on the cob.

After eating, otters commonly vomit up an abundance of fish scales and bones. This prevents a large number of valueless scales from passing through the entire digestive system.

The elongated body, webbed feet and powerful tapered tail allow the otter to be very quick in the water. River otters have been known to swim to 60 feet deep in the water, and they can swim at least a ½ mile while submerged. When an otter chooses to swim quickly, it undulates its entire body up and down in a whip-like fashion with their front legs held tightly to the body.

Commonly eaten foods include many types of minnows, sunfish, suckers, perch, and scultins in western habitats. Also eaten are crayfish (claws are not eaten), water snakes, frogs, and aquatic insects. Muskrats are eaten when available, as are mice.

Otters are not known to store food. Although an otter does not kill more food than it will eat, the high rate of metabolism keeps the furbearer hungry much of the time.

Young otters will often stay with their mother through their first winter season. Oftentimes, the young will follow the mother in a single file fashion, both on land and in the water.

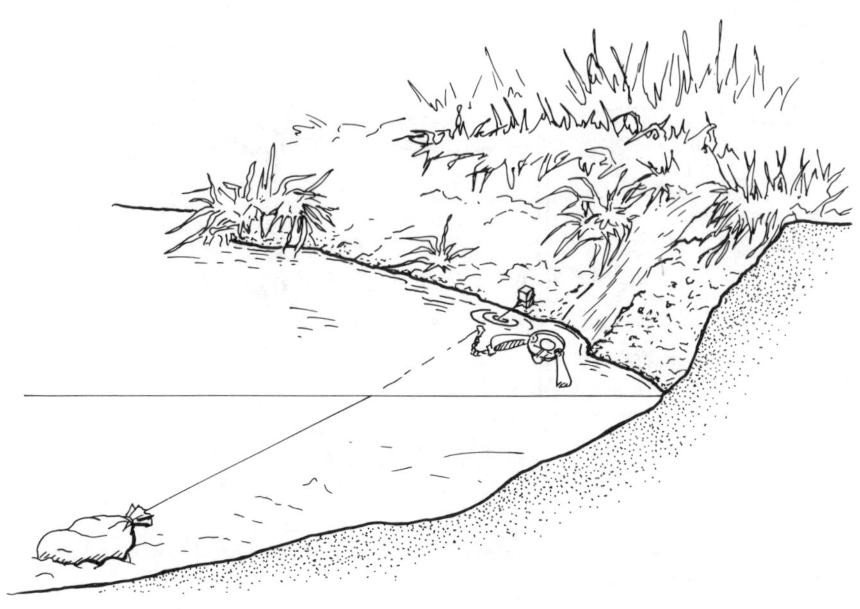

Overland trails and otter slides can sometimes be found, and these make excellent set locations.

Trapping

River otters are trapped with mid and large sized body gripping traps, and strong foothold traps attached to drowning slide wires.

Streams linking lakes are choice places to catch otters, and narrow places are often guarded with a submerged body gripping trap. The trap should be set so that the jaws close from top to bottom, and not from side to side, to take advantage of the stunning ability of the trap. When the water is deeper than the trap, most trappers prefer to set the trap right on the bottom. A log or crossing sticks are placed over the set trap to encourage the otter to dive to attempt to go through the trap.

Number 3 and number 4 foothold traps are also used by some trappers. These traps are usually concealed beneath the water where an otter is expected to enter or leave the water. These traps should be attached to a slide wire with a one way lock to allow the trapped otter to submerge in deep water while attempting to escape the trap.

Otters are powerful animals, and all sets must be constructed very strongly.

Good places to look for otter sets are near the ends of beaver dams, places where tracks indicate that otter are entering a hole in the ice to fish, or at the ends of culverts where many otters detour to go overland.

Fish are sometimes used to bait traps. As a general rule, the fish is used in shallow water and propped with stones or tied with a wire to make it appear as if it were alive.

Population densities of otters are difficult to estimate. The species is seldom abundant, and one otter per 20 square miles is considered a good population.

Otter travel patterns and habits are erratic, however, and a month of intense trapping pressure, or longer periods of lesser pressure are usually good conservation practices.

Dispatch

An otter is almost always dead when it is trapped properly. Live otters are usually dispatched with a shot into the brain with a .22 rifle or handgun.

Controls

Adult otters are rarely killed by other predators. Lynxes and wolves can kill them, and juvenile otters may also be vulnerable to predation by bobcats and coyotes.

Otters are relatively free of parasites due to infrequent uses of dens, constant traveling habits, and little contact with other otters that are not family members.

However, they are vulnerable to poisons which often show up in fish. Fish killed by acid rain may poison otters, and lethal amounts of DDT, PCB's, and mercury have been found in otters.

A significant habitat loss for otter has occurred over much of their historic range. Farming practices in many areas allow muddy and silty water with each rainfall, which discourages fish production as well as interfering with an otter's ability to locate food by sight.

Values

Although otters can and do eat trout, they usually help a trout stream by helping to contain populations of rough fish. Where fish are so abundant as to become stunted, predation certainly allows more food for the remaining fish.

Although otters sometimes kill muskrats and ducks, the numbers are so small as to be insignificant.

Otters can devastate fish farms. This is most apt to happen during the spring when a family of otters may be denned for 2 or 3 months.

Annual North American harvests yield about 50,000 pelts, with market values of between 1½ - 3 million dollars.

Fur Handling

An otter is the most difficult common furbearer to skin and flesh. If possible, have an experienced trapper help you skin, flesh and stretch your first otter pelt.

Otter furs are handled cased, with the fur on the inside. A knife with a drop point, or curved blade, is an aid when skinning otters.

The opening cut should be made from the inside of one hind leg to the other. Another cut will be necessary from this cut around the vent, and down the entire length of the underside of the tail.

After the opening cuts are made, the rounded knife should be used to cut the skin away from the hind legs. A cutting and slicing action will also be necessary down the length of the tail until the tail fur is completely separated from the tail bone.

The otter carcass can be suspended by the hind legs on a skinning gambrel to complete the skinning process. The pelt will not pull free, and cutting will be necessary to free the pelt over the entire length of the carcass.

Fleshing is best accomplished on a fleshing beam. The muscle and gristle attached to the pelt require both cutting and scraping. It is usually easiest to begin scraping the pelt on the belly side first, doing the sides next and the back last of all. The tail is also difficult to flesh, but it must be fleshed well all the way to the tip.

Otter pelts are usually stretched on wooden stretchers as the tail is tacked open with nails every inch or so all the way to the point. A wedge shaped belly board must be used to prevent the pelt from shrinking too tightly to the stretcher.

Otter pelts usually take a week or sometimes longer to dry properly. If the pelt appears greasy during drying, it can be wiped clean with a dry rag.

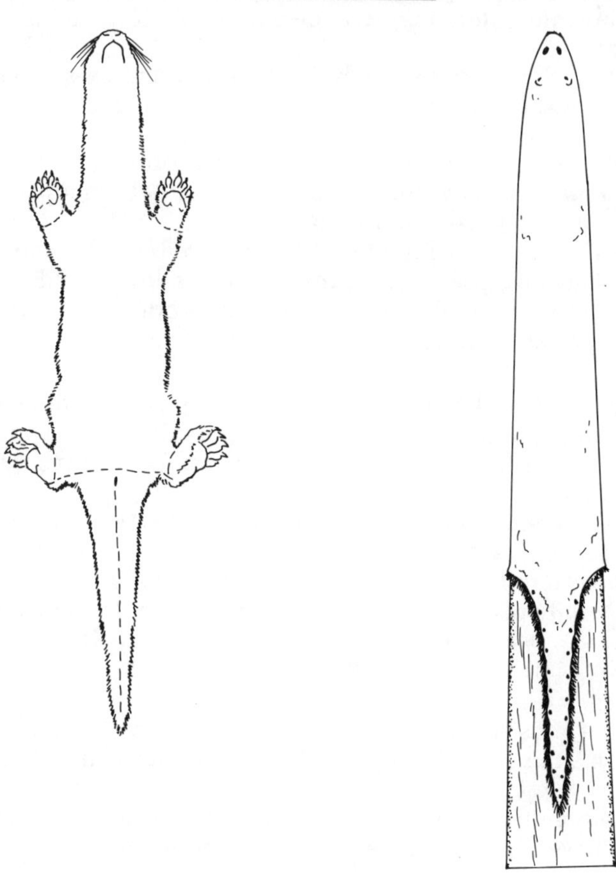

BOBCAT — Lynx Rufus

Order — Carnivora
Family — Felidae

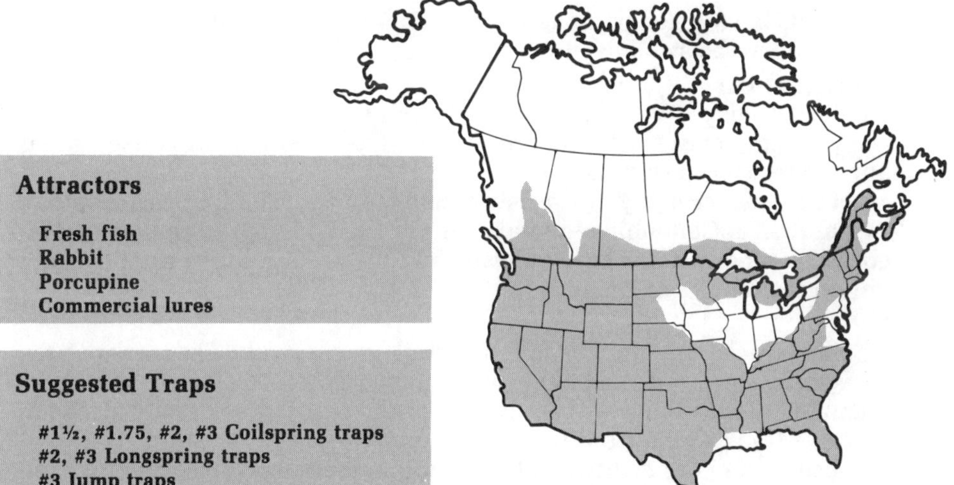

Attractors

- Fresh fish
- Rabbit
- Porcupine
- Commercial lures

Suggested Traps

- #1½, #1.75, #2, #3 Coilspring traps
- #2, #3 Longspring traps
- #3 Jump traps

The Bobcat

BOBCATS are widely distributed throughout the United States. Approximately one million bobcats live in a variety of habitats from dense forests, mountains, prairies, farmlands, and even deserts. They are rarely seen in the wild because the species normally travels by walking, and their keen eyesight and hearing are always on the alert for possible danger. Very capable predators, bobcats hunt by stalking their prey.

Description

Male bobcats are slightly larger and heavier than females. Most adult males weigh 20 to 22 pounds while females average 18 to 19 pounds. Individuals may be much larger at times, especially in the northern states, where many mature males may weigh 30 pounds. The heaviest recorded bobcat was taken in Maine, and weighed 76 pounds.

Bobcats have short tails of 5 to 6 inches in length. The underside of the tail is whitish, and there is a black spot near the end of the tail. Lynx can be confused with bobcats in northern areas, but the lynx tail is totally black, top and bottom, over the entire end of the tail.

The bobcat has a face ruff of longer fur, and slightly tufted ears. The back side of the ears are dark in color, with obvious white centers.

Overall coloration is reddish, greyish, or brownish on the backs, with lighter colored chins, throats, and bellies. Black spots are found on the front legs and bellies of bobcats, and some younger cats may be spotted almost all over the entire body. Spotting is less pronounced on older bobcats, which also tend to be darker in color.

Bobcats have retractable claws which do not show up in tracks. The claws are extended as the bobcat climbs a tree, catches prey, or defends itself.

Bobcats have 28 teeth, including four canine teeth. Meat is sheared off in sizes that can be swallowed whole, without chewing.

Distribution

Bobcats enjoy a very large range in the United States. The species is sparse or nonexistent in central farming regions, and urbanized areas along the eastern sea coast.

Bobcats adapt readily to a variety of habitat types. The species is found in several British Columbia mountain ranges, well down into southern Mexico. All southern states have bobcats, and the eastern range extends from Florida into southern Canada.

Sign

Bobcat tracks can often be found in trails or old roads. The track pattern seems to be a nearly straight line, with one footprint placed directly in front of another. The prints may be smudged as the rear foot is usually placed in the same track as the front foot.

Bobcat tracks are distinctive by their roundness, and absence of toenail marks.

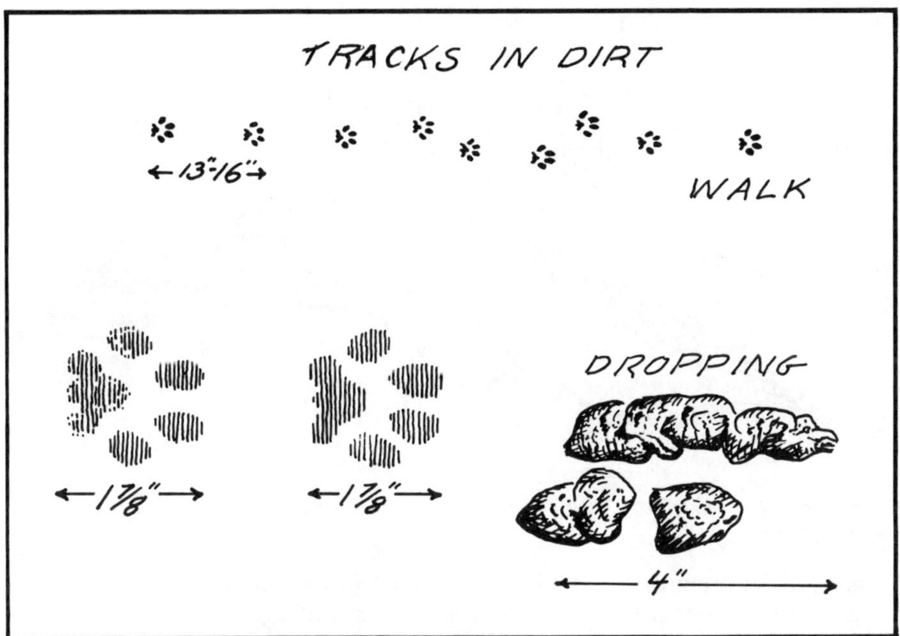

Scat is covered with scratchings at times, and left deliberately exposed at other times. Regular toilet areas may contain dozens of scats which are rather large, greyish, and contain rabbit fur.

Partially covered dead animals, such as deer or beaver, often indicate that a bobcat has been present.

Sheep killed by bobcats can usually be identified by evidence of feeding upon the nose, ears and lips.

Good places to look for bobcat sign include ridges through swamps, brushy river areas, rocky ledges, and dry washes.

Reproduction

Male bobcats do not breed as a rule until they are nearly two years old. Juvenile females are capable of breeding in their first year of life.

Litter sizes are usually 1 to 4, with 3 being an average litter.

Breeding normally takes place during February or March. Gestation is 62 to 70 days. Some female bobcats will raise two litters in a single year, and late born young often stay with the mother throughout the winter.

Breeding times can vary a great deal, and bobcats might be born in any month of the year.

Male bobcats are driven away after breeding, and the males seek other females. Females raise litters alone, which require that they leave the young unattended to hunt.

Underground dens in rocky places are usually selected as first choices for natal dens. If these are not available, the female bobcat can choose a hollow tree, or the underground den of another species as bobcats do not dig their own dens.

Bobcats are dependent upon rabbits in all areas. Bobcat population densities often follow the cyclic densities of these rodents. Most young bobcats are on their own by October, and significant mortalities occur when

Bobcats are attracted to large holes near their routes. Baits far back in the hole can be visible or lightly covered.

there are few rabbits for the young bobcats to prey upon.

Bobcats are considered to be old at 10 years of age.

Habits

Bobcats have keen senses of vision and hearing. The sense of smell is also developed, but bobcats are more dependant upon sight and sound to aid their particular style of hunting.

Territory sizes vary according to population densities, prey species densities, and region of the country. Males have much larger territories than females in all regions. A male bobcat's territory will often overlap several females as well as another male or two. A typical female will have a territory size of about 6 square miles, whereas a male's territory might be as large as 60 square miles.

Bobcats do not utilize all of their territories, but seem to have circuituous routes that are traveled regularly. This habit allows constant reproduction of prey species within the territory.

Many female bobcats will not travel further than one mile in a night. Both male and female bobcats stop traveling after enough food has been killed, and both sexes rest after feeding. For this reason, the times it takes a bobcat to complete its circuit varies a great deal. Most bobcats return to a particular point on their circuit every week to three weeks.

Bobcats do not fear the water as much as other cat species. Bobcats commonly wade and swim, and many bobcats do not hesitate to attack a beaver in shallow water.

Bobcats are skilled tree climbers, and they do not hesitate to bound up a tree to avoid persecution. When they are treed at night by dogs, they often do not stay long but jump at the first opportunity. When they are treed during the daylight hours, they are prone to staying in the tree for longer periods.

A good degree of curiosity indicates that bobcats are somewhat intelligent. However, a bobcat is also moody or indifferent at times, which may indicate that the species reponds most actively when it is hungry.

Bobcats are capable of good speed for short distances, but they normally walk while traveling. When a prey species is noticed, the bobcat will usually stalk the prey slowly until it is within leaping distance. At other times, a bobcat may conceal itself behind a rock or on a limb as it waits for a victim to come within striking distance.

Bobcats rely on cottontails, jackrabbits, or snowshoe hares for 75 to 90 percent of their diets. Venison is the next largest food item, followed by mice, ground squirrels, tree squirrels, and occasionally skunk, beaver, muskrat and birds.

Adult deer can be killed by bobcats. This is most apt to happen during winter months as other food items become more difficult to catch.

Trapping

Good traps for southern bobcats include 1½ and 2 coilsprings, and number 2 or 3 longsprings. Western and northern trappers usually favor number 3 traps of any design. Bobcats can also be caught in cage traps and medium or large sized body gripping traps.

A heavy bobcat will test a trap and its fastening. Bobcat traps should be staked solidly, and stakes should be driven beneath the soil to prevent the trapped bobcat from chewing off the stake.

In brushy areas, many trappers prefer to use a long chain of 5 or 6 feet with a grapple attached at the end. An extra swivel should be placed in the chain near the trap when grapples are used. Always be aware that a bobcat might climb a tree with the grappled trap.

Many trappers appeal to the bobcat's curiosity and attract it to the set location with a strip of cloth or a tin can lid suspended near the set with a piece of string. As the object flutters in a breeze, it will catch the attention of the bobcat and draw it toward the trap set. (Many state trapping regulations define and address "sight baits", so check your state regulations before you use any visible attractor to lure a bobcat.)

Cubby sets and hole sets are excellent bobcat sets when they are made close to where they will travel. Cubbies may be constructed of anything handy at the site. Many trappers favor large sized holes for hole sets which are often dug horizontally at the base of high banks or mounds. With either set construction, it is an advantage to place a piece of rabbit or other bait back into the cubby or hole to help entice the bobcat at the set. However, do make sure that the bait is not visible from above to prevent the attraction of predatory birds.

Bobcats do not make a lot of tracks at sets, but place their feet slowly and deliberately as a habit. For this reason many trappers place sticks or stones around the set trap to help guide the bobcat to step into the trap.

Lures can be very effective in attracting bobcats, depending upon the mood of the bobcat at the time it is near the set. In any event, lure applications do not seem to deter or repel bobcats from sets.

Bobcats are not particularly trap shy. Many bobcats have been caught in uncovered traps when they were placed exactly where the bobcat wanted to step. However, most trappers cover bobcat traps well in case a fox, coyote, or other valuable furbearer visits the set before the bobcat returns.

Male bobcats are much more vulnerable to trapping because their ranging habits are far greater than females. This allows for a conservative harvest in most areas as each remaining male will often mate with several females.

A teepee type cubby can be constructed easily. Be sure that the bait isn't visible from above to eliminate accidental bird catches.

Bobcats can be trapped somewhat selectively with fresh meat baits, lures with catnip, and set constructions made where visibility is obscurred by the landscape.

Bobcats are difficult to release safely from traps without the aid of a catch pole. Bobcats will fight, and each foot is to be respected as well as the teeth of the animal. To release a bobcat caught out of season, place the loop of the catch pole over the neck of the bobcat and choke it until it is unconscious. Release the trap as soon as possible, and quickly release the loop. Bobcats strangle much quicker than many other species. Always wear gloves when releasing a bobcat from a trap as scratches from claws often become infected and heal slowly.

An annual harvest of up to 30% of the total bobcat population is considered as not harmful to the species.

Dispatch

Trapped bobcats are usually killed by shooting in the brain area with a .22. To prevent any fur damage, place the shot at the base of the ear as the bobcat turns its head to the side.

Bobcats can also be killed with a sharp blow to the top of the skull with a metal trap stake, or suitable club.

Controls

Mountain lions and wolves occasionally kill adult bobcats. Predation by either species is not thought to be significant.

Significant mortalities of juvenile bobcats can occur during the first winter season. The young bobcats are not as skilled at hunting as the adults, and many do not survive their first winter when the weather is severe and rabbit populations are at a low cycle.

Juvenile bobcats are also vulnerable to predation by mature male bobcats, coyotes, eagles, and fishers.

Bobcats are vulnerable to rabies, feline distemper, mange mites, tapeworms, roundworms, lice, and bubonic plague.

Values

As significant predators of rabbits, bobcats help to stabilize rabbit population cycles which benefit many predatory species. More rabbits are killed when they are very abundant. During periods of low rabbit populations, many bobcats become malnourished and vulnerable to a variety of diseases and exposure to harsh weather conditions. These controls limit bobcat survival, and protect breeding populations of rabbits during these low cycles.

Adult bobcats do prey upon deer, especially when rabbits are sparse and the deer are most vulnerable during winter conditions of deep snow. A bobcat usually eats no more than 2 or 3 pounds of meat per day, and the deer carcass often serves as a food source for other species as well.

Some bobcats in western areas do prey upon sheep, and a single bobcat has been known to kill dozens of lambs in one night.

Bobcats do offer sporting values for hunters with dogs, predator calling, and trapping. Approximately 80,000 bobcats are harvested annually, and the bulk of these are taken by trapping. Values exceed 10 million dollars annually to fur harvesters in 32 states.

Fur Handling

Bobcat pelts are handled cased, with the fur on the outside. Skinning is accomplished by making a cut from the inside of one hind leg to the other. Another cut is then made from the base of the tail, around the vent to the first cut. Then the skin is peeled from the hind legs and separated from the hind feet.

At this point, many trappers suspend the carcass with a gambrel, and strip the tail off of the tail bone with the aid of a tail stripping tool, clothespin, or pliers. The skin can then be pulled down past the shoulders, where thumb pressure will allow the skin to be pulled down to the front feet, which are left attached to the carcass with a knife cut.

The skin can then be pulled down to the head area, where knife cuts will be necessary at the junctions of the ear canals, eyes, and nose.

Most bobcats need little fleshing, and this can be accomplished on a wooden stretcher with the aid of a single handled fleshing tool. Some bobcats are fatter than others. Exceptionally fatty skins can be scraped on a fleshing beam with a two handled fleshing knife using the dullest blade edge. Bobcat skins are rather fragile, and care should be taken to prevent tearing a hole in the skin.

If there are any holes in the skin, they should be sewed shut while the skin is still wet and pliable with a needle and thread.

The bobcat pelt should be stretched first with the fur on the inside. Either a wire stretcher or wooden stretcher can be used. If a solid wooden stretcher is used, be sure to use a wedge shaped belly board to prevent the skin from shrinking too tightly on the stretcher.

The pelt must be turned as soon as the leather side of the pelt is dry to the touch. Replace the fur on the stretcher with the fur on the outside for the final drying process.

Many bobcats are dry enough to turn fur side out in one or two days, and most pelts are fully dry after they have been on a stretcher for a week.

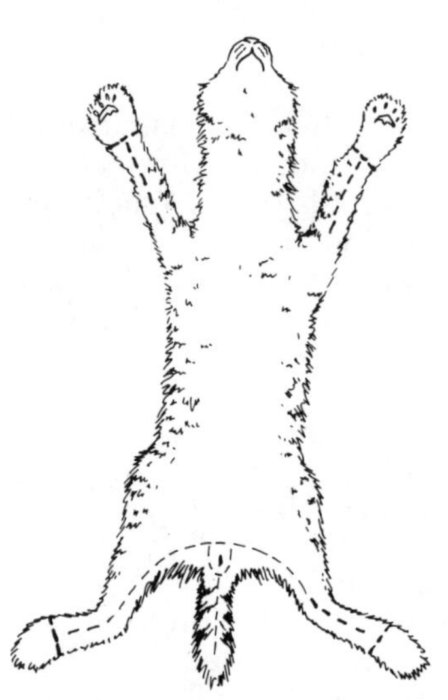

Selling Furs

THE markets and prices paid for American furs are not established by American fur buyers. The raw fur business is huge and flucuating market conditions are established and reestablished almost constantly with each international sale.

Although prices for many products are established as a result of the available supply and demand conditions, such is not the case with raw furs. Fur values are influenced far more by "fashion" and "demand" conditions in the international market places. Simply, a shortage of a particular type of fur does not make those furs worth more money, as the manufacturers who would normally buy that article will simply switch to another type of fur that is available.

Market conditions are certainly influenced by speculators who believe that a trend in fashion will shift to this fur or that fur. Millions of dollars are constantly invested in supplies of raw furs held in cold storage. These speculators are important in the raw fur business as they are able to offer furs to manufacturers on a year-round basis, and profit taking helps to stabilize the market and helps to prevent huge flucuations in prices.

Still, supplies of raw furs in storage can have a negative effect upon the market. Whenever a significant amount of particular types of furs are not sold before the next collecting season, buyers and speculators are hesitant to invest more money in an article that isn't selling well.

At times, the rural fur buyer gets blamed for poor prices, yet, the rural fur buyer is only a player in a complicated chain. Fickle markets rarely guarantee a profit in the American fur business. Many rural fur buyers provide important services to trappers by buying carcass animals, selling supplies, and offering advice on how to improve the appearance of handled pelts.

Regardless of prices being paid at the time, all furs bring the best prices when they are properly handled. Premiums are oftentimes paid for expertly handled furs, and the fur buyers have little choice other than to severely dock poorly handled furs. In turn, the rural fur buyer will be severely docked as he sells the same furs.

The sad truth is that millions of dollars are wasted each year by well meaning fur harvesters who do not know how to properly handle pelts. Everyone appreciates well handled pelts. You should always feel free to ask fur buyers or better trappers for advice or help to learn how to finish your own furs properly.

Some people are confused as to why a particular type of fur is wanted fur in, or fur out. There are reasons, and the bottom line is that fur buyers can determine best the true value of the particular type of pelt by examining either the skin side, or the fur side of the pelt. The fur of foxes and coyotes are finished fur side out so that the fur buyer, and his buyer, can see the depth of the fur and the color of the fur, and whether or not the fur has been damaged. On the other hand, the fur buyer can best determine the value of pelts of mink, raccoon, and muskrats by viewing the skin or leather side of the pelt. Primeness is easily determined by the coloration or pattern of coloration on the leather side of the pelt. Color can easily be determined by looking at the fur at the end of the pelt, and any bullet or bite holes are easily seen.

Pelts are usually wanted in long and somewhat narrow shapes today. Length always helps to sell a pelt. A relatively narrow stretch helps to prevent overstretching the pelt in the middle of the back. Furs that are stretched too widely thin the fur in the middle of the back, and this is the first place many fur buyers will look to determine value.

The proper fleshing of pelts is also important. Poorly fleshed pelts can either "grease burn" or "taint" before they can be tanned for use. Such pelts have little value as the fur is apt to "slip" or shed during the tanning process.

Furs that are not finished in the normal and wanted way will be downgraded. Fur buyers are uncompromising, and they have to be.

Furs are often graded as One's (I's), Two's (II's), Three's (III's), and Four's (IV's). Number One grades represent fully prime, well handled pelts. Number Two's represent the lower end that a good manufacturer will accept and be likely to use. Thirds are badly rubbed, unprime, or damaged pelts. Fourths are badly damaged pelts, and these pelts have little value.

There are several options for the fur harvester to consider when selling furs. These options include selling to a local or traveling fur buyer; selling at local fur auctions; shipping to brokers or buyers; and shipping to large auctions. All methods of marketing have advantages, and disadvantages, and there simply is no best way to sell.

Rural Fur Buyers

Rural fur buyers have been part of the American fur trade for hundreds of years. Fur buying is a sideline for some, and a full time job for others. Some of these small fur houses send representatives to different communities to buy furs, and others rely on walk in trade. Virtually all of these rural buyers provide valuable services to communities by buying carcass animals brought in as found road kills, as well as servicing hunters who shoot an occasional fox or coyote. Many rural fur buyers offer trapping supplies for sale, and most are quite happy to give you advice on handling your furs.

Some rural fur buyers operate on their own money, and others do not, but buy furs as agents for larger concerns.

Large collectors will sometimes pay a little more for the same furs, hoping to profit less on individual furs, but making a profit through volume. Some rural collectors or buyers have orders and contracts to fill, and at times, they have very good markets for certain types of fur.

One advantage of dealing with local fur buyers is that you can be present to accept or reject the bid. Another advantage is that if the check bounces, you will know where to go.

One disadvantage of dealing with rural fur buyers is that they have to buy many types of furs below the actual value. The buyer is certainly entitled to a fair profit, of course, and he does take a sizeable risk too. Still, the furs must be purchased somewhat below the real value in order for him to make a profit and stay in business.

Another disadvantage is that some fur buyers do contact each other and attempt to fix prices. This happens rarely, but it can and does happen at times.

It is always wise to check with several rural buyers when you decide to sell furs. Simply let the buyer sort and grade your furs without argument. Ask him to compute his best price, and advise him that you are accepting several bids on the exact same furs.

Whenever you sell to a rural fur buyer, you have an option to refuse the sale. A sale can be made only when the two parties agree to trade dollars for pelts.

Compared to shipping furs, rural fur buyers offer two real advantages. For one, you can make an immediate decision on whether or not to accept the bid. The other is that you can be paid instantly.

Local Auctions

Some trappers' associations offer fur auction services for their members. These auctions are held by a variety of methods, including open bids, sealed bids, lot numbers of entire collections, lot numbers of graded species, and so on. Like other methods of selling, there are both advantages and disadvantages for the sellers.

One important advantage in local auctions is that numbers of furs are assembled, and this is sure to cause the interest of large buyers and anyone interested in selected types of furs. Many times, these furs are bought at premium prices in order to fulfill contracts, providing a real advantage to some buyers who only want particular types or qualities of furs.

In some cases, trappers are able to establish a minimum price for their furs, and in other cases a trapper can bid openly on his own furs as they are being auctioned. The majority of small auctions operate this way today, and trappers who are present can prevent the sale of their furs when they feel that the offering is too small.

On the negative side, it is wise to know that fur buyers can get together before a sale and agree on who bids on what, and at agreed upon prices. Too, fur buyers may elect to boycott the sale in an effort to force more business at the local level.

These negative things rarely happen, and many trappers are happy with the results of prices paid at small fur auctions. Commissions are normally charged to finance and advertise the auctions, but the commission rates are usually offset by the prices paid in a spirit of competitive bidding.

Letters of bank credit or bonding are usually required for the buyers, and this helps to protect the auction service and the seller as the furs are traded for dollars.

When lot numbers are issued to establish the order of selling, early numbers often sell best for the same qualities of furs. As these buyers fulfill their needs, or credit limits, prices offered often decrease for comparable furs. During lengthy sales, high lot numbers may not sell at all.

Shipping To Brokers Or Buyers

Reputable buyers and brokers are located in many areas of this country. Goodly numbers of brokers and fur houses are located in New York, which has served for many years as a central collecting point for American furs. The bulk of the furs manufactured in America are processed in the greater New York area, where garment making skills have been passed from generation to generation.

Many speculators are involved in the New York raw fur business as cold storage facilities are available. Also, New York has always been a convenient place for European garment manufacturers to shop. As a result, the New York marketplace has always been attractive to shippers hoping to eliminate middle men in the selling chain.

However, many individual trappers have been disappointed after shipping furs to either brokers or fur buyers in different states. Many times, the prices actually paid are not the prices being advertised as being paid. At other times, the grading and evaluation differ between the seller and the buyer. The bottom line is that shippers have a very difficult time receiving their own pelts back if they are dissatisfied or reject the offering.

There certainly are goodly numbers of honorable and fair fur houses and brokers. Because anyone can submit an ad or send a price list, you are advised to check with other trappers or fur buyers to see if they believe that the fur house or broker you hope to do business with is reputable.

Brokers can sometimes get you the highest prices. Brokers do not buy your furs, but instead pay themselves a commission when the sales are made. Sales are usually made by private treaty with a manufacturer. One disadvantage is that you might not know when the sale actually takes place. As a result, shippers sometimes have to wait longer for their money than they would like to.

Anytime that you decide to ship furs to a fur house or broker, request that your furs be held separate until you accept the offering or appraisal. Have a letter copy made, and keep it for your own legal protection.

It is extremely unfortunate that an occasional, disreputable broker or fur house takes advantage of shippers. The better fur houses suffer as a result, and many of these better fur houses and brokers are in a position to pay the best prices for fur.

Consequently, shipping furs to brokers or fur houses can be more risky than other selling options.

Shipping To Large Auctions

Large American and Canadian fur auctions have been serving as important markets in recent years. Large numbers of furs and buyers are attracted to these events as actual markets are established for the different types and qualities of raw furs.

All of the large auction companies are bonded, and safe to ship fur to. Expenses and profits are made by charging for grading, cleaning, and commissions on sales.

Upon receipt of furs, the large fur auction companies clean and grade the furs according to rigorous standards. These individual furs are then sorted and placed into lots of identical furs for the convenience and inspection by potential buyers. The auction itself usually takes place with bidding on lot numbers only.

Due to the system of selling, it is impossible for the auction companies to keep individual shipments separate. However, excellent prices are often obtainable when large collections of identical quality furs are available for the convenience of large order buyers.

The larger fur auction companies do help to stabilize markets by refusing sales at artificially low prices. Furs not sold are then held over until the next sale.

Some large fur auction companies do advance money upon receipt of furs, and before actual sales are made. As a rule, they will advance only a partial payment of the estimated value, and interest is charged until the sale is made and the account settled.

Canadian auction companies do have bonded American brokers for the convenience of American shippers. Their salaries are paid by the auction companies, and it is wise to use their services to prevent the red tape complications of export permits, endangered species, and so on.

One of the keys for sellers in all regions to consider when selling furs is to try to get the furs where there will be numbers of the same types and qualities of furs for sale. Buyers can and do pay the best prices wherever there is a constant supply, and an abundance of the wanted articles to select from. Consequently, western furs are apt to bring the best prices in the west, and eastern furs are apt to bring the best prices in the east.

Other Products

MANY trappers overlook the fact that many of our common furbearers offer values other than their fur. In some areas of the country, a market exists for the meat of several species, including opossum, raccoon, nutria, beaver, and muskrat.

Taxidermists are always in the market for unusual animals. Furbearers with unusual markings or coloration often bring premium prices when sold. Many times, unusual animals have little or no fur value, so it is always a good idea to check with a local taxidermist whenever you catch an oddity. Examples might be a reddish opossum, raccoon, or skunk. A Sampson fox (without guard hairs) might have value to a local taxidermist, as might a greyback weasel (changing from white to brown or brown to white). In all cases with an unusual animal, do not skin it, but deliver it fresh or frozen for the taxidermist's consideration.

The glands of many species also have value, either for sale or for the trapper to make some of his own lures. Glands of particular value include beaver castor glands, musk glands of muskrats, weasels, mink and skunks.

The anal glands of foxes, coyotes and bobcats also have good value for lure making or sale.

Animal skulls make interesting collections. The claws of badgers are often used in jewelry to simulate bear claws, and the large incisor teeth of beaver are used in jewelry. Even fishermen who tie flys are in the market for some types of furs.

The meat of furbearers is wasted far too often. Meat is expensive, and it is a crime that millions of dollars worth of delicious and nutritious meat is wasted every year by our nation's fur harvesters.

The proper cleaning and preparation of wild meats makes all the difference in the world. Careful attention to detail will allow you to enjoy a valuable resource even more than just the pelt value.

There are two things that you should be aware of with all wild meats. First of all, check all livers. Whenever there is a discoloration, or spotting on the animal's liver, discard the entire carcass.

The second important thing to realize is that the "wild" or "gamey" flavors in wild games come from the fats, and not the meat, as a rule. For this reason, all fat should be removed from the flesh. All wild meats are much milder in taste when the fat is removed before cooking, and this can often be done easily with a paring or pocket knife. If fats or oils are necessary to keep the wild meats from drying while cooking, better flavors can be enhanced by using bacon strips, cooking oil, or butter.

Beaver

Beaver can be cleaned as soon as they are taken. A cut up the middle of the belly is needed to skin the animal anyway, so the animal might as well be field dressed. Pay careful attention to the liver, a large and dark colored organ behind the lungs and in front of the stomach. If the liver is spotted, or discolored, do not prepare the carcass for consumption.

The livers themselves are palatable, and people who like liver usually enjoy beaver liver. This liver is somewhat stronger in flavor than many other livers, so many trappers slice the liver thinner before frying along with onions.

The knife used to skin around the castor glands should not be used to skin the pelt away from the legs or back of the beaver. Use a clean knife, as a knife contaminated by beaver castor will effect the taste of the meat where it comes into contact with it.

Younger beaver are much more tender than older beaver. Younger beaver can be roasted whole. However, there is quite a bit of waste on an entire beaver carcass, and some trappers prefer to just remove the legs for cooking.

Many trappers prefer to soak the beaver flesh overnight in a saltwater bath. This will remove much of the blood from the meat.

There is a generous strip of meat along the sides of the backbone of beaver. This strip can be removed with a few simple cuts. On the older beaver, take these strips and tenderize them by beating them with the back edge of a cleaver or knife blade before cooking.

Beaver meat can be chunked and used in stews. It can also be broiled or roasted. Beaver meat can be made into beaverburger, and used in casseroles, meat loaf and spaghetti, with delicious results.

Beaver Recipe—Boil boneless pieces of young or tenderized beaver in salt-water until the meat becomes tender. Drain the meat well, roll in flour, and brown all over using bacon strips stuck on the meat with toothpicks. Use only a medium hot oven for browning, and serve while hot. Season to taste.

Bobcat

Contrary to some opinions, bobcat meat is very mild in taste. Young bobcats are more tender than the older bobcats. Many trappers prefer to use just the hams and front legs and shoulders for cooking. An overnight soaking in salt-water removes blood from the meat. The meat can be boned, cubed, or sliced, and fixed in a variety of ways. Bobcat is one meat that can be fried just like a chicken, and it is also good when made into roasts or stews.

Bobcat Recipe—Remove all fat from the flesh of the legs, and cut the bobcat flesh into serving sized pieces. Place the meat in a pan and cover it with milk. After it has soaked for 45 minutes, salt and pepper to taste, and roll in flour or cornmeal. Fry in hot bacon fat and serve hot.

Muskrat

Young muskrats are much more tender than older muskrats. The younger muskrats can be served in a variety of dishes, but the older muskrats are rather stringy in texture, so they are best made into stews.

The bulk of the edible meat on a muskrat is the hind legs and front legs including the shoulder area. The legs can be separated easily after skinning is completed, but be sure to check for a healthy liver. Legs that have been caught in a trap should be discarded.

Remove all fat from the meat, and soak the pieces overnight in a pan of salt-water to remove blood from the meat. Older muskrats can be tenderized to a degree by a pounding with the back of a meat cleaver or a kitchen knife.

Muskrat Recipe—Parboil muskrat legs in salted water in a covered pot. Include a sliced onion, bay leaf, and ½ teaspoon thyme. After boiling slowly for two hours, remove the meat and drain. Place the legs in a roasting pan. Add several pieces of bacon, 1 cup of water, and bake in a low oven temperature until tender. Serve hot.

Raccoon

Young raccoons are much more desirable than older raccoons for eating purposes. The older raccoons have a lot more fatty tissue, and this is very difficult to remove, giving the older raccoons a greasy and gamey taste. However, young raccoon are very good when they are cared for properly.

Raccoon Recipe—Trim all fat from a young raccoon, inside and out. Stuff the cavity with dressing, place the meat in a roaster, add two cups of water to the pan, baste with melted butter and roast until tender. Baste with butter occasionally during the roasting process, and serve hot.

Glands

The glands of several species are wanted by luremakers, and it would pay many trappers to investigate these sales possibilities whenever a large catch is expected. Trappers who take few furbearers should also save the valuable glands by freezing until enough glands are collected for a sale.

Beaver castors are wanted commercially, and they should be removed from the carcass carefully to prevent tearing. All membranes and flesh should be removed from the large glands, and they can be dried by hanging them over a rope or the bottom of a coat hanger. Castors take one year to dry completely, but they can be shipped when partially dry as long as they are packed in a ventilated box. The oil sacs have value to some luremakers too, so it is always wise to check with a luremaker to see if he has any needs that you can fulfill. Be sure to ask for directions as to how he wants the castors or oil glands handled.

The musk glands on spring caught male muskrats resemble small castors. These glands can be plucked from the carcass with your fingers. Generally, they are dried on a piece of screen, and used later to compound animal lures.

Skunk essence is also valuable, and it can be extracted from a dead animal easily with a syringe and needle. Probe the areas on either side of the anus until the glands are found, and then simply withdraw the syringe plunger to suck out the essence. It can be injected into a small bottle and sealed with wax for safekeeping or sale. Among other things, skunk essence is a valuable addition to many canine lures.

Few trappers catch enough mink to have enough mink glands to sell, and this need is pretty well filled by mink ranchers. However, a few saved glands can be used to enhance lures for mink and other predators.

The anal glands of foxes, coyotes and bobcats can be removed by making an encircling cut around the anus. The anus and attached glands are then pulled, and 3 or 4 inches of gut can be left attached to the anus. Any extra fur around the anus can be trimmed off with a scissors, and these glands can be either dried slowly in a cool place or frozen. If you decide to sell these glands, be sure to check with your buyer to see exactly how he wants them handled.

Lard can be rendered from animal fats, and although these lards are often too strong for cooking, they can be used to soften and waterproof leather shoes or boots. Badger fat makes an exceptionally good quality lard to treat leather with, and beaver lard makes a good lure base for canine lures.

To render lard, simply put the fat left over from the fleshing process into a pan, and simmer at low heat. The lard will liquify, and it can be poured into another container. As the lard cools, it will develop a paste like consistency.

Making a few simple lures is one way to enjoy the resources more, and many trappers enjoy experimenting with their saved animal glands.

A very simple and effective beaver lure can be made by grinding either fresh or dried beaver castors in a hand cranked food grinder. The dried castors grind easiest, and the grindings can be mixed in an electric blender with a 50-50 mixture of glycerine and water added until the desired consistency is obtained.

Gland lures for canines can be made by grinding the anal glands and covering the ground glands with canine urine. This concoction should be left in a dark and relatively cool place for several months before other ingredients such as beaver castor, muskrat glands, or mink glands are added for an added attraction. Many trappers prefer to stop the decaying process at this time with the addition of sodium benzoate, zinc valerate, or borax. The addition of glycerine or alcohol will often allow these lures to work in freezing weather.

For paste type lures, many formulas can be mixed with beaver lard.

Safety & Health

THREATS to safety and health can occur to anyone, and at any time. Still, basic preventative immunizations, a knowledge of first aid, and an application of common sense during a crisis can eliminate or minimize dangers.

People still die of tetanus, and there is really no excuse for that. After the initial series which are a pre-school requirement, all that is needed is a booster vaccination every ten years, unless a severely contaminated wound is suffered. Do check with your doctor, and completely eliminate this outdoor threat to your life.

The loss of blood from a wound can be a quick threat to life. Many people seem to forget that direct pressure to the bleeding site will control bleeding from most wounds. A piece of material from your shirt sleeve or shirt tail can be torn or cut in an emergency to be used as a compress. Do not dip the compress into a stream or lake, or you risk a much greater chance of infection.

Every trapper should take a short course in CPR (Cardiopulmonary Resuscitation). These courses are offered in many communities by the

Heart Association, the Red Cross, or a local ambulance service. CPR is especially useful in the case of drowning, and people have been successfully resuscitated after being submerged in cold water for as long as 20-30 minutes.

It is far better to know how to administer CPR, and never need it, than to not know how in an emergency.

Risk Taking

Risk is unavoidable in life, and each of us must constantly make decisions concerning our own safety. Accidents can and do happen to the most careful people, and traplines offer opportunity for dangerous risks. Importantly, cold temperatures during winter trapping conditions can impair a person's ability to recognize danger and make good decisions.

Dangers on a trapline can take many forms. Deep water, thin ice, slippery logs, firearms, and even live animals in traps offer almost constant hazards on traplines.

Experienced woodsmen differ from novices in that the experienced woodsman is constantly on the alert for danger. Every time you are presented with a decision that might be risky, stop, and consider the alternatives. Virtually every danger can be minimized or avoided with a little thought. Although it might be a little inconvenient to choose a safer route, or to take a hunter safety course, it is wise to know that it is much easier to stay out of trouble than to get out of trouble.

Safety should be your constant companion on a trapline. Dangerous risks are totally unnecessary, and a poor decision can cost you your life!

Clothing

The selection of proper clothing is one of the most important decisions that you can make that might affect your safety. A chilled body can cause you to make poor decisions, and common sense clothing can also save your life if you do make a poor decision. Long underwear, and wool clothing are essential choices for trapline wear in cold climates. Wool is not only a tremendous insulator, but it is far superior to synthetics because wool has an ability to shed water, and keep you warm even when it is wet. Although commonly worn, blue jeans are a very poor choice for pants. Blue jeans are very poor insulators, absorb water easily, and have little warming value when wet.

Layering is the wisest choice for active, outdoor people to keep warm. Two or more wool shirts worn under a tightly woven outer shell of nylon make a very versatile selection, as the wool shirts can be removed or added according to temperature and activity. The outer shells resist penetrating wind, and water from rain or snow, and many models have hoods which can be pulled over the head when desired. And for the sake of safety, bright colors are best for outer garments. Trappers have been shot by careless hunters. Brightly colored clothing greatly reduces this risk. Blaze orange outer garments have proven to be very effective in preventing accidental shootings.

Studies have proven that warm caps or hats greatly affect comfort in cold weather. Brightly colored caps improve safety, and it is a sure bet that you will make better decisions with a warm head.

Firearms

Many trappers use guns to dispatch animals, and an accidental discharge is certainly a threat to life. Owning, caring for, and using a gun is a huge responsibility. Many programs on gun safety are available today to help teach responsibilities and skills.

Every gun should always be treated by each individual as if it were loaded, without exception. A gun should never be pointed in the direction of another person.

Care should be taken to protect a firearm on a trapline, as mud or snow from an accidental falling can jam the mechanism or barrel. This can allow the firearm to explode as it is fired.

Many guns can be loaded and carried without a cartridge in the firing chamber. This is the safest way to carry a loaded gun, and the cartridge can always be advanced into the firing chamber when it is needed.

Dogs

A trapped dog always presents a threat. Even when the dog appears docile and friendly, the dog might bite you as you try to release it from the trap. For the sake of your own safety, you should use a catch pole to pin the dog to the ground as you release the trap from its foot. At the very least, hold the dog's muzzle shut with one hand as you release the trap. In the excitement, the dog may not realize that you are helping it, so you should always use caution.

Wild dogs are sometimes mean and very aggressive in traps. Whether these dogs should be released is a judgmental decision. However, if it is possible that the dog might be someone's errant pet, it should always be released.

Aggressive dogs can be released easily after they are subdued with a catch pole. With an exceptionally aggressive dog, you might have little choice other than to choke the animal unconcious before you can release the trap. Always pin the necks of these aggressive animals with your knee as you release the trap, in case the animal revives prematurely.

Precautions

At every spot on your trapline, you should know the shortest direction for help. Whenever you need help, don't be ashamed to ask for it. Most people will help you, or let you use their phone, if they realize that you are in trouble.

Protect your eyes at all times while trapping. One common mistake is for one person to follow another too closely in the woods or brush. Limbs swinging backward behind the first person can injure the following person's eyes. Learn to keep a safe distance at all times when following another. Sunglasses do help to protect eyes from objects, and certainly ease eye strain on bright days.

Axes are important tools to some trappers and some types of traplines. Because they are heavy and sharp, it is always wise to consider how they are used. An axe should never be carried without a sheath in a packbasket. If the trapper should trip and fall, there is opportunity for the axe to cut the head or neck of the fallen man. It is much safer to carry the axe with one hand gripping the axe right below the axe head. If a tripping occurs, the axe can be easily controlled.

An axe should always be carried by a trapper when he is on ice. A spot of unsafe ice can occur anywhere, and many trappers have saved their own lives by swinging the axe head into the ice so that they can pull themselves from the frigid water.

There are many precautions that can be taken to minimize dangers, and prevent dangers on a trapline. Snowshoe bindings can be selected that are rubber and elastic enough to allow the trapper to pull his feet from the bindings if he should fall through the ice. Waterproofed matches and a candle should always be carried along with a dependable fire starter in wilderness areas. Extra clothing can be stored in a trapline vehicle, and gas tanks should always be kept filled. A CB radio is a wise investment, and a call on channel 9 might put you in direct radio contact with qualified help.

Do not, under any circumstances, ever feel around through a hole in the ice to locate a trap. Currents and animals can dislodge set traps, and trappers have died after being caught in their own traps under these conditions. Any under ice trap checking should be done with a stick or axe handle.

Every trapper who expects to trap from a canoe or boat should learn water safety skills during mild weather. Water safety programs are regularly sponsored by the U.S. Coast Guard, and many state game departments have similar programs to help prevent needless accidents.

The time to learn boatmanship and canoemanship is not during the cold water conditions of trapping seasons. One accidental dunking can be life-threatening at this time.

Diseases

Diseased animals can also pose a threat to humans. Several important diseases that are carried by furbearers can be transmitted to man, and among these, rabies is the most serious.

Rabies

Rabies is a virus which grows and multiplies in the nervous tissue of warm blooded mammals. During the later stages of infection, the virus is also present in the saliva. Disease transmissions to healthy animals commonly occur when an infected animal bites another. Some rabid animals are aggressive, foam at the mouth, and attack without provocation or reason, but many rabid animals simply get sick and crawl off into a hole to die. As a result, it is possible for any warm blooded mammal to have rabies, and be infectious, without showing any obvious symptoms.

It is a known fact that the rabies virus can live for a period of time suspended in air that is not exposed to ultraviolet light. Laboratory experiments indicate that rabies transfer is possible by breathing rabies contaminated air. Two men have been known to have died of rabies after exploring a cave where rabid bats were present, even though neither man was known to have been bitten.

Fortunately, the sun provides sufficient quantities of ultraviolet light, even on cloudy days, to kill the rabies virus within minutes.

Some species are much more prone to become infected with rabies. Very vulnerable wild species include bats, skunks, raccoons, coyotes, foxes, and bobcats. Very vulnerable domestic species include cows, horses, dogs, and cats. Opossum and rodents such as mice, rabbits, beavers and muskrats rarely get rabies.

Rabid striped skunks are a particular problem because this species has demonstrated that it can have rabies, and spread rabies, without dying of the disease, and without any visible symptoms. The problem is acute because many skunks share communal dens, and there is ample opportunity for one infected skunk to contaminate the air being breathed by the others. As a result, it is possible for all of the skunks in the den to contract rabies, and spread it to the skunks in other communal dens.

In theory, it is reasonable to expect that the air emerging from underground skunk dens could contain sufficient amounts of the live rabies virus to infect a dog, raccoon, fox, bobcat, or even a stray house cat which might investigate the den entrance as a normal hunting activity. Also in theory, it would seem possible that a cow or horse grazing at the den entrance could be infected as well before the ultraviolet light kills the live virus.

For that reason, trappers are urged to not kneel and set traps at known skunk dens.

Because all striped skunks should be treated as rabies suspects, never shoot the animals in the head or spinal column. These areas have massive amounts of nervous tissue, and a bullet might expose the live virus directly into the air. Skunks should always be shot from an upwind position. A shot piercing the heart and lung area is far safer.

The risk of getting rabies from skinning an animal can be reduced by skinning the animal the day after it was killed, instead of the same day. The rabies virus does not live long in a dead animal at normal temperatures. Although the rabies virus will live in a frozen animal, there is thought to be little risk in handling a frozen animal because the virus is immobilized by freezing.

The rabies virus is not known to live in an animal's blood, urine, musk, or droppings. However, it is possible for a fur handler to cut into nervous tissue while skinning a furbearer, and the living virus could enter the human body through an open sore or cut on the person's hands. Therefore, latex dish washing gloves can be worn by the fur handler as a significant safety precaution.

Laboratory tests have shown that a washing with soap and water greatly reduces the probability of rabies innoculation. Washing with soap and water is the first aid treatment of a wound after a person has been bitten by a known or suspect animal. Fur handlers should always wash their hands and arms after skinning animals.

All dogs and cats owned by trappers or fur handlers should be vaccinated for rabies, and it is equally important to follow the booster shot recommendations of the veterinarian. Both pet dogs and cats often come into contact with furbearers that might have rabies, and an infection of the pet could take place as the pet nuzzles or touches the nose or mouth of an infected furbearer.

Rabies infected house cats are probably a greater threat to human life than rabies infected dogs. While both dogs or cats will die within a few weeks after contracting rabies, the death or disappearance of house cats is seldom given much consideration. The "dumb" form of rabies is far more regular than the "furious" form, complete with the erratic behavior, foaming at the mouth, and aggressiveness. A transfer of rabies is possible from a pet dog or cat by sneezing, or licking on the human's face near the eyes, nose or mouth. While the rabies infected dog would probably get sick and die at home, causing a concern and investigation, many house cats with rabies are not recognized because of their habit of wandering off to die.

House cats appear and disappear as a normal activity, and it is highly likely that far more house cats have died of rabies than dogs.

As a result, rabies vaccinations of pets is not only a protection for the pets; it is a common sense safety precaution for people as well.

In recent years, a rabies vaccine has been developed that is providing excellent immunity for humans. Known as "Human Diploid Cell Vaccine" (HDCV), this vaccine is now being recommended for all persons who commonly come into contact with wild or domestic animals that might have rabies. The pre-exposure vaccinations can be administered by any doctor. A series of three vaccinations is currently recommended, and a simple blood test will confirm immunity levels.

HDCV is administered into the patient's arm, and it hurts no more than any other vaccination. Importantly, patient reactions are very rare.

The threat of rabies is very real. Thousands of animals have been tested annually as rabies positive in recent years, and the sheer number of wild animals prevent any effective control programs. The truth is that our nation's trappers are the only control of rabies in wildlife. Striped skunks with rabies are a huge problem, and these animals are contained by trappers who trap them deliberately, or catch them just the same in sets designed for other species.

The rabies incubation period in humans varies widely. Symptoms of the disease can appear in as little as a week, or take a year or longer. However, by the time that rabies can be diagnosed, death is virtually certain.

If You Are Bitten

1. Attempt to kill the animal without damage to the skull if it is a wild animal.
2. If the animal is domestic, insist that the offending animal be penned and observed for at least 10 days to see if it gets sick or dies.
3. Cleanse the wound as quickly as possible with soap and water.
4. Keep the dead animal cool, but do not freeze it.
5. Call your doctor. He or she will make a decision based on the type of offending animal; whether or not the animal escaped; whether or not the animal might have felt provoked; the type and location of the bite; and whether or not rabies is likely in the area. You may be required to deliver the animal carcass to a veterinarian for processing and shipping to a laboratory for analysis.

Leptospirosis

Leptospirosis is another disease that can be transmitted to humans from biting animals. This disease can be fatal, but it is usually treatable when diagnosed in time. Symptoms vary widely with infected individuals. Many infected people experience illness about a week after contracting the disease.

Leptospirosis organisms often live in stagnant water. Infection can occur with trappers who don't wear protective rubber gloves over hands with open sores or cuts.

Plague

Bubonic plague is a constant threat to the health of trappers in the Rocky Mountain and western states. This disease is primarily a rodent disease. Transmission to a human can occur via flea bites from infected rodents, or fleas from predators who have been in contact with infected rodents. Coyotes, bobcats and foxes are infested with fleas in western states. These furbearers should be placed in plastic garbage bags and sprayed liberally with an insecticide immediately after they are killed. This safety measure kills the fleas before they decide to leave the cooling body of the host animal, and greatly reduces the possibility of a disease transmission to the human.

Plague organisms are present in the blood of infected animals, so it is possible that a fur handler can get the disease simply by skinning an infected animal whenever he has a cut or sore. Wearing latex dish washing gloves to skin western predators is a safety measure, and can prevent the skinner from becoming infected.

Symptoms of plague develop rapidly. Swelling occurs in the lymph glands within two to six days after coming into contact with a plague infected animal. "Knots" often form under the armpits or in the groin area, followed by high fever, irregular pulse, mental confusion, delirium, coma, and even death.

Bubonic plague in humans can often be treated successfully. But, it is extremely important to seek medical help as soon as any symptoms appear.

Tularemia

Tularemia is an infectious disease which normally infests rodents and rabbits. Muskrats and beaver are susceptible to this disease. Evidence of tularemia is white spots on the animal's liver.

Tularemia can exist in epidemic proportions, killing masses of muskrats and beavers. The danger of people getting tularemia is much greater under these conditions. Human innoculations can take place with the bites of woodticks or deerflys. It is also possible to get tularemia from eating incompletely cooked rabbits, muskrats or beavers.

Tularemia organisms are also present in the blood of diseased animals, and fur handlers can get the disease when skinning infected animals with an open sore or cut on their hand. As a safety precaution, latex dish washing gloves can be worn when skinning, and animals suspected of having the disease should not be skinned.

Tularemia organisms can survive for several months in the carcasses of dead animals, and the same length of time in mud or water.

The tularemia incubation period in humans is very short, and an infected human can experience symptoms in one to ten days after exposure. Symptoms include stiffness, weakness, lethargy, increased respiration, coughing, and diarrhea.

Tularemia is treatable in humans, and a doctor's care should be sought as soon as symptoms appear.

Giardiasis

Beaver in many areas of the country host a parasite that can contaminate water for human consumption. Giardiasis is widespread and further complicated by large populations of beavers in many states.

The beaver serves as a host to this parasite, and expels Giardia cysts with bowel movements. As a normal activity, beavers evacuate their bowels in water, and this simply releases the cysts. The Giardia cysts are too small to be filtered economically, which presents problems for reservoirs where drinking water is stored.

Giardia cysts multiply in the intestinal tracts of humans, often provoking severe diarrhea for weeks or months if not treated and killed with antibiotics.

Giardiasis can be prevented by using water from wells, or springs where beaver are not present.

Hypothermia

Hypothermia is a condition which occurs when the body temperature drops to a subnormal level. Hypothermia is a major cause of death among outdoorsmen who are poorly clothed, ill prepared, or exhausted. Deaths reported as "exposure" are usually caused by hypothermia.

Hypothermia can occur to persons of all ages. It can occur any month of the year, and at moderate to cold air temperatures.

The condition of hypothermia is caused by exposure to water, cool air, or very often, a combination of the two. As the chilled body begins to shiver, the energy reserves of the body become depleted. Internal body temperatures drop as the body loses heat faster than it can develop it. Vital internal organs begin to lose their ability to function, and judgement and reasoning power are seriously impaired as the brain begins to cool. Mental confusion and loss of memory occur before the hypothermia victim loses consciousness. Death may follow.

Trappers are very vulnerable to hypothermia because accidental dunkings in cold water can and do happen. A further complicating risk is the fact that trappers are often tired from carrying the weight of traps, and many traplines are in areas far from help.

Therefore, it is critically important for trappers to recognize symptoms of hypothermia, and it is equally important to know how to treat hypothermia in an emergency situation.

Symptoms of Hypothermia

1. Uncontrollable spells of shivering.
2. Slurred or slow speech, incoherent or vague statements.
3. Memory lapses.
4. Fumbling, stumbling, lurching.
5. Drowsiness.
6. Exhaustion.

Treatment of Hypothermia

Hypothermia is extremely serious, and even a mild case requires immediate treatment. Victims may not realize or may even deny that they are in trouble, so trust the symptoms rather than opinions.

1. Move the victim of hypothermia as quickly as possible to shelter. Do not be afraid to ask for help, and take advantage of any home or cabin that is reachable.

2. If shelter is not readily available, a fire **must** be built. If you realize that you are a victim, concentrate your every effort to build a fire. Resist every temptation to nap, and collect as much firewood as you can to feed the fire.

3. Regardless of temperature, all wet clothing **must** be removed as soon as the fire is sure.

4. The victim **must** be warmed. Warm packs can be used, such as hot water bottles, warm and moist towels, or blankets. A sleeping bag can be used at a camp, and another person should enter the sleeping bag to provide additional warmth.

5. The hypothermia victim can be given warm fluids during recovery. Do test the fluids to be sure that they are not too hot, as the fluids will seem hotter to the victim. Do not give a hypothermia victim alcohol.

The ability to build a fire is incredibly important if help is not within reach, you are wet, and you realize that you are suffering the symptoms of hypothermia. Waterproof matches or a dependable butane lighter and a candle, along with pieces of pitch wood or other fire starters, should always be carried by trappers in remote areas as basic lifesaving equipment. While it is very disagreeable to remove wet clothing in severe temperatures, the wet clothes must be dried by the fire.

Prevention of Hypothermia

Most situations that could lead to hypothermia can be recognized and avoided by a safety minded trapper who is constantly on the alert. Taking a chance on thin ice, crossing a stream on a slippery log, or wading in unknown water depths are all risks which can lead to life threatening hypothermia.

The use of common sense attitudes, and common sense clothing, greatly diminishes any chance of hypothermia occurring. Always remember that hypothermia is caused by chilling and exhaustion.

Common Sense Rules

1. Avoid any unnecessary risk.
2. Wear adequate clothing, preferably wool.
3. Rest every time you are tired, preferably out of the wind or rain.
4. Always know where you are, and where to go for help.
5. Always carry waterproof fire building materials.

Photography

MANY trappers enjoy taking pictures on a trapline to serve as records and pleasant memories. There is always a lot of pleasure in looking through old photographs, remembering your first fox, where you used to live, or how you used to dress. Even poor photographs bring joy as you grow older.

There certainly are a wide variety of cameras to select from for trapline use. Inexpensive and simple cameras take acceptable pictures under certain conditions. Better quality pictures are possible with the more expensive 35 mm camera. Which type of camera is best for you depends upon what you are satisfied with, and what you can afford. Still, it is far better to have pictures from an inexpensive camera than none at all.

The care of a camera can be a problem on a trapline. Dirt, sand or water are always present on a trapline, and any of these on or in the camera can certainly cause problems. Some sort of protection must be used to protect the camera when it is not in use. A waterproof camera bag can fill this need nicely, and if you don't have anything else, a camera can receive some protection if it is placed inside a clean, heavy, wool sock.

Films are vulnerable to heat, and a common mistake is to place a loaded camera or film on the dashboard in a vehicle. The light coming through the windshield can be very hot, even on mild days, and cause the chemicals on the surface of the film to deteriorate, ruining the photographs. It is far better to carry the camera under the seat, or in the glove compartment of a vehicle.

Regardless of the type of camera you have, learn to evaluate the scene through the view finder of the camera before you take the picture. Pictures say a lot of things to different people, and your first consideration is to ask yourself how others might interpret the picture.

Pictures of live animals in traps often do not please others, and you should certainly avoid taking pictures of live animals that might appear to be stressed or in pain. Although a picture of an animal in a trap can be used to teach others, many people would view the photograph as distasteful.

Live animals in traps do offer opportunity for good pictures. Many animals in traps are not in pain, or unduly stressed, and there is certainly nothing wrong in showing a trap on an animal's foot as long as the photo would be interpreted correctly by others.

Better photos of animals in traps can often be made by taking the picture from a low angle. The low camera angle gives the trapped animal a more dignified appearance than a photo taken at a downward angle. Some animals are confused when the photographer lays down, and many trapped animals will pose by sitting or standing erectly. Some animals will move around somewhat, and this can give opportunity to get pictures without the trap showing as well. A horizon beyond the animal is also possible from a low camera angle, and this can add a lot of interest and dimension to the photograph.

Getting close to the animal makes a stronger picture than another taken from a further distance. You should always stay a safe distance away from the animal as a safety precaution. Your view through the camera view finder might not indicate the true distance, so constantly be aware of exactly how close you really are when you position yourself.

Tricks to try to get more interesting pictures of live animals in traps include "squeaking", or throwing your hat in another direction. If you make a squeak with a loud kissing sound, many animals will perk up their ears, or cock their heads to locate the sound, giving you opportunity to snap a more interesting picture if you are quick enough. The act of throwing your hat off to one side will often cause the animal to look in that direction, or to change poses.

Although pictures of animals are interesting, better pictures include the trapper. People are as interesting as animals, and a combination of the two greatly helps to explain the picture. This usually requires the presence of someone other than the trapper to take the photograph, although some trappers with timers on their cameras are able to prop the camera, activate the time switch, and include themselves in the picture.

Again, a low camera angle often gives the strongest photograph. Some thought should be given to composition, and many times a better photo is possible if the trapper moves this way or that, or assumes a kneeling position. Above all, allow the trapped animal all of the dignity possible. Never take pictures with a gun raised at the animal, or any situation which others might interpret as teasing the animal.

Dead animals with people also make interesting photographs. Again, interpretation can vary, so it is important to consider the dignity of the dead animal. Misinterpretations of the trap can be eliminated by removing the trap from the animal's foot before the picture is taken. Another trick is to display the animal by holding it with the head up, and not down. Animals held with the heads held high simply seem more dignified, and a good photograph shows both dignity and pride on the trapper's face.

Brightly colored clothing improves pictures taken in color. The colors of the landscape, and the colors of the furbearers themselves, are often quite drab during trapping seasons. A colorful jacket or hat certainly attracts attention, and adds snappiness to pictures that would be dull otherwise.

Photos of people in sunglasses are uncomfortable to look at. After all, photo viewers want to see the person's face, and sunglasses distract and detract from the quality of the photograph. If the trapper being photographed complains about the brightness of the sun, simply move to one side to take the picture. Great photos can be made when the lighting is from one side, and you can avoid a picture of an uncomfortable, squinting subject.

Hats or caps worn on a trapline add a lot of character to a photograph. But, be sure that your subject lifts the cap bill or hat brim so his or her eyes are visible.

Pictures taken on water traplines are always interesting. The photographer rarely knows how the water will turn out in the finished print. Clear water can appear as green or blue in the picture, and there is always a lot of light bouncing off of the water to create special effects on either color or black and white films. Simply stunning photographs of water scenes happen quite regularly, and completely by accident.

Water also lends itself well to show movement. A trapper splashing through the water often makes a good picture, especially if the trapper is carrying a load of traps or a furbearer or two. For some pleasing effects, you might try a few exposures from the sides and back of the traveling trapper. There is no need to position the moving trapper right in the center of the photograph, and better shots often leave space in front of the moving person. That is a consideration for the viewer, who is more interested in where the trapper is going than in where he has been.

Photos of drowned animals in traps rarely turn out well, however, an interesting photograph can be made of the trapper removing the animal from the trap, or better yet, holding the animal aloft after the trap has been removed. Great shots can be made when the trapper is holding the animal to one side while looking at it rather than the camera. One good trick is to take several photographs as the trapper lifts the dead animal out of the water. Very often, a trickle of water from the wet furbearer will be visible in the photograph, creating and adding interest.

Order is also important to a good picture. A picture of a pile of dead animals is not only disorderly; it is also subject to a lot of misinterpretation. Other than improving a picture of this type with the addition of a person, a more pleasing order can be established by separating species. Separated species, arranged with some sort of order, show more pride on the part of the trapper, and add integrity to the dead animals. Large catches of foxes, beavers or muskrats look better when all the heads or tails are in one direction. The tailgate of a pickup is useful for pictures of this type, and usually there is room on the tailgate for the trapper to sit. Another alternative is to have the trapper sit, kneel or squat behind the animals.

The background in a picture can enhance, or detract from the finished picture. Many photographers make the mistake of only "seeing" the subject itself through the view finder of the camera. The camera will record whatever is there, whether you noticed it through the view finder or not. Distractions, such as a telephone pole, power lines, or shiny objects certainly detract from a picture, and they can usually be avoided by a different camera angle. The key is to see the distractions before the picture is taken. There is something very uncomfortable about looking at a photo of a young trapper holding up his first mink, with a telephone pole seemingly growing out of his head.

Excellent portraits of trappers are possible on a trapline. Cloudy days, and the softer light of morning or evening often give the best results. People should be recorded as they are, and in their proper environment. Trappers are happiest in their trapline clothes, and on their trapline. Some portrait tricks include turning the trapper's shoulders slightly to the left or the right, rather than letting him or her stand squarely in front of the camera. Try to put the trapper's hands to good use by cradling an animal, holding a trap, or even folded across the chest. Try a few different angles, and get in close with the camera. It isn't necessary to get the entire animal in the picture, but do include its head for ready identification. Above all, consider the background, or anything that might attract undue attention.

Good photography can be simple, or extremely complex. Many excellent books on photography are available today at camera shops, bookstores, and public libraries.

Traplines do offer many opportunities for great photographs. After all, traplines are interesting, animals are interesting, and trappers are interesting.

Knowing what not to take a picture of is as important as knowing what to take a picture of. But remember that you sure won't have any pictures if you don't take any. A good photograph allows you to enjoy a pleasant memory over, and over, and over again.

The Social Threat

TRAPPING is under a constant and vicious attack. Legislative bills to prevent trapping appear regularly in our nation's capitol, as well as many state legislatures. Foothold traps are a primary target in many of these bills. Well financed and political forces are determined to remove the only acceptable, non-lethal, economical and efficient tool that fur harvesters have to control wild furbearers and predator populations.

It is sad to realize that the harvests of wildlife are ever a political issue at all. Yet, politicians without training, or expertise, constantly introduce legislation that would void the highly successful game and furbearer management programs in every state. Ignored, or debated, are the biologists and scientists who have the experience and training necessary to make the best decisions concerning our wild species.

It is saddest of all to realize that a small minority of special interest sportsmen also attack trapping. That attitude is based upon a hope for less competition for select species, or unfounded fears of traps.

A number of organizations have preyed upon the public to solicit donations to "help" wild animals. Emotional appeals and dramatic photographs are used regularly to deceive gullible people into contributing to finance programs to "save this" or "save that". The presentation of truth or facts rarely gets in the way of these emotional campaigns to finance operations. Numerous campaigns to "ban the steel trap", or "save the baby seals" have generated millions of dollars from gullible people.

Some of these organizations are actually big businesses. Staffs are paid, publications are distributed. Some of these businesses invest in real estate and stocks and bonds. Money generated is often used to finance more emotional campaigns or programs designed to attract the media for even more progpaganda value.

Although many thousands, even millions of dollars have been contributed in good faith to help wildlife as a result of these professional campaigns, an evaluation of public inspection copies of corporate tax returns indicate that stocks and bonds are more apt to be purchased with these donations than are used to help wildlife directly.

In all fairness, some of these organizations do contribute to programs to control pet populations, but money spent to actually help wildlife with emergency food, habitat improvements, research, management or control can be totally nonexistent!

That financial burden falls squarely on the shoulders of American sportsmen, and the American sportsmen have always paid this bill willingly.

In a free society, it is reasonable to expect that these organizations will continue to exist, at least as long as the public and our elected representatives will tolerate the publishing of misrepresentations, half-truths, and outright deceptions. The stakes are high for the career administrators of these anti-trap organizations, and include prestige, money, power, and the desire to dictate or legislate personal values.

Without a doubt, many well-meaning but poorly informed people have been attracted to join and support these organizations in the belief that they are actually helping wild animals.

The vocal anti-trap organizations have little concern for the small minority of people who are the harvesters or producers of our land. As is evidenced by an almost total lack of contributions to help wildlife, it would surely seem that the professed concern for wildlife is not even real.

The foothold trap and trapping are destined to remain constant issues because both the trap and trapping are viewed by the antis as the weak spot in wildlife management. The total number of trappers in America amount to about ½ of one percent of the entire population. That tiny minority has few resources, little political power, and poor communications. Therefore, trapping is not only the easiest target, it is the first real target for the organizations committed to stopping not only trapping, but hunting and fishing as well.

It is not even reasonable to expect the "Animal Welfare" organizations to disintegrate if they are successful in outlawing trapping, or the foothold trap. These organizations need a "cause" in order to justify their own existence, and it is logical to expect them to use the same tactics to persecute fur ranchers, hunters, and anyone thoughtless enough to impale a worm on a fish hook.

The battleground is public opinion. Public opinion translates to votes, and the antis know full well that elected politicians feel compelled to honor the opinion polls from back home as they cast their important votes.

The vast majority of Americans are either against trapping, or don't even realize that trapping exists today. A recent university survey indicates that 77% of Americans are against trapping. Many believe that common species like mink, beaver, foxes and coyotes are endangered species. Obviously, the American public is ignorant of the true status of wildlife, and of the important role of game managers to maintain and control wild populations in harmony with other land needs.

There is a sharp division in the view of trapping between urban and rural people. Most rural people live much closer to the land, and have a better perspective of wildlife, and the needs to control wildlife. A lifestyle closer to the land allows many rural people to better understand the complexities of nature, and to appreciate the many products that are harvested annually from the land, including crops, firewood and wildlife.

As a result, the attack on trapping is often focused in cities. After all, a vote is a vote, and the anti-trap propaganda is directed to the huge masses who are either poorly informed, or don't care.

Due to the continuous barrage against trapping, many trappers and friends of trappers have been and will continue to be organized at both the state and national levels to represent and defend the needs of the species, as well as the rights of Americans who choose to participate in beneficial harvests.

This organization has been essential in the constant fight against the idle, and the wealthy, who would impose their own sense of values upon the good, hard working, producers of this land.

All outdoor sportsmen can take notice and be proud to see trappers form a line of defense. Trappers do have a lot of friends, and that is critically important in the determined fight against overwhelming odds.

Trapping survives, and trapping must survive if significant numbers of animals are to enjoy quality lives, and quality deaths.

A Brotherhood

ACCUSATIONS and criticisms against trapping and trappers have caused many who do trap to join together in organizations in recent years. The constant battle to save trapping is a contest to preserve a basic human right — the freedom of choice.

The ownership of animals are identified by law. The needs of the species to be controlled are scientifically and firmly established. Our furbearing species, like all other natural resources, have value, and the use of that value is easily defendable because furbearers are one of our few natural resources offering an annual surplus. Excesses of furbearers not cropped are simply wasted, and threaten the health of others of the same species.

But the fact remains that trapping can be abolished with the stroke of a pen. All trappers are therefore joined together to suffer or enjoy a common destiny. Trappers are brothers, united by a common love.

The character of a person who traps is constantly demeaned by anti-trap propaganda. Trappers are accused of being brutal, uncaring, uneducated, lower class, and mercinary individuals who exploit animals for profit. In truth, such is not the case at all, and recent studies confirm without a doubt that trappers are purely and simply — just people.

There are only two distinctions that separate an average trapper from another average citizen. For one, a trapper is more likely to live in a rural area. The second is that the trapper is apt to have a better knowledge of wildlife, a better respect for wildlife, and a better love of wildlife.

People of all walks of life are attracted to trap. Students trap, as do some doctors, lawyers, farmers, laborers, and even housewives. Many Congressmen trapped in their youth, and Congressman Donald Young of Alaska considers himself to be a professional trapper. Iowa Governor Harold Hughes trapped mink while he was living in the Governor's Mansion, and it seems safe to suggest that important affairs had to wait when a mink needed to be skinned.

The suggestion that trappers trap for a profit is only partially accurate. Profits are certainly enjoyed by trappers during years when fur prices are comparitively high, but only about 6% of the total number of trappers trap mainly for the money. Profits in trapping are far from sure, and nearly 90% of all trappers trap because they enjoy the outdoor experience, the challenge, and the excitement as the major reasons.

A person who chooses to trap is inclined to enjoy other outdoor sports, including hunting and fishing. There is little doubt that trappers buy many licenses and permits to support game management. It is possible that trappers pay more for wildlife management than any other identifiable group of sportsmen.

Considering the realistic threat to trapping today, it is incredibly important for the small minority of people who happen to trap to join the National Trappers Association. Members, and money, are constantly needed for a variety of noble purposes. Representing trappers in Washington, D.C. is expensive and the NTA testimony certainly has a greater impact as it represents the interests of more and more members. The NTA publication is also costly, but necessary in the effort to inform trappers. Other benefits of NTA membership include the opportunity to buy health and life insurance at group rates. Advertising in the NTA publication allows many trappers to shop for prices on equipment in the convenience of their own homes. There are often contests with significant prizes.

The NTA is also active in the individual states when it is asked and needed. The experience of NTA officers is helpful when testimony is needed. Significant amounts of NTA money have been given to state trapping associations when there is a justifiable and real need.

The annual NTA Convention is a real thrill to attend. The largest group of trappers ever known to assemble do so at these conventions. Interesting speakers, contests, and demonstrations by accomplished trappers are helpful to many. Real trapping supply bargains are available as large numbers of trapping supply dealers gather to sell their wares.

The important person in the NTA is the member. The individual member is a part and equal owner, and each member has opportunity to influence policy, and cast his or her conscience in a vote.

The Officers and Directors of the NTA are constantly trying to build a bigger and better NTA. The need to defend trapping is immediate. There is also an abundant opportunity to help others who are trappers.

If you do not belong to the NTA, then the NTA cannot count you or represent you.

Membership in your state trapping association is equally important. Scores of anti-trap bills are introduced annually in state legislatures. The various state trapping associations monitor legislative bills, and provide a determined effort at providing testimony and lobbying. Congressmen and Senators are interested in how local people feel or might be affected by legislation, and a strong state trapping association can provide both excellent representation, and political clout.

State trapping associations also provide numerous benefits to members. There is always opportunity to comment on proposed trapping regulations, and your opinions can have a real impact on trapping seasons. If you believe that a trapping regulation needs to be changed, you will have opportunity to present your suggested change for the discussion of the membership. The discussion of your brother trappers will determine if your recommendation has merit, and good suggestions are usually adopted by a voting process. Game Commissioners certainly appreciate this democratic process. The recommendations of the state trapping associations are always evaluated and often honored.

Trapper and trapping education programs are offered by many state trappers associations. Conventions and meetings offer a lot of opportunities for you. It is a sure bet that your state trappers association cannot count you, or represent you, if you are not a member either.

Both the NTA and the state trappers associations are constantly searching for more help, and more talent. There are many jobs, and many roles to fill in the effort to help each other, and educate the public. The chances are excellent that you can help in his noble purpose. There is a satisfying pleasure in helping others, and all that you have to do is volunteer.

If you care enough about your rights as a free American, it is important for you to be an active member in your trappers association. One of the single, most important things that you can do is to write your legislators when you are asked to by trapping leaders. It is a fact that your personal letter will be read. Don't forget for one minute that you represent only about one-half of one percent of the population as a trapper. You can be sure that massive anti-trap letter writing campaigns are being implemented to revoke your rights. As a result, you really don't have a choice other than to write too.

A poor letter can be damaging, so it is important to know how to write your legislator. It is important to know what to say, and it is also important to know what not to say. For that very reason, please refer to the following guide whenever you write your legislators:

Legislative Letter Guideline

Do be timely with your letter. The time to write is when issues are being considered, and your trapping leaders will encourage you at the proper times.

Do be positive in your approach. If your approach is negative, it will be reacted to with negativism.

Do be accurate. Do be sure that you mention the proper bill number, and check your spelling and punctuation.

Do consider the legislator. Your letter should be typed if at all possible. If not, readable penmanship may determine whether your letter will be read at all.

Do keep it short. Your letter to a legislator should address only one subject. Better letters are only one page in length, clear, and concise.

Do emphasize how you would be adversely affected. Your representative cares about your well being, and he is entitled to know how proposed legislation might impact your life.

Do ask for your representative's position. You have every right to know how your representative might vote on an issue, and you certainly can ask your representative to reconsider his position if you know that he favors poor legislation.

Do include your full name and address. Your letter must be signed, and you should include your name and address on the envelope as well as at the bottom of your letter.

Do not be intimidated. Congressman are not high and mighty. Congressmen are just people. Your elected representatives deserve respect, and they are entitled to form opinions. But you deserve respect, and are entitled to opinions too. Your letter will have an impact.

Do not use a form letter. Form letters and postcards are rarely considered, and certainly do not have the impact of a personal letter.

Do not mention that you have been asked to write. There is no need to mention that you belong to a trappers association. Your letter would have less impact if the Congressman suspected that you were directed to write.

Do not mention party affiliation. Wildlife matters are not divided along party lines, and whether you happen to be a democrat or republican doesn't matter at all.

Do not mention that you are a taxpayer. You are expected to be a taxpayer.

Do not present official information. Official information will be presented through the proper channels. Health officials and game departments have access to the best information, and these officials have the authority and responsibility to present an account of how proposed legislation might alter existing conditions.

Do not argue. Do not ever be caught in an emotional argument, especially about whether or not the foothold trap hurts. The behavior of animals in traps suggests that wild animals are stressed more by being restricted in traps than any pain related stress. But this is difficult for non-trappers to understand. Instead, emphasize the species needs for control, and point out that the foothold trap is the only alternative as a live trap for many species.

For information on finding out who your state Senator and Representatives are, check with your local library, post office, or newspaper. Your U.S. Senators and U.S. Representatives can be reached at the following addresses:

The Honorable (Name)
U.S. House of Representatives
Washington, D.C. 20515

The Honorable (Name)
United States Senate
Washington, D.C. 20510

The following letter example is not to be copied. It is printed as an example of a good letter to a U.S. Representative, and it might be helpful for you to consider the form of the letter to aid you when you have a need to write.

(Date)

The Honorable John M. Smith
U.S. House of Representatives
Washington, D.C. 20515

Dear Representative Smith,

I sincerely believe that H.R. 1797 is a bad bill, and that I would be directly and adversely affected by the passage of this bill prohibiting foothold traps.

My son and I take our annual vacations every fall to harvest muskrats in a few marshes in the 12th District, as did my father before us. We find that we need foothold traps to accomplish this harvest properly, and there simply isn't an alternative tool for this needful harvest.

The muskrat harvest has been scientifically managed by our state game department for many years, and I assure you that our modest profits have been an important source of income for our families.

Please consider opposing this bill on its own merits, and kindly inform me of your position on this important matter.

Sincerely yours,
Robert E. Jones
P.O. Box 100
Midtown, PA 17345

cc: Senator Thomas E. Brown

The TV Networks

Anti-trap sentiments are common on many TV programs. These sentiments are sometimes subtle, and sometimes very direct and damaging to the character of trappers.

Many times, the networks excuse or try to justify the slander by stating that the offending programs are designed for entertainment, and that damage wasn't really done because these programs are accepted by the public as fictitious entertainment.

Yet, damage is done every time a trapper is portrayed to be dirty, mean, or barbaric.

Equal time to correct slander is usually not possible with these attacks, as equal time can only be demanded according to law by political candidates with opposing views.

However, you do have a right to write the local TV stations as well as the networks to register your complaint. Be brief, identify the program and the situation you wish to object to, and be courteous. The pulse of the public is important to TV executives. Constructive letters can have an impact on future programming.

ABC
Programming Department
1330 Ave. of the Americas
New York, NY 10019

CBS
Programming Department
51 West 52nd Street
New York, NY 10019

NBC
Programming Department
30 Rockefeller Plaza
New York, NY 10019

Your Newspaper

Many newspapers devote space for readers to express opinions, and anti-trap letters commonly appear. For that reason, you should continually read these letters or opinions. You will likely find that you will be allowed to rebut an anti-trap opinion if you can present good information in a kind manner.

If a strong anti-trap message appears in your newspaper, one of the first things that you should do is to send a tear sheet of the article to your state game department. Include all of the information, such as the name of the newspaper, the publication date, the editor's name, the proper address, telephone number, etc. Ask your game department to respond to the anti-trap material. Your game department has access to official information, and an official response will be viewed as credible.

You have a right to an opinion too, and a short, clear, accurate response can have a lot of impact upon the readers.

Many anti-trap letters are printed as a result of an illegal trapper who doesn't check his traps regularly, or sets his traps where he doesn't have authority. If you decide to give your view, do not, under any circumstances, ever defend an illegal trapper. Instead, carefully point out that a law has been broken, and that the thoughtlessness on the part of one individual certainly does not reflect upon all trappers.

At times, the controversy will center around a view that the foothold trap is cruel, or inhumane. Your response should not center around whether or not the trap might cause pain to the trapped animal. Although many animals do not appear to suffer pain in a foothold trap, the public won't accept that argument because it doesn't "seem" reasonable. Instead, carefully point out that the foothold trap is a live trap, and that it is **needed** to control furbearer and predator populations.

Some anti-trap letters suggest that trappers catch significant numbers of non-target species. You do have the right to question the authenticity of those printed numbers. Highly inflated numbers of non-target animals caught in traps is typical anti-trap propaganda without basis in fact or truth.

Always be aware that your letter might be edited. Try to keep your thoughts concise, with one thought to a paragraph, to prevent an editing which might take your response out of context.

Above all, be timely, calm and courteous. An angry response from you is discrediting, and does far more harm than good.

Many anti-trap letters to editors are called for by professional anti-trap people, so don't bother wasting your time to try to convert the offending letter writer. Remember at all times that the public has very little knowledge of trapping, and the needs of the species. The opinion of the public is important, and honorable editors feel a responsibility to present both sides of a view.

Give every consideration to the local editor, and type your letter if you can. Otherwise, good penmanship is a must.

Always sign your letter to an editor, and clearly print your address. Unsigned letters are never printed, and you can ask that your name be withheld if you wish.

As brothers in trapping, we all help each other when we trap properly, respect the rights of others, abide by the law, and defend the needs of the species. If you would call yourself a trapper, then you are honor bound to represent your brother trappers in your own community.

Please do it well.

National Trappers Association

Preamble

We, the trappers of North America, prompted by a feeling of profound respect and gratitude toward the many valiant Fur Trappers who have gone before us, whose courageous deeds and exploits will forever embellish the pages of our Nation's early history, and being duly grateful for the rich legacy of wildlife bequeathed by our predecessors associate ourselves for the following purposes: to promote sound conservation legislation and administrative procedures; to save and faithfully defend from waste the natural resources of the United States; to promote sound environmental education programs; and to promote a continued annual fur harvest using the best tools presently available for that purpose.